The Fictional Lives of Shakespeare

Modern biographies of William Shakespeare abound; however, close scrutiny of the surviving records clearly show that there is insufficient material for a cradle to grave account of his life, that most of what is written about him cannot be verified from primary sources, and that Shakespearean biography did not attain scholarly or academic respectability until long after Samuel Schoenbaum published *William Shakespeare A Documentary Life* in 1975.

This study begins with a short survey of the history and practice of biography and then surveys the very limited biographical material for Shakespeare.

Although Shakespeare gradually attained the status as a national hero during the seventeenth and eighteenth centuries, there were no serious attempts to reconstruct his life. Any attempt at an account of his life or personality amounts, however, merely to "biografiction".

Modern biographers differ sharply on Shakespeare's apparent relationships with Southampton and with Jonson, which merely underlines the fact that the documentary record has to be greatly expanded through contextual description and speculation in order to appear like a Life of Shakespeare.

Kevin Gilvary received his Ph.D. in English Literature from Brunel University London in 2015. He also holds a BA and MA in Classics as well as an MA in Applied Linguistics from the University of Southampton. He taught at Barton Peveril College in Hampshire, UK, for twenty years.

Routledge Studies in Shakespeare

For a full list of titles in this series, please visit www.routledge.com.

The Fictional Lives of Shakespeare

Kevin Gilvary

Routledge
Taylor & Francis Group

LONDON AND NEW YORK

First published 2018 by Routledge

2 Park Square, Milton Park, Abingdon, Oxfordshire OX14 4RN
52 Vanderbilt Avenue, New York, NY 10017

Routledge is an imprint of the Taylor & Francis Group, an informa business

First issued in paperback 2019

Library of Congress Cataloging-in-Publication Data
CIP data has been applied for.

ISBN: 978-0-8153-9443-3 (hbk)
ISBN: 978-0-367-89159-6 (pbk)

Typeset in Sabon
by codeMantra

Contents

Early Editions of Shakespeare's Works

Rowe Nicholas Rowe. 1709. *The works of Mr. William Shakespear; in six volumes. Adorn'd with cuts. Revis'd and corrected, with an account of the life and writings of the author. By N. Rowe, Esq.* (Second impression 1709; new edition 1714).

Pope Alexander Pope. 1723–5. *The Works of Shakespear: 6 vols.* (Volume 1 containing the prefatory material is dated 1725; the remaining volumes are dated 1723.)

Theobald Lewis Theobald. 1733. *The Works of Shakespeare: In Seven Volumes.* (Further editions in 1740, 1752, 1757, 1762, 1767, 1772, 1773, and 1777 made it the most reprinted edition of Shakespeare in the eighteenth century).

Hanmer Thomas Hanmer. 1744. *Works of Shakespeare. 6 vols.* (Re-printed 1745; 1747; 1751 and 1760. Second edition 1770–71).

Warburton William Warburton. 1747. *The Works of Shakespear in Eight Volumes.*

Johnson Dr. Samuel Johnson. 1765. *The Plays of William Shakespeare, in Eight Volumes.*

Capell *Mr William Shakespeare his Comedies, Histories, and Tragedies 10 vols.*

Steevens George Steevens. 1773. *The plays of William Shakespeare* (known as Johnson-Steevens 1). Revised editions, 1778 (Johnson-Steevens 2); 1785 (Johnson-Steevens 3); 1793 (Johnson-Steevens 4); 1803 (first variorum or Johnson-Steevens 5); 1813 (second variorum or Johnson-Steevens 6).

Malone Edmond Malone. 1790. *The plays and poems: of William Shakspeare, in ten volumes.*

Boswell Edmond Malone & James Boswell Jr. (eds) 1821. *The Plays and Poems of William Shakspeare* 21 vols. Third variorum.

Abbreviations

Quotations of the works of Shakespeare are taken from Stanley Wells & Gary Taylor, eds. (1986) *William Shakespeare: the Complete Works.* Oxford: Clarendon Press.

The following abbreviations are used:

WS   E. K. Chambers. 1930. *William Shakespeare: A Study of Facts and Problems.* 2 vols.

ES   E. K. Chambers. 1923. *The Elizabethan Stage.*4 vols.

EMI   *Every Man in his Humour* (Play by Ben Jonson, first performed *c.* 1598).

EMO   *Every Man Out of his Humour* (Play by Ben Jonson, first performed *c.* 1599).

List of Tables

List of Plates

Acknowledgements

This book is the outcome of many years of study, which resulted in my doctorate being awarded at Brunel University London in 2015. I owe a special debt of gratitude to my supervisor, Bill Leahy for overseeing my research, and to Sean Gaston, Tom Betteridge, and Philip Tew of the School of English & Humanities. Emma Jolly gave me constant help throughout my studies. I have also been grateful for advice from Ros Barber, Bob Griffin, and Steve Rollins, and in particular Bob Bearman of the Shakespeare Centre Library and Archive at Stratford-upon-Avon.

I myself learned a considerable amount from many speakers who gave papers at conferences held in London, Stratford-upon-Avon, (especially at the Shakespeare Institute), Washington D.C., and Ashland Oregon. The efficient staff at the British Library, the Bodleian Library, The National Archives, the London Metropolitan Archives, the Shakespeare Centre Library and Archive at Stratford-upon-Avon, Southampton University Library, the Hampshire Archives, the Hampshire Public Libraries, and the Folger Shakespeare Library in Washington have all greatly assisted my research. The editorial team at Routledge under Michelle Salyga have been particularly helpful and understanding.

I recall many, many other teachers, actors, and scholars who have enhanced my appreciation of Shakespeare. Among these, Mark Rylance has been an inspirational figure at Shakespeare's Globe in London, both for his outstanding performances and for the many meetings which he organised. In addition, my wonderful colleagues in the English Department at Barton Peveril College, Hampshire, gave me great assistance. Finally, none of my research would have been possible but for my wife's total support and encouragement throughout my studies.

Finally a note on Authorship. Throughout this study, I have accepted the traditional attribution of the plays and works to William Shakespeare of Stratford-upon-Avon, endeavouring to show that no biography of his life is possible. The question of authorship is entirely separate and any reader who wishes to pursue this interest might usefully begin with *Shakespeare Beyond Doubt*, eds. Stanley Wells & Paul Edmondson (2013) and *Shakespeare Beyond Doubt?* eds. John Shahan & Alexander Waugh (2013).

Kevin Gilvary

Introduction
The Fictional Lives of Shakespeare

> What, will the line stretch out to the crack of doom? Another yet!
> *Macbeth*, 4.1.130

Like Macbeth confronted by the interminable line of Banquo's progeny, any person wanting to investigate the historical William Shakespeare must be astonished at the huge number of modern biographies about the Bard. In 1998, the popular film *Shakespeare in Love* depicted a playwright with an unattested love interest of the fictional Lady Viola de Lesseps, against an invented antagonist, Lord Wessex, while following the unlikely advice of Kit Marlowe for *Romeo and Juliet* without recognising the source of the play in Arthur Brooke's poem *The Tragicall Historye of Romeus and Iuliet* (1562). Since *Shakespeare in Love* there have been over twenty-five full-length biographies, some written by eminent academics such as Katherine Duncan-Jones, Stephen Greenblatt, and Lois Potter, others by established biographers such as Anthony Holden, Peter Ackroyd and Michael Wood. The number of these biographies is all the more surprising when we recall that no new information about Shakespeare has emerged from any contemporary document since 1931 when Leslie Hotson published his transcription and analysis of the Langley writ of 1596. Before that, the last new information about Shakespeare was discovered in the court records of the Bellott-Mountjoy case, and published by Charles Wallace in 1910.

Modern biographers vary considerably in their portrayal of the Shakespeare of their own imaginations. Edmond Malone was the first critic to investigate historical records for Shakespeare from which he made biographical inferences. He could not envisage that "a man of such sensibility, and so amiable a disposition, should have lost his only son, who had attained the age of twelve years, without being greatly affected by it." To this he added another inference, this time from the works, in proposing that Constance's lamentations for her son (*King John* 3.4 16–106) "may perhaps add some probability that this tragedy was written at or soon after that period." At least Malone offered a note of caution in these claims. Modern biographers however make similar assertions with no sign of doubt, often identifying a speech, a character or an idea with

Shakespeare himself. Some writers claim to identify Shakespeare's Protestant outlook (e.g. Honan, 79–80; Ackroyd), others assert his partisan Catholic affiliations (e.g. Greenblatt, 102–103; Wood). A few find republican ideals in the plays (Hadfield), a majority find monarchical tendencies (Saccio). Echoing the sentiments of T. S. Eliot, Blair Worden explains:

> In modern times, we have had a monarchist Shakespeare and a republican Shakespeare, an aristocratic Shakespeare and a bourgeois Shakespeare, Terry Eagleton's Marxist Shakespeare and Michael Portillo's Tory Shakespeare.... each interpretation tells us more about the interpreter, not the interpreted.
>
> (29–30)

Similar differences emerge over descriptions of his supposed relationships with his wife, his patron(s), his colleagues and his rivals. These differences of interpretation, well summarised by David Bevington (2010), tend to indicate that there is no reliable basis for such interpretations. For any reader wishing to know more about Shakespeare and how he came to compose his works, the difficulty lies in choosing between these competing biographies: which one portrays the "real" Shakespeare? Which one tells the story most accurately? The answer is none of them. The few historical records do not reveal his personality or describe his "life trajectory". What passes for Shakespearean biography offer extensive description of the historical, developed by the dubious practices of speculation, using uncorroborated posthumous anecdotes, and making biographical inferences from the works.

The critical reader will of course always bear in mind the distinction between primary and secondary sources. A primary source is a "document, image or artefact that provides evidence about the past. It is an original document created contemporaneously with the event under discussion" (Robert Williams, 58). A primary source must directly and unambiguously reference the subject to be considered part of the biographical material. On the other hand, a secondary source may present an anecdote or a claim which cannot be verified in the primary sources. If the anecdote is repeated, it becomes a myth which "comes down from the past whose truth is popularly accepted but cannot be checked" (Merriam-Webster). Myths are propagated for their significance to the culture of a people rather than for their historical accuracy. E. K. Chambers referred to such unevidenced claims as the "Shakespeare-mythos". He lists fifty-eight writers between 1640 and 1858 whose comments about Shakespeare cannot be verified with regard to contemporary or near-contemporary records (*WS* ii. 238–302). Biographers of Shakespeare often claim the authority of an "early source" or a "credible tradition" to justify a line of interpretation when there is no basis in contemporary documents.

The next stage for the reader anxious to investigate the life of Shakespeare is to seek the contemporary records on which biographies are (or should be) based. Actual transcriptions are hard to find. Instead, biographers offer summaries and interpretations as E. K. Chambers observed of the biographies by Sidney Lee and J. Q. Adams (1923): writers using continuous narrative "do not set out *in extenso* the original documents on which they are based. These are summarised, and subjective interpretations [are] added" (1946, 7). This observation remains true of modern biographies.

The inquisitive reader will eventually make use of documentary collections, such as the two volume study by Sir Edmund Chambers, *William Shakespeare: A Study of Facts and Problems* (1930). Chambers generally published accurate transcriptions of records held by offices such as the Shakespeare Birthplace Trust at Stratford-upon-Avon, the British Library in London, the PRO (now The National Archives at Kew), the London Metropolitan Archives at Finsbury, and the Folger Shakespeare Library in Washington, D. C. While Chambers's organisation is helpful and analytical, he often merges his report of the records with his own discussion and interpretation, especially when dating the plays. In short, Chambers allowed his own subjective interpretation to intrude into his presentation of the historical record, as he himself recognised later (1946, 8).

Starting with a critical examination of biography and literary biography as a genre in Chapter 1, we find that biography is typically defined as a narrative account of a person's life; while a literary biography attempts to relate the works of a writer to a life. In western literature, biography emerged in the classical period when the lives of powerful men were described by biographers such as Suetonius and Plutarch. Medieval monks added a second class of subject, the biographies of saints, as exemplars of the holy life. Both of these types of subject are evident in the emergence of English biography during the Tudor period with Hall's *Chronicle* (1547) and Foxe's *Book of Martyrs* (1563). Literary biography only became established in England during the eighteenth century when Dr. Johnson added the lives of writers as a third major subject for biographers. These elements converge when the biographies of Shakespeare emerge in the Victorian period: a writer, who was an important person and divinely inspired. The New Biography of the twentieth century, however, attempted not only to show a more rounded view of subjects by mentioning their failings, but also offering a more intimate description of a subject's life. Techniques such as the speculative reporting of the subject's personal thoughts, experiences and motives were increasingly used by biographers in the 1920s and 1930s. Although these practices were dismissed by Durling and Watt as 'biografiction' (1941, 2–3), they remain visible in many modern biographies, especially those dealing with Shakespeare.

The extant biographical data for Shakespeare is assessed in Chapter 2, "Gaps in our Ignorance", not just with regard to the extent of the surviving records, as has been attempted by many biographers such as Chambers (*William Shakespeare* 1930) and Schoenbaum in *Shakespeare's Lives* (1970, 3–72), but more importantly with regard to the limitations of the material and the lack of key records. The small number of historical documents which reference William Shakespeare offer no insight into the poet's thoughts and motives, but consist mainly of legal documents. References in printed texts allude to an author in print or to his works. Nor do the records support any reliable chronology of his works. Thus every attempt at a biography of Shakespeare lacks a framework for his literary career and any indication of the playwright's personal thoughts, experiences and motives.

Biographical comments about Shakespeare in the seventeenth and eighteenth centuries are considered in Chapter 3, "Inventing the Myths," where it is noted that without firm evidence about the Bard, various claims were made which have not been verified subsequently from extant sources. The only scanty notice of Shakespeare's life at this time was written by Nicholas Rowe for his new edition of the works in 1709. Rowe's anecdotes can be shown upon scrutiny to be false or unfounded. Although widely republished in the following 150 years, Rowe's *Account* was held in very poor repute by subsequent editors, such as Dr. Johnson. The biographical investigations of Edmond Malone form the subject of Chapter 4, "Doubting the Myths". Malone discovered many new documents concerning the life and times of Shakespeare, but rejected many of the unfounded assertions made by previous critics such as Rowe. He cautiously offered a chronology of the plays which has been very influential but its reliability is uncertain. Malone's great ambition was to write a life of Shakespeare, but this was never achieved.

Popular narrative biographies in the period from 1803 to 1975 are considered in Chapter 5, "Filling in the Gaps," where the main focus was to produce an exemplary biography worthy of the National Poet. Much of the description of Shakespeare's life was either derived from an uncritical acceptance of the myths first attested in the eighteenth century or through selective biographical inference from the works. This chapter then traces the influence of the New Biography in the twentieth century (up to 1975). At the same time, there was a strong current of skepticism as to the value of a Life of Shakespeare. This doubtful outlook was re-affirmed when the biographical approach to literature was dismissed as a fallacy by the New Critics such as Winsatt & Beardsley (1946) as deriving from each reader's subjective estimation of the author's character and personality. In the twentieth century, it was widely accepted that there was insufficient material for a biography of Shakespeare based on contemporary records.

Samuel Schoenbaum's *William Shakespeare: a Documentary Life* (1975) is considered in Chapter 6, "Re-Imagining the Life". This was a pivotal work in changing the previous perception that no biography was possible. Few modern biographers look any earlier than this work when citing sources. It begins with the claim that there are more records than popularly supposed and gives large scale reproductions of over 200 documents. These are used to support a linear narrative of the life of Shakespeare. However, only a quarter of the documents contain contemporary references to Shakespeare. By linking events and situations in an imaginative way, interpreting as he progresses. Schoenbaum perpetuates many myths: that Shakespeare spent his childhood in Stratford where he received his education; that he was patronised by Southampton; that he inspired envy in Jonson; and that he retired to Stratford. None of these assertions can be verified from primary sources. Chapter 7 "After Schoenbaum" reviews a wide range of modern biographies on Shakespeare. These show a commendable desire to understand the poet and the playwright, and to share their insights regarding the great works. However, they rely on a range of historically dubious techniques to embellish and expand the established narrative outline.

The final chapters are concerned with two supposed relationships of Shakespeare, both important for any literary biography. Chapter 8, "Inventing a Patron," reviews the thin evidence linking Shakespeare with the Earl of Southampton. Accepting the myth that Shakespeare enjoyed this aristocrat's patronage, biographers project the playwright into the earl's life, often by identifying him with the 'fair youth' of the sonnets and the underlying subject of *Venus & Adonis*. The wide variety of interpretations concerning their relationship are shown to be without foundation. Chapter 9.

"Inventing a Rival," (Chapter 9) considers how Ben Jonson is cast as the antagonist to Shakespeare, intimately acquainted and full of admiration but ultimately consumed by envy. These views are shown to have no basis in primary sources.

While Shakespeare never mentions Jonson and alludes only rarely, if at all, to his works, Jonson's comments in The First Folio are found to be in line with other commendations, or literary puffs for which he was likely to have been paid. In his own writings and private conversations, his rare comments serve only to disparage Shakespeare.

The extant records give a very limited framework for the life of William Shakespeare. They are lacking in detail and offer no insight into his character or personality. The literary and theatrical records are so fragmentary that no reliable account of Shakespeare as a playwright can be constructed. Moreover, no direct connection between any of the plays and any events in Shakespeare's life, such as the deaths of his son, father or mother, can be reliably demonstrated. The records do not provide sufficient material for an evidence-based biography of Shakespeare. David Bevington notes that Shakespeare's silence on himself and his outlook "positively invites speculation" (2010, 13). This may be so, but it is not justified in biography.

The main gaps in the records concerning Shakespeare are Table 0.1:

Table 0.1 Gaps in the records for Shakespeare

---

a absence of personal papers written by Shakespeare such as letters, diaries, notes or journals;

b absence of personal records about Shakespeare by friends, acquaintances, neighbours or colleagues;

c absence of allusion in the Stratford records to his work as a poet and playwright. The public records in Stratford state his birth, marriage, children's births and their deaths. The records indicate his increasing wealth and standing there.

d absence of records of William Shakespeare from his birth in 1564 until his marriage at the age of 18;

e absence of records about William Shakespeare from the birth of his twins in 1585 until the possible allusion in a 1592 pamphlet;

f absence of records that he was in London between 1604 and 1612; he attended the Bellott-Mountjoy case at Westminster Hall on 11 May 1612 – the only record to locate Shakespeare to a particular place on a particular day in his life;

g absence of dates of composition for his poems and plays; no document records any sequence of composition;

h absence of full performance list, including premières. The extent records are fragmentary and ambiguous (e.g. the play witnessed by Platter in 1599 might not have been Shakespeare's play);

i absence of records concerning his working practices: there is no evidence as to whether he worked on one play or one poem at a time, whether he ever revised his own works either for the stage or for publication, whether he ever revised the works of others, whether he ever actively worked alongside other playwrights, whether his works were initially intended for performance at court, or what he might have thought about other poets and playwrights;

j no insight into the person among the allusions to Shakespeare as a poet and/or as a playwright, which only attest his reputation.

Overall, modern biographies of Shakespeare have only a small factual framework. There is insufficient material upon which to construct a coherent linear account of the subject's life. Scarcely any of the claims made about Shakespeare as a writer can be verified by reference to historical records. As a result, the biographies of Shakespeare only offer historical fact in their treatment of the context and in dealing with a few of the external events of his life. For the inner man, these narratives accounts are entirely conjectural. The only acceptable methodology for considering Shakespeare's life is to undertake skeptical examination of those discrete topics for which there are primary sources. Any picture of Shakespeare will thus be very limited, but will at least have the merit of being historically based, verifiable, and not simply fiction.

1 Biography
Much Practice, Little Theory

No words or thoughts, motives or actions, should be ascribed to the subject without evidence. The sources of the evidence should be clear and verifiable.

—Anne Chisholm (2001)

A biography is widely understood to give the "the record of the life of an individual written by someone else" (*OED*) providing a factually based account of a life in a linear narrative. Literary biography, as a recognised subgenre, offers not just an account of a subject's life, but also shows how the author's writings came into being and traces an author's development. Biography has been a recognised genre from the classical period and became established in early modern England with the primary intention of describing exemplary lives. In the early twentieth century, exponents of the New Biography put emphasis on a more realistic appraisal of a subject, often enhanced by reporting their inner thoughts and feelings. During this period, the subgenre of psychobiography emerged with an assessment of the subject's childhood experiences and influences. The chapter finally considers the background to biographers, some academic, others professional, as well as publishers whose main concern is good business. Biography is a profitable genre for publishers and writers.

There is broad agreement that a biography gives "a narrative history ... of the life of a notable individual from birth to death" (*Oxford Dictionary of Literary Terms*). Margaret Drabble notes that a good biographer maintains "high scholarly standards" combined with "imaginative insight and narrative skill" (*Oxford Companion to English Literature* 1985). Literary biographers likewise offer a narrative history of a writer's life and development. *The Concise Oxford Companion to English Literature* (1996) emphasises the external person, literary, and other influences on the subject. The other approach considers their internal development, recreating the creative imagination and the artistic process of the writer. A critical literary biography, such as Jocelyn Baines's study of Joseph Conrad (1960), also contains discrete analysis of the subject's literary works. While the broad definitions of biography and literary biography are widely accepted, the formal characteristics of biography as a genre have been formulated less often. Sir Michael Holroyd notes that there are "no absolute rules – each subject differs in the opportunities and problems he or she offers, and what works best is what appeals instinctively and calls forth our most original and potent language" (*The Guardian* 1 June 2002).

From classical times until the end of the Edwardian period, the emphasis in biography was to reveal personality in a portrait, on the assumption that character was fixed. With the advent of the New Biography after World War I, there was greater interest in a life story; the need for a coherent narrative has assumed greater importance. Today a literary biographer attempts to offer a continuous and coherent account of the life of a writer, with the biographer's own insights and evaluations.

For an account of someone's life that is both narrative and historically accurate, there must be sufficient primary sources from which a narrative can be constructed. The requirement of a historically documented basis for biography was stated by John Garraty, general editor of the *American National Biography* (1999). He explains how factual accuracy is the highest priority for every one of the entries:

> After the staff at Columbia University had approved an essay, it was factchecked under the supervision of the *ANB* staff of Oxford University Press in Cary, North Carolina. The Oxford factcheckers generated well over a hundred thousand queries, and their work has immeasurably strengthened the factual foundation of our understanding of the American past.
>
> (Garraty, Preface, *ANB*)

For any literary biographer, it is essential to establish a factually accurate framework of an author's life, including dates and times of composition of their works, whether and when any revisions were made, and the date(s) of publication. Only then can the literary biographer begin to relate biographical material towards a critical appreciation of their texts.

1.1 The Western Tradition of Biography

Biography emerged as a genre in the Roman period, when Suetonius described the lives of Julius Caesar and the first eleven Emperors. While following a chronological account, Suetonius also sought to relate any anecdotes, especially from the childhood of the subject which would illuminate the subject's character. Suetonius influenced Plutarch, a younger contemporary who wrote twenty-three pairs of *Parallel Lives* in which he linked the biographies of illustrious Greeks with famous Romans (e.g. Alexander and Julius Caesar). Plutarch announced his intention to reveal character in his most important subject:

For it is not Histories that I am writing, but Lives; and in the most illustrious deeds there is not always a manifestation of virtue or vice, nay, a slight thing like a phrase or a jest often makes a greater revelation of character than battles when thousands fall, or the greatest armaments, or sieges of cities.

(*Life of Alexander*, 1)

The tendency to reveal the subject's character had a moralising element, which remained a strong element of biography until the early part of the twentieth century. After the Roman Empire became Christian, biography became divided between panegyric in praising emperors and hagiographic in the description of the holy man. Hagiography flourished during the medieval period especially as literacy the preserve of clerics.

In early modern England, the advent of print culture and the growth of literacy led to interest in biography. Biography was used for political and nationalistic purposes. Thomas More consciously followed classical models in his *History of King Richard III* (first printed 1543). Hall's *Chronicle* (1547) was organised around the lives of English kings. Medieval hagiography survived after the Reformation: English writers such as John Foxe began to reformulate religious history so as to forge a Protestant past. His *Acts and Monuments* (1563–1583), often fictitiously, described the exemplary lives and deaths of many Protestant martyrs. Thomas North's translation of *Plutarch's Lives* appeared in 1579. All of these writers exerted a strong influence not just on Shakespeare but on later biographers.

While the emphasis of biography was still mainly on powerful rulers, literary biography began to emerge when Izaak Walton (1593–1683) described the lives of religious writers, such as John Donne (1640). A much wider treatment of great Englishmen was attempted by Thomas Fuller (1608–1661) in *The History of the Worthies of England* (1662). Taking each county in turn, Fuller included brief descriptions of local saints, clerics, politicians, authors, and landowners. Within this framework, Shakespeare was accorded a few comments. John Aubrey (1626–1697) compiled notes about a wide range of people between 1669 and 1693, but showed less interest in the biographies of men of national significance than Fuller had done. Like Fuller, Aubrey included brief mention of Shakespeare.

John Dryden was the earliest English writer to use the terms 'biography' and 'biographer'. For his edition of *Plutarch's Lives* in 1683, Dryden prepared a life of the author from explicit comments which Plutarch made about himself.[1] Biographical dictionaries emerged in the late seventeenth century and expanded in the eighteenth. Shakespeare is given an increasingly important entry in these but more from a sense of nationalistic appreciation rather than for any contribution to the biographical material. The first such dictionaries in English, compiled by Edward

Phillips in 1675 and Gerard Langbaine in 1691, combined literary appreciation with some biographical content, which was often derivative, undocumented, and anecdotal. This approach influenced Nicholas Rowe in his introduction to the works of Shakespeare (1709) and remained evident in the literary dictionaries of Giles (1719–1720), Cibber (1753), and especially the six-volume *Biographia Britannica* (1747–1766). In these works, Shakespeare's significance as a national poet was increasingly established before anyone had actually investigated his life. Dr Johnson helped to establish the popularity of literary biography in the latter part of the eighteenth century. His Prefaces, Biographical and Critical, compiled mainly from secondary sources, originally served as introductions to selections of poems but were soon collected and published independently as *Lives of the Most Eminent English Poets* (1779–1781). Dr Johnson followed the western tradition of biography in seeking a mundane fact or hidden story as the key to understanding the character as a whole.[2] His achievement was to formalise the biographical approach to literary appreciation, relating criticism to a chronological framework of each writer's life and situation. There was a further boost to the popularity of the genre after the death of the great doctor as Johnson himself was the subject of many biographies, by among others Thomas Tyers (1784), William Shaw (1785), John Hawkins (1787), and most famously James Boswell (1791).

The first monograph to deal with biography as a genre was James Stanfield's *Essay on the Study and Composition of Biography*, which emphasised the didactic purpose in "developing the principles of man's active and moral nature" (1813, v). This approach continued to dominate the genre throughout the Romantic and Victorian periods. Thomas Carlyle (1795–1881) at this time enunciated the significance of the biography of great men. His lecture, "The Hero as Poet: Dante and Shakespeare," showed his greater interest in a writer's reputation than in his life: "Consider what this Shakespeare has actually become among us. Which Englishman we ever made, in this land of ours, which millions of Englishmen, would we not give up rather than the Stratford Peasant?" (Carlyle 1841, 132). One major development during this period was increased interest in childhood, especially with the publication of novels by Charles Dickens. With no record of Shakespeare's childhood between his baptism and the issue of a marriage licence, Victorian writers such as Charles Knight (1843) and John Payne Collier (1844) chose to invent one, a utopian vision of a warm and caring family, described in exceptional detail. From this flowed the national campaign to purchase of the 'Birthplace' in 1847. The process of national celebration through biography reached its zenith with the publication of the *Dictionary of National Biography*, beginning in 1885 and amounting to 63 volumes by 1900. Both the first of the two editors, Leslie Stephen (the father of Virginia Woolf) and Sidney Lee, warned against the Victorian tendency towards unconditional hero worship. Lee saw his role as a narrator, not a moralist, and he insisted on the investigation of primary material (1911, 25–26; 41). His *Life of Shakespeare* (1897, 1898, 1915), restrained by the standards of the day, is examined in Chapter 5. Despite the observations of Lee and the emergence of the New Biography, uncritical eulogy has remained evident in celebrity biography into the twenty-first century, and nowhere is this more evident than in biographies of Shakespeare.

New Biography and New Criticism

The emergence of a "New Biography" after World War I has been attributed to Lytton Strachey's publication of *Eminent Victorians* (1918), in which he attempted to debunk some of the more extreme myths surrounding Victorian heroes such as General Gordon and Florence Nightingale. In the preface, Strachey rejected the majority of existing biographies for "their tone of tedious panegyric, their lamentable lack of selection, of detachment, of design" (1918, viii). The New Biography was characterised by a demand for factually based judgements, selectively used. The second feature was interest in the subject's failures and failings. Third, he was keen to reconstruct the thought processes of the subject, in line with the stream of consciousness as a narrative mode in fiction. Virginia Woolf in *The Art of Biography*, written in 1939, noted that reliable, personal material was indispensable for any biography showing interior thought processes. Contrasting Lytton Strachey's portraits of Queen Victoria in *Victoria* (1921) and Queen Elizabeth in *Elizabeth and Essex* (1928), Woolf explains:

> it is clear that the two Queens present very different problems to their biographer. About Queen Victoria everything was known. Everything she did, almost everything she thought, was a matter of common knowledge. No one has ever been more closely verified and exactly authenticated than Queen Victoria. The biographer could not invent her, because at every moment some document was at hand to check his invention… [Of Queen Elizabeth] very little was known – he was urged to invent.
>
> (Woolf, *The Art of Biography*, edn. 2008, 119)

Woolf then concluded that biography "must be based upon fact. And by fact in biography we mean facts that can be verified by other people besides the artist" (2008, 120). Woolf was aware that fiction was common in biography in the 1920s. Many exponents of the New Biography were deplored by Durling & Watt for an assumed ability to "read his [sic] subject's mind, freely using the interior monologue or stream of consciousness made popular by novelists" so that the biographer "not only manipulated deeds for dramatic effect but supplied an accompaniment of speech, motives, and audible thoughts as well" (1941, 2). They also criticised the use of novelistic techniques such as the "tricks of suspense and surprise, climax and anti-climax" to establish a narrative or by imposing a single interpretation on a subject. For Durling & Watt, however, these deplorable evils – the use of inference, conjecture, and unwarranted coherence – amounted to 'biografiction' (1941, 3).

Amongst literary scholars during the twentieth century, however, there was little enthusiasm for literary biography. T. S. Eliot, in his review of *Ben Jonson* by Gregory Smith (1919), expounded the purpose of literary biography: to show how the life of the poet informs the work. Eliot simply noted that little if anything in Smith's biography added to the critical understanding of Jonson's works. Eliot's interest lay in textual analysis and he became a major influence on the New Critics, reducing interest in literary biography among academics. Wimsatt & Beardsley (1946, 470) likewise rejected interest in the author when approaching literary appreciation: "The design or intention of a work is neither available nor desirable as a standard for judging the success of a work of literary art." They accordingly ignored any external evidence about a work of literature and identified as a fallacy that a literary work could be taken as a guide to the author's own experience.

Another approach to biography emerged in the twentieth century: psychobiography was as an attempt to show the inner life, by relating internalised experience especially from childhood to the subject's later motives and behaviour. The starting point for this was Sigmund Freud's study of Leonardo da Vinci in 1910. While Freud has been criticised for errors in this study, Elms (1994) shows that fundamentally Freud's approach was tenable because there was suitable biographical material – in Leonardo's case, his description of recurrent dreams. Psychobiography became especially popular after the Great War: notable examples include Edmund Wilson on Ben Jonson (1948) and Walter Bate on Samuel Johnson (1977). Psychobiography relies for its usefulness on suitable personal material and responsible use of appropriate psychological theory. The main difficulty for any psychobiography is to find dependable, documentary evidence for childhood experiences. The psychiatrist, Anthony Storr, accepts that a psychoanalytical approach can be useful if childhood experiences or mental disorders were documented (e.g. Dickens's bipolar episodes) but very misleading when used in undocumented speculation about supposed infantile experiences.[3]

Biography from the Late Twentieth Century Onwards

Publishers from the late twentieth century onwards have witnessed a huge increase in the sales of biography. Many modern biographers are professional writers who depend directly on sales to the public for their livelihood. These include Michael Wood, Peter Ackroyd, and Bill

Bryson, who have all included a life study of Shakespeare among their publications. They rarely give explanations as to why a new biography is needed or why they feel more competent than others to conduct such a study. What is important is a good narrative style. Ultimately, a deal for any biography is made only if the publisher believes that there is a good business case – not because it offers fresh research, exciting new insights, or attempts to correct previous mistakes, misunderstandings or misinterpretations. The late twentieth century has also seen a revival of academic interest in literary biography. Using approaches such as Marxist readings, cultural materialism, and new historicism, academics are increasingly inclined to relate a text to its author and the social conditions in which it was produced. Literary biography has become even more popular at the turn of the twentieth-first century, with Charles Dickens, Jane Austen, George Eliot, the Brontës among the favourites, all of whom have been eclipsed by Shakespeare.

1.2 Coherence and Linear Narrative in Biography

Coherence is a central feature of biography because of the human need to find coherence in each individual, even though few lives demonstrate coherence (Ellman 1971, 19). Until a century ago, writers sought coherence by describing the subject's character as a fixed entity. Often, an anecdote from childhood or a prophecy at birth foreshadowed a subject's great (or vicious, or holy) deeds. The reader's expectation for a single explanation is welcomed by writers who wish to simplify a subject's character and provide a 'rosebud assumption' to the life of the subject.[4] At first sight, a single interpretation is most possible in literary biography as a writer is the person most likely to leave journals and letters which reveal their inner thoughts, feelings, and motives. Michael Wood (2003) uses this approach when claiming that Shakespeare was a closet Catholic, which he used as the key to his character and life. However, many biographers are aware of the paradox: Virginia Woolf in *Orlando* (1928, 295) makes the protagonist comment: "a biography is considered complete if it merely accounts for six or seven selves, whereas a person may well have as many thousand." Richard Holmes describes how writers struggle "to find shape and meaning within the apparent randomness of the subject's own life and work" (2002, 16–17). Some writers present a subject "full of contradictions" as if this were unusual for a human being.[5]

Coherence is also expected in a narrative account. While delineation of character was the central approach, Suetonius also gave a life story of each emperor's life. He began each *Life* by showing how he rose to power; then he described what he did in power; and finally, what he was like in private. This paradigm was used by Plutarch and medieval biographers. The use of a linear narrative to describe someone's life first emerged in autobiographical novels, such as Defoe's *Robinson Crusoe* (1719).

Dr Johnson was the first in English to describe a real person's life using a linear narrative in his *Life of Mr. Richard Savage* (1744). With the advent of New Biography, the main emphasis has been to tell the story of someone's life, to report the life trajectory. Readers, it is assumed, look for order; they do not expect a chaotic presentation of data about a subject but a coherent account often using foreshadowing or flashback to indicate cause and effect. The result is a tendency towards fictional biography – when writers place more emphasis on the narrative trajectory of a life which derives from their own imagination, rather than on documentary evidence (Parke 2002, 29). Even if the "facts" are documented, the process of presenting them in a narrative form often distorts them for the sake of coherence. Fictional biographies thus arise from the use of "factual materials about real people and events and developing them by applying fictional narrative techniques" (Erickson 1993, ii. 313–14).

The generic structure for English biography was laid down by James Stanfield (1813, x–xi): each biography should begin with a historical review of the period and then give an account of the subject's character. The subject's life should then be described in the following stages: infancy, childhood, adolescence, youth, manhood, and declining age. The biography should connect the "distinct characteristics of each with the general progression of the whole." The biography should finish with the "professional biography" of the subject's career and contribution to his field of specialisation. The German psychologist, Charlotte Bühler, followed a similar pattern of life divisions as: youth, trials, early maturity, full maturity, and decline (1935, 405–9).

Table 1.1 A biographical paradigm

I.	Introduction	The significance of the subject of the biography and the reasons for the biographer to attempt the life.
II.	Family and background	Involves treatment, often extensive, in which the biographer attempts to identify key influences in subject's family, the family connections, and their cultural milieu.
III.	Birth scene	Frequently described in detail.
IV.	Life	The narrative then proceeds through a series of episodes, as the subject settles upon an objective to follow, a quest, which is usually achieved in some kind of climax.
V.	Death	For many biographers, the Death Scene often has a key significance, as noted by Hermione Lee (2005) in her chapter 'How to end it all'.
VI.	Surviving family	The subsequent history of a widow(er), children, etc.
VII.	Significance	A final verdict of the importance of the subject.

Most modern biographies follow Buhler's pattern for the life but with particular emphasis on key moments or turning points in the subject's life. Biographers frequently follow the journey of a hero as put forward by James Campbell in his 1949. The central element is the subject's call to action, a decision to follow a course of action leading to success and recognition, followed by retirement. This pattern usually involves a mentor at the outset, to give advice on the challenges facing the hero, the assistance of an unlikely friend, antagonism usually in the shape of a person opposed to the hero's quest but also as obstacles to be overcome.

James Campbell came to this paradigm after analysing many fictional accounts of heroes from a wide range of cultures and was able to establish a series of elements in his study *The Hero of a Thousand Faces*. Campbell's structure corresponds closely to the phases (up to thirty-one) of the hero's adventure as proposed by Vladimir Propp in *The Morphology of the Folk Tale* (1928).

This narrative paradigm, whether consciously or not, is followed in many biographies. Biographers of course like to 'set the scene' and dwell on details of the subject's family and home, identifying the influential "environmental forces" on the development of the subject; for a writer this might be a relative with similar talents or a great teacher. At some point, biographers identify one moment in their subject's life, which sets

Table 1.2 Campbell's Narrative Structure: *The Hero of a Thousand Faces* (1949)

Hero's Journey

Departure
 1 The Call to Adventure
 2 Refusal of the Call
 3 Aid of a Mentor
 4 Crossing of the First Threshold
 5 Belly of the Whale

Initiation
 6 The Road of Trials
 7 The Meeting with the Goddess
 8 Woman as Temptress
 9 Atonement with the Father
10 Apotheosis
11 The Ultimate Boon

Return
12 Refusal of the Return
13 The Magic Flight
14 Rescue from Without
15 The Crossing of the Return Threshold
16 Master of Two Worlds
17 Freedom to Live

them off on their route to success (or failure or notoriety as the case may be), which Campbell identifies as the first stage of the hero's journey. Biographers then identify the assistance provided by some kind of friend. The second major phase of the subject's life concerns the hero's initial efforts and failures. Biographers like to portray "the trials of life and spiritual tussles" out of which, they claim, great writers are made. After these setbacks, doubts, and trials, the hero overcomes the difficulties and achieves his due success, before returning home to further acclaim. The death scene has held even more significance for biographers partly because there is usually some historical record alluding to the event, e.g. Marlowe's inquest, Shakespeare's will, but also so that the narrators can interpret their subject according to their own views.

While paradigms, such as those described by Campbell and by Propp, offer a strict coherence to a fictional narrative, they are not easy to impose on the lives of real people. First, great literary figures such as Charles Dickens show no sudden call to become a writer; rather, it is something instinctive which is recognised as a special quality at an early age. Second, there is rarely one single crowning moment when an artist such as Mozart or Michelangelo achieves their goals. Frequently they continue their work as an artist until their deaths. Third, there is a tendency among biographers of adopting a deterministic view of their subject, as one born to succeed. Michael Benton has been critical of following such a linear narrative: modern literary biography invariably adopts "a unidirectional, teleological reading of a literary life" (2009, 65).

It often seems that biographies are derivative. James Clifford's advice for would-be biographers is to read all accounts of the subject before embarking on fresh research (1970). The obvious danger is for successive biographers to be following an established narrative, merely offering minor variations. Any writer adopting Clifford's strategy would be influenced by previous biographies, which Glen Jeansonne (1989, 64) has called the "inertia of literary myth." Jeansonne extends this to readers and publishers who are only prepared to accept small changes to an established narrative (1989, 63–64). Similarly, David Gates in his *New York Times* review (3 November 2011) notes that "the recent biographies [of Dickens] are remixes of familiar episodes and anecdotes." Gates drew particular attention to an apparent meeting in 1862 between Dickens and Fyodor Dostoyevsky. In a letter, Dostoyevsky recalled their detailed conversations. The meeting was included by Malcolm Andrews in his study of Dickens (2006), by Michael Slater in his biography of Dickens (2009), and by Claire Tomalin in hers (2011). Gates's comments drew interest and criticism from various Russian experts who had never heard of the letters or ever suspected such an encounter. The letters had first come to academic attention in the west in a short article in the *Dickensian* by one Stephanie Harvey in 2002. Harvey quoted a Soviet scholar, K. K. Shaiakhmetov, who had apparently reported it in a Kazak journal *Vedomosti Akademii Nauk Kazakskoi SSR* (Alma Ata 1987)

'News of the Academy of Sciences of the Kazakh SSR'. Despite research in Moscow and Alma Aty, there was no record of any such journal, no record of an academic called Shaiakhmetov, and no record of the letters. The article was a hoax, apparently perpetrated by a male writer, A. D. Harvey, and its acceptance by such distinguished writers as Andrews, Slater, and Tomalin simply shows how derivative biographies can be.[6]

1.3 Types of Biographical Material

When talking about his editorship of the *DNB*, Sir Sidney Lee asserted that "the biographer begins his [*sic*] task by sorting heaps of written or printed papers, by exploring official records; by ransacking many a dark and dismal cavern of research." The biographer then has to "sift his sweepings" before giving "essential form" to his findings. Lee makes an important distinction: "Unlike the dramatist or the novelist, the biographer cannot invent incident to bring into relief his conceptions of the truth about the piece of humanity which he is studying" (1918, 8). This point was emphasised in a slightly different context by the German philologist, Paul Maas, who stated: "To present what is doubtful as certain is to remain further from the goal than if one were to confess one's doubt."[7] Modern readers have the same expectations, according to the biographer, Alan Shelston, who states that the research biographer inevitably takes as his standard 'truth of fact' (1977, 69). As we have seen, the editors of the *American National Biography* (1999) also made factual accuracy the highest priority of each entry. Philip Furbank agrees:

> [A] biography is expected to supply dates, information about family trees and about birth, marriage and death; a chronological progression; and various other practicalities. Readers and critics, further, tend to speak, in Boileauesque fashion,[8] as though there were 'rules' as to how a biography should be written.
>
> (Furbank 2000, 18)

Another biographer, Anne Chisholm, made a similar case for factual accuracy:

> The biographer can, and should, select and arrange the facts about the subject's life; but the facts themselves should be demonstrably true. No words or thoughts, motives or actions should be ascribed to the subject without evidence. The sources of the evidence should be clear and verifiable.
>
> (Chisholm 2001)

Without suitable and sufficient materials, any account of a subject's life results in "fictional biography" in which the author "relies on secondary sources and treats the life of the historical subject as a novelist would treat a character, adding and inventing as the author sees fit" (Clifford 1970, 84–87). The first step towards the preparation of any biography, therefore, is to review the biographical material to see if a biography is possible. The prolific biographer, André Maurois, recognised this in his 1928 *Aspects de la bibliographie* (Jack Kolbert, *The Worlds of André Maurois* 1985, 88–89). Only then would he undertake careful reading of the subject: sifting through archives, records, the subject's own notes and scribblings, and any manuscripts or unpublished works.

Such records are not equally valuable and David Schwalm, a specialist in life-writing then at UC Berkeley, drew up the following list in order of significance for the would-be biographer (1980, 26, n. 2):

i   autobiographical documents (e.g. letters, diaries, literary works);
ii   testimony of witnesses;
iii official documents (e.g. parish registers, county records, contracts);
iv   physical objects (e.g. clothes, furniture, residences, neighbourhoods, institutions);
v   images (e.g. contemporary portraits, photographs);
vi   biographer's first-hand experience of the subject, e.g. private interviews (unless deceased or unreachable).

Of these, autobiographical documents are thought to be the most valuable for imparting insight into a subject's character. Autobiographical documents are not always reliable: subjects may not be fully aware of their own motives and feelings, or they might be misrepresenting them. With regard to a writer's literary output, Wimsatt & Beardsley (1946) rejected any author's own testimony as reliably useful towards an understanding of their work. The second major source of material comprises testimony of witnesses: personal opinions about the subject (e.g. diaries, correspondence, and judgements) expressed by others. The biographer has to make similar judgements about their accuracy. It is not easy to decide how dependable such records are. Holmes notes that "memory is fallible, memoirs are inevitably biased; letters are always slanted towards their recipients; even private diaries and intimate journals have to be recognised as forms of self-invention" (1995, 17). Thus the biographer has to evaluate every detail in any diaries, correspondence, and personal opinions expressed by or about the subject.

The third major source of biographical evidence is found in public records and archives, e.g. births, marriages, deaths, contracts. Biographers trawl through such records and give a framework to the life. Some biographies only report the archival record and have been labelled by James Clifford as "objective biography" (1970, 84). Examples of this style, also known as the 'dossier' approach, include the 2001 biography of William Blake by G. E. Bentley Jr. However, no such biography can ever be completely objective, as biographers have to select, omit, and organise material about their subject for the biography. A fourth major area of biographical evidence concerns context, which includes physical objects (e.g. clothes, furniture, possessions) and physical remains (e.g. the house and locality where a subject grew up). Norma and June Buckley's 2010 *Walking with Wordsworth* proves very popular for those wishing to "follow in the Lakeland laureate's footsteps by the lakes and tarns, rivers and valleys he celebrated in verse." The biographer may broaden this to include institutions where the subject may have been education or worked. Schwalm puts images (e.g. portraits) into a fifth category, knowing that these were open to manipulation and mediation. Finally, he places the writer's first-hand knowledge of the subject, which he considers least reliable as the writer is likely to use a biography for partisan purposes.

Notes

1 John Dryden, ed. 1683–1686. *Plutarch's Lives.* 5 vols. Dryden's Life of Plutarch appears in volume 1, 1–126.
2 Dr. Johnson's comment appeared in *The Rambler* 60, 13 October 1750, 31 (reprinted in James Clifford, ed. 1962. *Biography as an Art: Selected Criticism 1560–1960*, 1962, 39–45).
3 Storr, Anthony. "Psychiatry and Literary Biography." In *The Art of Literary Biography*, ed. Peter Batchelor (1995) 73–80.
4 The term 'Rosebud Assumption' was used by Louis Menand, Professor of English and American Literature and Language at Harvard University in his review of three books about biography (*New Yorker*, 6 August 2007). In the 1941 classic film *Citizen Kane,* a young reporter sets out to find the significance of the subject's last word 'Rosebud', hoping to find a single explanation to understand a complex life.
5 The phrase has recently been used by Daniel Schreiber in his biography of Susan Sontag (2014).
6 Eric Naiman gives a detailed account of the hoax in 'When Dickens met Dostoyevsky' in the *TLS*, 10 April 2013.
7 Paul Maas, *Textual Criticism* (1958, translated from the second German edition of 1949 by Barbara Flower). Oxford: Clarendon Press, 17.
8 The French critic, Nicolas Boileau-Despréaux (1636–1711), tried to prescribe rigid rules for literary genres in the manner of the ancient writer, Longinus (Jules Brody, *Boileau and Longinus*. Geneva: E. Droz, 1958).

2   Gaps in Our Ignorance
The Biographical Material for William Shakespeare

Anyone with a normal threshold of evidentiary sufficiency will have to want very much to believe in order to find such a work [as a biography of Shakespeare] credible.

—David Schwalm (1980)

[There are] huge gaps in knowledge that make any biographical study of Shakespeare an exercise in speculation.

—Stephen Greenblatt (2004)

Is there enough biographical material for a coherent, narrative account of Shakespeare's life? Shakespeare's biographers accept that there are gaps but overall that there are sufficient contemporary records for a reconstruction of his life. Like many other biographers, Maguire and Smith (2012) state that "it is not true to say that the records are scant" (106). After a very brief review of what is known, they add: "We lack comparable information for many of Shakespeare's Elizabethan and Jacobean contemporaries" (107). This claim may be true, but biographers of Shakespeare are not attempting a series of life studies about "many" early modern dramatists or indeed about any other playwright, but one study of one particular writer. More general commentators, those who have studied the lives of writers more widely than just Shakespeare disagree with Maguire and Smith: Richard Altick in his review of English literary biography believes not, stating that the "available solid facts" would merely fill up a half dozen pages but "would tell us nothing of what we would most dearly wish to have information about, his character and personality" (1965, 15).

We need to assess the primary material for Shakespeare not just to its extent (as invariably happens) but more importantly as to its limitations. The material is mainly confined to his lifespan (1564–1616), but some consideration is given to allusions after this date. We can then consider different types of evidence concerning Shakespeare and what these records can indicate. Our search begins with Shakespeare in the Public Records (both in Stratford and in London), followed by allusions in literary and theatrical records, which concern performances and publication of Shakespeare's works in London. Finally, we can examine allusions to Shakespeare in print.

Until recently, scholars have referred to E. K. Chambers, *William Shakespeare: A Study of Facts and Problems* (1930), who discusses and evaluates the material in volume I, and presents transcriptions of most documents in an orderly manner in volume II. However, to commemorate Shakespeare's death, the year 2016 saw the launch of an exciting new online exhibition called Shakespeare Documented at www.shakespearedocumented.org. In general, this website provides immediate access to a wide range of documents. Most entries offer a diplomatic transcript of the document, usually after a reviewer's (personal) explanation of the record. That is to say, the reviewer gives the interpretation before the evidence. A second weakness in the design of the site is that many documents (as with Schoenbaum's *Documentary Life*) turn out to be contextual; they do not name William Shakespeare – instead they detail topics such as the family in Stratford or the theatres in London. Third, the actual contemporary handwritten records which directly and unambiguously reference the subject, about one hundred in total, must be accessed in a link 'Manuscript mention of Shakespeare in his lifetime'. The lack of an overall list of these documents prevents any easy examination of their date range. As websites can be ephemeral, I continue to refer to Chambers's two-volume study. Outline lists of the allusions are included in Appendix A.

2.1 Source Material for Shakespeare

Using the list drawn up by David Schwalm (1980, 26, n. 2), we can assess the source material for Shakespeare as follows.

(i) Autobiographical Documents, e.g. Letters, Diaries, and Literary Works

Autobiographical documents are the most important for understanding a subject's character and experiences. From study of intimate sources of biographical data, biographers attempt to explain motive and rationalise the subject's life decisions. For a life of Shakespeare, this is an insurmountable problem. He left no letters and no journals of his own, neither personal nor business; he expressed no opinions about anybody or anything, whether family members, neighbours, townsmen, business associates, colleagues, rivals, or patrons. Unlike Jonson, Shakespeare did not refer to himself explicitly in any of his works. Schoenbaum was well aware that this deficiency renders impossible any attempt to reconstruct Shakespeare's thoughts and motives: "What would we not give for a single personal letter, one page of diary!... A certain kind of literary biography, rich in detail about (in Yates's phrase) the momentary self, is clearly impossible" (1970, 767). To overcome this lack of personal account, biographers resort to making inferences from the works. Such inferences remain entirely subjective due to the lack of explicit testimony either from Shakespeare or from a close friend or family member.

There are some personal documents, but they are not particularly revealing. Two short dedications to the Earl of Southampton for the narrative poems in 1593 and 1594 appeared in print. These dedications use the form of self-abatement common at the time (as will be seen in Chapter 8). Shakespeare's final wishes were recorded in his will in 1616, in which he distributed his possessions, mainly to his daughter Susanna and her husband, Dr John Hall. He mentioned bequests to his wife, and to his second daughter, Judith. He leaves small bequests to various friends and acquaintances in Stratford: he left his sword to Thomas Combe; five pounds to Thomas Russell; £13 6s. 8d. to Francis Collins; 20s. in gold to his godson, William Walker; and 26s. 8d. each to Hamnet Sadler, William Reynolds, Anthony Nashe, and John Nashe, who were neighbours in Stratford. There is also an interlinear addition, in which he leaves "to my fellows John Hemings, Richard Burbage, and Henry Condell" 26s. 8d. to buy mourning rings.

The will indicates a man of considerable property, with specific intentions for its distribution. It makes no mention of anything literary: no books owned or borrowed; no manuscripts, not even a printed quarto of one of his plays. To overcome the lack of anything literary in the will, biographers resort to speculation, saying that he did not need to mention any books or manuscripts as they would have been listed separately (for which there is no evidence). Shakespeare asked for his soul to be commended to God and "my bodye to the earth whereof yt ys made." He left no provision for any monument. Bill Bryson sums up: "It cannot be emphasised too strenuously that there is nothing – not a scrap, not a mote – that gives any certain insight into Shakespeare's feelings or beliefs as a private person" (2007, 17).

There is one manuscript which is said to contain a section handwritten by Shakespeare. MS Harley 7368 consists of a play script entitled *The Book of Sir Thomas More*. The actions deals with the rise of Henry VIII's lawyer and his ultimate fall for refusing to recognise the religious supremacy of the King. About six different scribes have been identified, with marginal notes added by Edmund Tilney, Master of the Revels. One section, comprising 147 lines, has been assigned to a scribe known as Hand D, who is often claimed to be Shakespeare himself. This section depicts a scene in which More delivers a speech to quell a riotous group of citizens. The identification was first suggested in 1871 by Richard Simpson on the basis of spelling, vocabulary and ideas. Later, the handwriting was compared to Shakespeare's known signatures and pronounced to be Shakespeare's in studies published in 1923 and 1983.

The Arden Shakespeare issued an edition of the play, with Hand D attributed to Shakespeare in 2011.[1] Not everyone accepts the attribution. It was rejected by among others a handwriting expert, R. A. Hubler, in 1961 and by Carol Chillington, a historian of the Elizabethan theatre, in 1980. Most recently, Diana Price has reviewed the identification and noted among other points that no such play was ever attributed to Shakespeare; even if the style and content can be attributed to Shakespeare by matching similar passages in plays such as *Coriolanus*, the actual script may be the work of a copyist; finally that there is so little of Shakespeare's handwriting extant (merely six signatures dating from 1612 onwards), that there is not sufficient basis to make a meaningful comparison of the Hand.[2] Nevertheless, Hand D continues to be identified by some as Shakespeare's autograph.

(ii) Testimony of Witnesses

The second most informative material comes from the records of witnesses who recorded personal opinions about Shakespeare (e.g. in diaries, correspondence, and judgements). Only a small number of contemporary witnesses pay testimony to Shakespeare: firstly in 1598 one of his townsmen was in London in 1598 and hoped that Shakespeare would loan him £30. There are a few letters about this topic which are extant. A second document, dated 11 September 1611, contained a list of about seventy Stratford citizens who were prepared to promote a Bill in Parliament for highway repair; the name "Mr William Shackspere" seems to have been added in the right margin. Thirdly there was an issue about the proposed enclosure of lands around Stratford; one of his townsman, Thomas Greene, made notes and recorded his hopes that Shakespeare would oppose them. Shakespeare is named five times between January 1614 and September 1615. Greene makes the only record of a conversation between Shakespeare and anyone:

> [17 November, 1614]. my Cosen Shakspeare commyng yesterday to towne I went to see him howe he did. He told me that they assured him they ment to inclose noe further then to gospel bushe & so upp straight (leaving out part of the dyngles to the Field) to the gate in Clopton hedge & take in Salisburyes peece.
>
> (WS ii. 142–47)

The actual relationship implied by "cosen" is unclear. Although we know that Greene was in "towne," i.e. London, we do not know exactly where the two men met. The exchange sheds little or no light on Shakespeare's character, simply that he wished to protect his interests (Bearman 2016, 138–45). From these few witnesses, we only find out that Shakespeare was an affluent citizen of Stratford.

There are some references to Shakespeare as a member of the Chamberlain's Men: in March 1595, he received payment along with Kempe and Burbage for a performance at court in December 1594. However, the record does not state whether he was paid as an author, an actor, or as an officer of the company. Another reference of limited value is a 1602 diary anecdote, in which, John Manningham described how Shakespeare managed to secure the delights of a lady before the arrival of Richard Burbage (*WS* ii. 212). The brief account does not state when or where the incident took place and adds only a very little to the biographical knowledge of Shakespeare. Another instance of the name 'Shakespeare' handwritten in connection with some plays appears in unsigned jottings in the Northumberland Manuscript (1598–1603), attributed to the little-known Adam Dyrmonth. The scribblings suggest that Shakespeare was the author of *Richard II* and *Richard III* (which had already been published under the name of Shakespeare in 1598), but the scribbler makes no personal comments about the author.

A different category of witness involves printed allusions. Chambers lists fifty-three allusions to Shakespeare from 1590 to 1640 (*WS* ii. 186–237) but only eighteen of these allude to Shakespeare by name before 1616; many others refer to one of the poems or the plays. The earliest allusion in London is taken to be in Greene's pamphlet *Groats-Worth of Wit*, which was edited for publication by Henry Chettle after Greene's death in 1592. Greene warns others (playwrights?) to beware of 'those Puppets (I meane) that spake from our mouths, those Anticks garnisht in our colours', and continues:

> Yes, trust them not: for there is an vpstart Crow, beautified with our feathers, that with his *Tygers hart wrapt in a Players hyde,* supposes he is as well able to bombast out a blanke verse as the best of you: and being an absolute *Iohannes fac totum,* is in his owne conceit the onely Shake-scene in a countrey.
>
> Greene, *Groats-Worth of Wit,* 1592

Since 1787, many critics have followed Edmond Malone by interpreting Greene's warning as an accusation that Shakespeare was a plagiarist when revising the plays of others.

The reference to "shake-scene" is widely taken to indicate that Greene is referring to Shakespeare. The phrase "Tygers hart wrapt in a Players hyde" is a near quotation of a line from *The True Tragedy of Richard Duke of York* (published in 1595; the line also occurs in the expanded version *3 Henry VI* in the First Folio). This may even be an example of a lifted line which caused Greene to complain. So almost all authorities call this the earliest reference in print to Shakespeare as a playwright. Nevertheless, the allusion is ambiguous: the addressees are not named; the warnings are capable of many interpretations; the 'upstart crow' might allude to Shakespeare as an actor, as a playwright, or as a company member; or it might allude to someone else altogether. Even

Greene's authorship is in dispute: clearly, every printed document was mediated by the stationer and the typesetter; in this case, Greene's manuscript had also been mediated by Henry Chettle, who concedes:

> I had only in the copy this share; it was ill written, as sometime Greene's hand was none of the best. Licenced it must be ere it could be printed, which could never be if it might not be read. To be brief, I writ it over, and as near as I could, followed the copy...
>
> Henry Chettle, *Kind-harts Dreame,* December 1592

Chettle in his Address to the Gentleman Reader, prefaced to *Kind-harts Dreame* asserted that he did not wish to cause offence to some unnamed person who was known for his "uprightness of dealing,... honesty, and... facetious grace in writing." Some commentators believe that Chettle is accurately describing Shakespeare in such glowing terms (e.g. Schoenbaum 1987, 154–55; see Section 6.3). Of course, with Greene dead, *Groats-Worth* may even have been written by Chettle, according to Jowett ("Johannes Factotum" 1993). Lukas Erne (1991) argues that the upstart crow is not Shakespeare, while Vickers (2017) believes that Greene was simply repeating a criticism against actors who depended on playwrights while enjoying more prestige and greater financial reward.[3] Altogether, the allusions might or might not reference Shakespeare, they might or might not indicate that he was a plagiarist, and they might or might not suggest that he was a fine writer.

All the other allusions to Shakespeare in print occur after 1593 (e.g. *Willobie His Avisa,* 1594), when Shakespeare published the first of his narrative poems. The most important allusion was by Francis Meres (*Palladis Tamia* 1598), who named twelve plays of Shakespeare, which indicate that these plays were in existence (although *Love's Labour's Won* has not been identified with certainty). Meres compiled a balanced list of six comedies with six histories and tragedies; he did not produce a definitive list of all works composed by Shakespeare to date. Meres's favourite writer was Michael Drayton who is accorded five paragraphs and is mentioned twelve times. He seems only to be acquainted with Drayton's reputation ('...is helde for...'). He praises Shakespeare and mentions him nine times in three paragraphs but gives no personal information and does not even use his Christian name, unlike his reference to 'my friend master Richard Barnfielde'. Meres lists about seventy contemporary writers. So it is unlikely that he was personally acquainted with all of them during his residence in London. Meres does mention Shakespeare's 'sugred Sonnets among his priuate friends, &c', which were not published for another eleven years. But we hear nothing about who those friends were; nor do these unnamed friends ever report any Shakespeare sonnets in manuscript. Meres knew the name 'Shakespeare' in connection with a variety of genres but not any actual person who wrote them.[4]

In 1599, the poet John Weever, pays homage to "Honie-tong'd Shakespeare." Weever shows no special interest in, or knowledge of, Shakespeare as only one epigram out of 160 mentions him (1599, iv. 22) out of about 160. There are further impersonal references to an author called Shakespeare in *The Pilgrimage to Parnassus* and *The Return from Parnassus*, Parts I and 2 (1600–1601). Another mention, by Henry Chettle in *England's Mourning Garment* (1603) chides him as one of a number of poets who did not lament the death of Queen Elizabeth, another indication of absence, again as a famous author in print. Similar allusions to a published author were made by William Covell (1595), Richard Barnfield (1598), John Bodenham (1600), the otherwise unknown Anthony Scoloker (1604), William Camden (1605), John Davies (1610), John Webster (1612), Richard Carew (1614), Thomas Freeman (1614), Edmund Howes (1615), and Thomas Porter (1615). These allusions only confirm Shakespeare's reputation as an author in print, either as a published poet, or as a dramatist; they give no information about the man.

Although Jonson makes more comments about Shakespeare than any other writer does, he did not make any mention of Shakespeare before 1616. In his *Works,* he did not dedicate any of his 133 epigrams to Shakespeare, implying that they did not have any close relationship. Jonson's contradictory opinions – he was publicly fulsome in the First Folio (1623) but privately dismissive when conversing with Drummond in 1619 – are only documented after Shakespeare's death in 1616. Jonson's view of Shakespeare is considered in Chapter 9. Other writers of commendations, such as Digges, Mabbe, and Holland in the First Folio (1623), only offer conventional praise to Shakespeare as an author; few biographers claim they show any particular insights into the person.

(iii) Official Documents, e.g. Parish Registers, County Records, and Contracts

The third major source of biographical evidence is found in public records and archives, e.g. births, marriages, deaths, and contracts. Biographers investigate such records so as to give an objective framework to the life. There are various official documents which record Shakespeare's baptism, issue of a marriage license, property dealings, court cases, tax evasion, and burial. However, these extant records are mainly legal and public, giving some outline to his life. But they impart no insight into his personality or motives. These official records are considered in detail later in this chapter.

(iv) Physical Objects

Objects such as personal possessions, his house, and localities known to the subject have limited significance. Regarding actual objects, there is no surviving material for Shakespeare. None of Shakespeare's manuscripts, no books owned, no books borrowed, no clothes, no chairs rocking or otherwise, no beds, no cutlery, no crockery, and no mulberry trees have survived. The titles of two recent studies suggest that many of objects of Shakespeare have survived, but these are merely common objects from the early modern period, some of which are mentioned in the works. These objects do not relate to anything Shakespeare actually owned (Plates 2.1 and 2.2).[5]

Plate 2.1 Shakespeare's 'Birthplace' a Victorian Reconstruction.

Plate 2.2 Mason's Croft: an authentic medieval building in Rother Street Stratford-upon-Avon.

Regarding buildings, a late medieval house within a longer terrace on the north side of Henley Street has since the eighteenth century been associated with Shakespeare's birth. The 'Birthplace' was fully established as such in the nineteenth century when the owners came to sell. Following a public subscription, a pair of houses were purchased for the nation on 16 September 1847 (Thomas 2012, 60–90). In 1866, they were presented to Stratford Corporation.[6] Because Shakespeare is held in such high regard as a kind of 'secular deity', the cottage which was reconstructed in the Victorian period serves as a suitable place for Shakespeare lovers to commemorate him. Into the twenty-first century, the 'Birthplace' has been marketed in the following manner:

> William Shakespeare was born in this house and grew up here with his parents and siblings. He also spent the first five years of his marriage living here with his wife Anne Hathaway. John and Mary Shakespeare were wealthy enough to own the largest house on Henley Street. John Shakespeare lived and worked in this house for fifty years. When he married Mary Arden she came to live with him....
>
> Shakespeare Birthplace Trust website,
> accessed 3 June 2017

These statements are advanced with astonishing certainty, yet none can be supported with reference to contemporary documents. All claims that this building was actually the place where Shakespeare was born need to be treated with caution. First, any medieval timber-frame building has over the centuries undergone maintenance with regard to the fabric, some of which may have to be replaced at any time. The pair of houses in Henley Street was no exception. However, these houses were completely restored after their purchase in 1847 such that the 'Birthplace' is in fact a Victorian replica, with the clean, straight lines of machined wood.

By contrast, Mason's Court in nearby Rother Street dates to *c.* 1450 and retains its original curved beams and undulating roof. At most, the 'Birthplace' is a house on the site of a building where Shakespeare might have been born. Next, the adjoining houses were demolished in 1857 possibly due to fire risk (as Levi Fox reports), giving the detached buildings a more impressive aspect.[7] Most importantly, there is great uncertainty over the location of the Shakespeare family house as Sidney Lee reports:

> Some doubt is justifiable as to the ordinarily accepted scene of his birth. Of two adjoining houses forming a [now] detached building on the north side of Henley Street, that to the east was purchased by John Shakespeare in 1556, but there is no evidence that he owned or occupied the house to the west before 1575. Yet this western house

has been known since 1759 as the poet's birthplace, and a room on the first floor is claimed as that in which he was born.

Lee A Life of Shakespeare, 1899, 8

Chambers reviews the mention of properties in the Stratford records owned or leased by the Shakespeares (*WS* ii. 32–34). In 1552, William's father John was fined xij^d (along with Humphrey Reynold and Adrian Quiney) for leaving a *sterquinarium* (refuse heap) outside his property in Henley Street, without stating where this property was located. Two records in 1556 state that John Shakespeare bought the lease for a house in Greenhill Street and a lease for another house in Henley Street. This record does not confirm where exactly these houses were, whether the property in Henley Street was the same as the one he was occupying in 1552, or indeed if he ever lived in any of these properties. In 1575, John Shakespeare paid £40 for leasehold for two houses on Henley Street (identifiable from the 1590 Survey of the Possessions of the Earl of Warwick with those sold in 1847). In 1582, John let a house out to William Burbage, known from the court records of a dispute over the rent (1588–1592). So any house out of a number of properties might have been the family home in 1564: one in Greenhill Street, two or three in Henley Street, and possibly another in Henley Street which Burbage came to occupy (Thomas 2012, 60–95). As to the actual place of birth, there was no record: the family might have been living in any one of a number of properties in Stratford, which they owned or rented. Or his mother might have been staying at the Arden family farm at Wilmcote for her confinement. Or she might have gone into labour unexpectedly when visiting other people. Few of these possibilities are mentioned by biographers.

In 1597, Shakespeare bought a large house in Stratford known as New Place for £60, possibly because fire had damaged the family house(s) in Henley Street (Bearman 2016, 84). New Place was bequeathed to his daughter Susanna who in turn passed it on to her daughter Elizabeth. George Vertue made a drawing of it in 1737, showing an impressive gabled house. However, a later owner, the Reverend Francis Gastrell, demolished it in 1759 as he did not wish to pay the local taxes levied on town houses. Shakespeare also bought a property in London, the Blackfriars Gatehouse, which was purchased in 1613 and immediately mortgaged. This house was demolished in 1655, but would have burnt down in the Great Fire of 1666. It is not known whether Shakespeare bought the Blackfriars Gatehouse to live in or to rent out.

One building, which must have been known to Shakespeare is the Parish Church of the Holy Trinity. This impressive medieval stone church survives along with its register of baptisms, marriages, and burials. Within the church is a monument to Shakespeare. Another building to survive, but without any documented connection to Shakespeare is the

King's School at Stratford; but its records for the period do not survive. So there is no record that William or his brothers actually attended there. It lies very close to the site of New Place, which is assumed to be where Shakespeare was living until his death. In his will, Shakespeare makes no mention of the school.

(v) Images

While there is no certain likeness of Shakespeare, three representations have been "tacitly acknowledged" as accurate portraits. In the chancel of Holy Trinity Church at Stratford, there is a monument showing the bust of a man with an upturned moustache holding a pen in one hand and some paper in the other hand. There are no documents concerning its commission or construction. Whereas John Combe left £60 in his will for a "convenient tomb," Shakespeare left no instructions or money for any monument. This has led Bearman to suggest that the monument may have been commissioned after his death by the King's Men, perhaps when they visited Stratford in 1622 (2016, 173). Most commentators accept that the monument appears today much as it was in its original form. However, William Dugdale drew a very different portrait some-time between 1634 and 1649, depicting a thinner man with a downward moustache, with hands placed downwards on a woolsack a woolsack.[8] This sketch was copied into a more detailed engraving by Wenceslas Hollar (or his assistant R. Gaywood) for the image in the *Antiquities of Warwickshire Illustrated* (1656, 520). Strangely, the monument (in neither version) does not actually name William Shakespeare or give his dates. A Flemish engraver, Michael Vandergucht, copied Hollar's en-graving for Nicholas Rowe's edition of 1709. The difference in appear-ance might be explained, as C. C. Stopes notes, because many church monuments were defaced during the Civil War. Stopes adds that liter-ary tourists might have taken mementoes from the monument. She also mentions that in 1691, the chancel where the monument is located was repaired in 1691 (Plates 2.3–2.5).[9]

The monument was described by John Aubrey in the 1670s as de-picting Shakespeare in a "tawny satin doublet I think pinked and over that a black gowne like an undergraduates at Oxford."[10] This descrip-tion could apply equally to the Dugdale draming or to the present ap-pearance. However, Lewis Theobald in 1733 describes the monument as representing him with "a cushion spread before him with a pen in his right hand and his left rested on a Scrowl of paper" (1733, i. xi), the first written description which conforms to the modern appearance.

Almost all modern commentators follow E. K. Chambers who stated, without citing any evidence, that the monument was restored without change to its original form (*WS* ii. 183–85). Katherine Duncan-Jones in *Portraits of Shakespeare* rejects the Dugdale drawing and the Hollar

Plate 2.3 Hollar's Engraving of the Shakespeare's monument in Dugdale's
   Antiquities (1656).

engraving as authentic likenesses stating that Dugdale did not make the
sketch at Stratford until after it had been restored in 1649 and that both he
and Hollar made many mistakes in their portraits (2015, 35–38). Somewhat surprisingly, the sketch by Dugdale and its reproduction in 1656 are
absent from the National Portrait Gallery's expensive publication *Searching for Shakespeare* (2006). This omission was lamented by Peter Beal
in a letter to the *TLS* (16 June 2006). In reply, Jonathan Bate dismisses
Dugdale's drawings as "more or less worthless" (letter to the *TLS* 23 June
2006). However, Brian Vickers disagreed, noting that "when Dr. William
Thomas republished the *Antiquities* in 1730, having personally checked
all the church monuments represented, he found that only one of Dugdale's sketches needed correcting in its main detail" (Letter to the *TLS* 30
June 2006). Overall, it is quite possible that Dugdale made an accurate
sketch of the monument in its original form and that it was remodelled
into its present form, perhaps in the early part of the eighteenth century.
   A second portrait with some claim to authenticity occurs on the title page of the First Folio of 1623, a large engraving signed by Martin
Droeshout, who was then in his early twenties and unlikely ever to have met

Plate 2.4 Droeshout's Engraving: Title Page of First Folio (1623).

Shakespeare. It is said that there would have been enough people involved in the publication of the First Folio who would have known Shakespeare personally and would therefore require a reasonable likeness. This portrait has been heavily criticised on a number of counts and has been

Plate 2.5 Monument to Shakespeare: Holy Trinity Church, Stratford-upon-Avon.

dismissed as an unreliable representation of Shakespeare (Cooper 2006, 48).[11] Opposite this engraving in the preliminary matter to the first folio is a short poem by Ben Jonson in which he suggests that the "figure" was for (not of) Shakespeare and that the Reader should "look Not on his Picture, but his Book." The suggestion is that the portrait cannot capture the poet's wit, implying also that it is not a realistic likeness. It is not known if Droeshout used a source image for his engraving. Leah Marcus considers the portrait and Jonson's accompanying poem in about fifty pages (1988, 1–50) and finds the juxtaposition very strange. She concludes that the Droeshout portrait is an iconoclastic image that contradicts itself.

According to Cooper, the Chandos Portrait, acquired by the NPG when it was established in 1856, is the "the only portrait of Shakespeare that has a good claim to have been painted from life." Duncan-Jones agrees saying that it "is widely accepted as genuine" (2015, 75) due to its continuous documentation. However, the lengthy provenance was first asserted as a likeness of Shakespeare in 1719 (Malone 1790 i. ii. 126–7; Cooper 2006, 54). Another painting, the Cobbe Portrait, has recently been claimed by the Shakespeare Birthplace Trust as a likeness (Wells 2009). However, most scholars follow Tarnya Cooper, curator of sixteenth century portraits at the National Portrait Gallery, who believes this portrait is more likely to be a study of Sir Thomas Overbury (Higgins 2009; Duncan-Jones 2015, 109–14). Many other portraits have at times been claimed as likenesses of Shakespeare, among them the Grafton and the Sanders, but with no overall agreement. Thus, we have no reliable representation of Shakespeare's appearance.

(vi) Biographer's First-Hand Experience of the Subject

For Schwalm, this was the least trustworthy type of evidence. Malone lamented the fact that those who might have known Shakespeare or his family left no record of their acquaintance: Malone repeats a complaint that previous writers had missed the opportunity to interview surviving relatives of Shakespeare: "our poet's grand-daughter, Lady Barnard, who did not die till 1670. His sister, Joan Hart, was living in 1646; his eldest daughter, Susanna Hall, in 1649; and his second daughter, Judith Queeny, in 1662" (1821, ii. 7). Modern biographers believe Shakespeare speaks to them through the works, and hence feel qualified to describe his personality, feelings, and motives.

After listing various types of evidence which form biographical material, David Schwalm comments on the lack of biographical data regarding Shakespeare:

> A serious lack of information about a biographical subject (e. g., Shakespeare) makes it rather difficult for us to feel that the man has been accounted for, and biographies of such subjects can contain little but "must have's" and "probably's" based on virtually no hard evidence at all. Anyone with a normal threshold of evidentiary sufficiency will have to want very much to believe in order to find such a work credible.
>
> Schwalm, 1980, 27, n. 7

2.2 Public Records: Stratford-upon-Avon

About eighty handwritten records mention Shakespeare by name or refer unambiguously to him during his life time, with about thirty Stratford records held at the Shakespeare Centre Library and Archive at Stratford-upon-Avon (Bearman 1994).[12] Some documents relevant to William's life in Stratford are held at the Worcestershire Archives (concerning his marriage) and at The National Archives (property documents and will). The Parish Register at the Church of Holy Trinity in Stratford-upon-Avon contains entries regarding baptisms, marriages, and burials for the period from 1558 to 1600. They were written by just one scribe, probably the Vicar, Richard Byfield, acting in accordance with government instructions, probably about the period 1598–1600. All of the dates in the Register followed the Julian calendar (now referred to as Old Style) which remained in force in England until 1752. The baptism of "Guliemus Shakspere" was recorded on 26 April 1564. There is no record of the actual date of William's birth. Sidney Lee stated (without any supporting evidence) that it was common practice for infants to be baptised three days after birth (1925, 8). So it remains widely believed that William was born on 23 April, St. George's Day.

William is not mentioned again until he is aged eighteen. The Worcester Diocesan Register records the granting on 27 November 1582 of a marriage licence to "Willelmum Shaxpere et Annã Whateley de Temple Grafton." The next day a pledge for a surety was signed on behalf of a proposed marriage between "Willm Shagspere" and "Anne Hathwey of Stratford in the diocese of Worcester maiden" (*WS* ii. 41–42). Almost all biographers take these names as referring to the same man and the same woman. The next two records which mention William concern the births of his children: the Parish Register of Holy Trinity record the baptism of Susanna daughter of William Shakspere on 29 May 1583 and of Hamnet and Judith Shakspere on 2 February 1585 (*WS* ii. 2–3). On 11 August 1596, the Parish Register records the burial of "Hamnet filius William Shakspere" (*WS* ii. 4). There is no record of the cause of death and no further record concerning Hamnet.

From 1585 until 1598, there is no mention of a William Shakespeare (or variant on it) until 1598 when aged 33, he is listed among townsmen holding malt, in his case ten quarts (*WS* ii. 99–100). In 1595, the Privy Council had ordered the Justices to regulate the trade of corn and require excessive stocks to be sold. Shakespeare's name did not appear on an earlier list of corn-holders (7 December 1595), possibly because he was not a householder until he bought New Place in 1597. As Shakespeare became one of the more affluent citizens, he and his family were able to store a reasonable amount of malt during a time of shortage. Not all biographers accept that his holding was excessive enough to constitute "hoarding."

There are no extant letters by Shakespeare to any recipient. The only extant letter to Shakespeare concern business in the correspondence of Richard Quiney dating to 1598–1599 (*WS* ii. 100–3). Quiney received two letters from Abraham Sturley suggesting that "Mr Shaksper" / "Mr Wm Shak," then in London be approached for the loan. Quiney duly wrote a letter requesting £30 for an unspecified cause. As the letter was found among Quiney's possessions in Stratford, it seems that it was not delivered – although of course the extant letter may have been returned or it may have been a draft.

William Shakespeare acquired various properties in Stratford. Two documents – recording his purchase of New Place in 1597 for £60 (*WS* ii. 95–97), and 107 acres of arable land and 20 acres of pasture at Old Stratford in 1602 at a cost of £320 (*WS* ii. 107–111) – were drawn up in London. In 1602, he also bought a cottage in Chapel Lane in 1602, close to New Place (*WS* ii. 111–12). This cottage oddly pertained to Rowington Manor, and may explain why a 'William Shakespere' appeared as a landholder in the records for Rowington Manor in 1605. According to the will, his daughter Judith had to surrender any claim to the Chapel Lane property to her sister (*WS* ii. 175). In 1605, William is recorded as purchasing a half-interest in a lease of "Tithe Lands in Stratforde vpon Avon, Olde Stratforde, Welcombe and Bushupton" from Ralph Hubaud for £440 (*WS* ii. 118–22). This acquisition of property show that Shakespeare a fairly affluent citizen, giving him an annual income of perhaps £100 (according to Bearman, 2016).

Shakespeare appears in a few petty court cases in Stratford. The earliest was in 1604, when he sued the apothecary Philip Rogers for 35s.10d. plus 10 shillings damages; four years later, he is mentioned eight times in seven documents when he sued John Addenbrooke for the small debt of £6 (*WS* ii. 113–18), in a case which dragged on for almost a year. In 1611, Shakespeare and others went to court to try to make William Combe pay more for the rents attached to the Stratford tithes (*WS* ii. 122–27). A kinsman of William Combe, John Combe, left Shakespeare £5 in his will in 1613. Shakespeare in turn bequeathed his sword to another member of the family, Thomas Combe (*WS* ii. 127–41).

In 1611, Shakespeare seems to have made a late contribution towards promoting a Bill in Parliament for the improvement of highways around Stratford as his name is added in the right hand margin to a list of contributors. It is not known how much (if anything) he contributed.

William Shakespeare was buried at the Holy Trinity Church on 25 April 1616, having died on or about his 52nd birthday (*WS* ii. 8). There is no record of the cause of death. Two tributes to him can be found in the Holy Trinity Church at Stratford, first noted by Dugdale in a visit of 1634 and published in 1656.[13] The main tribute occurs on the wall of the chancel:

Judicio Pylium, genio Socratem, arte Maronem
Terra tegit, populus maeret, Olympus habet.

[A Pylian in judgement, a Socrates in genius, a Maro in art, The earth buries him, the people mourn him, Olympus has him.]

Stay, passenger, why goest thou by so fast?
Read if thou canst, whom envious Death hath placed
Within this monument Shakespeare: with whom
Quick Nature dide; whose name doth deck his tomb
Far more than cost; sith all he had writ
Leaves living art but page to serve his wit.
                              Obiit ano doi 1616. Aetatis 53. Die 23 Ap

[He died in the year of our Lord 1616, in his 53rd year, on 23 April.]
    Neither tribute indicates any literary activities. Dugdale also mentioned that "neare the wall where this monument is erected lyeth a plaine free stone underneath which his body is buried, with this epitaph."

Good friend for Jesus sake forbeare,
To dig the dust enclosed here.
Blessed be the man that spares these stones,
And cursed be he that moves my bones.

In his will, Shakespeare gave detailed instructions as to his final wishes (*WS* ii. 169–81). The first page was dated March 1616; pages 2 and 3 were dated January 1616. It is thought that he may have decided to amend his will after the marriage of his younger daughter, Judith, to Thomas Quiney in February 1616. Each page is signed "William Shakespeare" though not in a consistent manner, suggesting that at least one signature was made by a legal clerk. The bulk of Shakespeare's bequests went to his eldest daughter, entailed to her eldest male heir. His younger daughter was to receive £150 on certain conditions. His sister Joan and her three sons were remembered in the will. A variety of small bequests were made to ten other people. In an interlinear addition, he left his wife "my second best bed with the furniture." In another interlinear addition, he assigned xxvis. viijd. each to "to my ffellowes John Hemynges, Richard Burbage and Henry Cundell xxvis. viijd. A peece to buy them Ringes." The will was probated in London on 22 June 1616. It is often stated that there would have been an inventory of his goods, presumed to include manuscripts and books, which would have been lost in the Great Fire of London 1666, but there is no mention of any such inventory.
    Other records show that his wife, Anne, died in 1623 at the age of 67, which would have made her about eight years older than her husband.

Their elder daughter, Susanna, married Dr John Hall in 1607 and died in 1649, aged 66. Their younger daughter, Judith, married Thomas Queeny in 1616 and died in 1662, aged 74. Susanna's daughter, Elizabeth, was born in 1608 and was married twice, first to Thomas Nashe in 1626 (who died in 1647) and second to Sir John Barnard in 1649. She died without issue in 1670 aged 62 (*WS* ii. 4–13). Malone reports that another, Thomas Hart, sixth in descent from Shakespeare's sister Joan, was still living in Henley Street in 1788 (1790, i. ii. 180, n. 5) (Table 2.1).

The major gap in the records at Stratford concerning William Shakespeare, which precludes the possibility of writing a coherent narrative account of his life, is the absence of any record from his baptism until the issue of a marriage licence in 1582. There is no confirmation that he was even in Stratford at any time during his infancy, childhood or youth. Thus any comments about Shakespeare's childhood, youth, and education are speculative. Most writers believe that he lived a normal life in Stratford, studied at the local grammar school and was inspired by the visits of travelling players, either at Stratford or at Kenilworth. None of these assumptions is documented. It has been argued by Gray (1926) and by Honigmann (1985) that Shakespeare did not spend his childhood entirely at Stratford.

In fact, for the first thirty years of his life, only five records in the midlands actually mention William by name. After his baptism, he is mentioned in the Worcester marriage records (1582), and then twice in the Stratford Parish records as the father of children (born in 1583 and 1585). His place of birth is a fiction, since there is no record where it took place and the family home at the time cannot be established with any exactitude. Another fiction concerns his possible education at the King's School. There are no records for the period and so no confirmation that Shakespeare attended this school (or any other school) or what he might have studied there if he did. Any comments about Shakespeare's

Table 2.1 Years when There Are Documented References to William Shakespeare in Warwickshire 1564–1616

1564	-	-	-	1604	1614
-	-	1585	-	1605	1615
-	-	-	1596	1606	1616
-	-	-	1597	-	-
-	-	-	1598	1608	-
-	-	-	-	1609	-
-	-	-	-	-	-
-	-	-	1601	1611	-
-	1582	-	1602	1612	-
-	1583	-	-	1613	-

education depends on contextual inference of the kind performed by T. W. Baldwin in *William Shakespere's Small Latine and Lesse Greeke* (1944). Baldwin gathers an enormous range of information about school education in England during the Tudor period and generalises into a kind of National Curriculum, as if this was being uniformly followed throughout England. Many of the documents cited by Baldwin indicate aspirations – what it would be good for students to learn – rather than a reflection of what they were actually learning. Jonathan Bate in *The Genius of Shakespeare* then makes the connection with a passage from the plays as follows:

> The lesson of Sir Hugh Evans in *Merry Wives* is based on the standard school text of the period. It is all the evidence we need that William Shakespeare attended the King's Free School of Stratford-upon-Avon.
>
> Bate *Genius of Shakespeare* 1997, 8

The school text was William Lily's *Lily's Grammar of Latin in English* which was authorised in 1542 for the teaching of Latin in England. The passage from the play merely shows that the author had experience of a Latin teacher, not how, where or when he gained such experience. Many other commentators have made the same leap of faith as Jonathan Bate.

There are two further obstacles against constructing a life of Shakespeare: the lack of any contemporary reference in Stratford to William Shakespeare as a man; no personal letters to or from him, and none concerning his family or friends. Thus it is not known in which years he was in Stratford, when he left, how often he visited or for how long. Nor is it known whether his wife and children ever accompanied him to London; it is usually assumed that they did not, but J. Q. Adams thinks they did (1923), a tenable view. It is not known whether he was present at the death or burial of his son (died 1596), or of his father (died 1601) or of his mother (died 1608) or whether their funerals were conducted according to the Catholic or Protestant rite.

The third gap in the Stratford records is the lack of any reference to him as a writer. The epitaphs in the Holy Trinity Church do not mention him as such and the earliest depictions of the monument (1634, 1656, and 1709) show the subject holding a woolsack, not a pen. Shakespeare does not claim to be a writer in his will and mentions nothing literary by way of his manuscripts of eighteen or so unpublished plays, any books owned or borrowed or any reference to any other literary figure. He did not remember the King's School in his will. In all, there are only passing references to him by his fellow townsmen concerning finance and property: a possible loan, the improvement of the highway, and the possible enclosure of land.

Most biographers fill these gaps with unfounded assertions about his family life, his youthful experiences, and his education. Discussion then develops about topics such as whether he was born or died on St George's Day, whether he only conformed outwardly to the Church of England, and how he came to leave his wife only his "second best bed." There is little attempt to explain how he came to finance the purchase of New Place (£60), the land at Old Stratford (£320), and the share in the tithes (£440). Overall the documents in Stratford only indicate William Shakespeare's growing prosperity and his standing as an affluent citizen of Stratford. They give no indication of his thoughts, experiences, motives, or literary activities.

2.3 Public Records: London

The Public Records in London which concern William Shakespeare show his avoidance of small tax payments and involvement in minor court cases (including being bound over to keep the peace). There are about thirty-five handwritten documents mentioning William Shakespeare at The National Archives in Kew, London, reviewed by David Thomas (1964).

The earliest allusion to William Shakespeare in London occurred in 1588–1589, in a complicated legal suit heard at the Queen's Bench (*WS* ii. 35–41). William is mentioned in a case against John Lambert signifying that he was the legal heir to the plaintiffs. The allusion does not constitute evidence as to his location at the time. The next mention of William Shakespeare in public records in London occurred in the Langley Writ of 1596 when William Wayte took a case to the Judge of Queen's Bench saying that he feared for his life from William Shakspere, Francis Langley, and two women. The magistrate ordered the Sheriff of Surrey to produce the accused "who had to post bond to keep the peace, on pain of forfeiting the security." The document, discovered and published by Leslie Hotson in 1931, is the most recently discovered document bearing Shakespeare's name which actually adds to our knowledge of Shakespeare. This case suggests that Shakespeare and Langley were involved in violence and possibly extortion, but is usually overlooked by commentators. Five documents in London state that Shakespeare was a defaulter on tax, providing evidence as to where he was living in the parish of St. Helen's, Bishopsgate in 1597–1598, and on Bankside 1599–1600 (*WS* ii. 87–90)

Shakespeare's name does not appear in any other ward apart from Bishopsgate. After 1600, Shakespeare has not been traced on any further subsidy rolls (whether in London, Surrey, or Stratford) and there is no record of any tax payment by him in the Royal Household, for which he was a minor officer from 1603.

Three records in London confirm his purchase of property in Stratford: New Place in Stratford for £60 in 1597 (*WS* ii. 95–9); 107 acres of arable land and 20 acres of pasture in Old Stratford for £320 in 1602 (*WS* ii. 107–11); a share in the Blackfriars Gatehouse for £140 in 1613 (*WS* ii. 154–68). These documents contain two of the six known Shakespeare signatures to survive. The documents concerning Shakespeare's tax avoidance are puzzling as to why he should put his liberty at risk for so small an amount of tax (less than a pound) in 1597 when he was paying £60 for New Place in Stratford and helping to set up the Chamberlain's Men at the Globe in 1599. In 1596, John Shakespeare applied for a coat of arms and a record documents his career in Stratford and his family background, but add no knowledge about William's career. Two later documents from 1602 concern a complaint against Sir William Dethick, the Garter King-of-Arms, and his associate William Camden (Clarenceux King-of-Arms). In this complaint, William is described as "ye player," not as a poet or playwright (*WS* ii. 18–31).

In May 1603, a royal warrant followed by letters patent authorised "our Servauntes Lawrence Fletcher, William Shakespeare, Richard Burbage, Augstyne Philippes, Iohn Heninges, Henrie Condell, William Sly, Robert Armyn, Richard Cowly" to establish the King's Men. In March 1604, the Account Book of Master of the Wardrobe recorded issuing four yards of scarlet-red cloth to members of the King's Men including Shakespeare. Another record confirms payment in August 1604 for the King's Men to attend the Spanish delegation at Somerset House, but Shakespeare is not specified. In 1605, Augustine Phillips left money in varying amounts to his colleagues, including 30*s*. in gold 'to my ffellowe william Shakespeare' in his will, but this confirms nothing about Shakespeare's whereabouts or activities at the time.

There is a gap from 1604 until 1612, when Shakespeare's name next appears in contemporary public records in London. For the lawsuit Bellott v Mountjoy, held in 1612, Shakespeare was called as a witness to certain dowry arrangements. His name occurs eighteen times (*WS* ii. 90–95). The relevant documents were discovered by Charles Wallace in 1909–1910 and have been represented and contextualised by Charles Nicholl (2007). These Bellott v Mountjoy documents contain one of the six known Shakespeare signatures to survive. These signatures vary so much as to suggest that he was in failing health, e.g. he may have suffered a stroke; a few people suggest that the signatures may have been made by legal officers. However, these twenty-five documents add little to his biographical materials. He was described as "William Shakespeare of Stratford vpon Aven in the Countye of Warwicke gentleman of the age of xlviij [aged 48]" – this much was already known. The Mountjoy's maid, Johane Johnsone, affirmed that Shakespeare "laye in the house" in Silver Street, near Cripplegate, about ten years previously – a new item of information. Neither the exact date nor the duration of Shakespeare's stay with the Mountjoys was recorded. In his deposition, Shakespeare was unable to provide any information to help settle the case. This is the only occasion when Shakespeare can be unquestionably located to any particular place on any particular day in his entire life: he made his deposition on 11 May 1612 in Westminster Hall. The records of the Bellott-Mountjoy case add little to the biographical material and are treated sparingly by biographers.

2.4 Literary and Theatrical Records 1593–1623

The literary and theatrical records which concern Shakespeare as an author, actor or sharer and/or his works derive from the Stationers' Register (SR), the Revels Accounts, Henslowe's Diary, and various court records. The title pages of plays convey much information about a range of topics: the playing company, occasionally venue(s) of performance, the author's name (increasingly during the 1590s), and the place, date, and printer of the work. The title pages of Shakespeare's plays do not reveal when a play was composed and (unlike Jonson's *Works* 1616) do not indicate when it was first performed. Printed records, such as title pages and allusions to Shakespeare, are not strictly primary sources as to some extent they have been mediated.

The name "William Shakespeare" is first associated as the author of a literary work with the publication of the narrative poem *Venus & Adonis* in 1593. The name does not appear on the title page but below a dedication to the Earl of Southampton. The same arrangement occurs the following year with the publication of *Lucrece* and is repeated in them many subsequent editions. In 1609, a collection of 154 sonnets was published entitled *Shake-spears Sonnets*. Between 1594 and 1600, at least nine plays were published anonymously that were subsequently attributed to Shakespeare. The name "William Shake-speare" (or a variant spelling) appears on the title page of a play for the first time in 1598 for reprints of *Richard II* and *Richard III* and for the earliest known version of *Love's Labour's Lost*. His name appeared on the title pages of thirteen different plays published in his lifetime. See Appendix A for a brief outline of Shakespeare's printed works 1591–1623.

Henslowe's Diary is a document of great importance for the early modern theatre but sheds little or no light on Shakespeare's career. The theatre owner, Philip Henslowe, kept a notebook from 1591 to 1609 in which he recorded payments to playwrights, actors, costume makers, carpenters, and the Master of Revels. He mentions 27 playwrights but never Shakespeare. He records payment for many plays but never for any Shakespearean titles. He cites 280 plays including seven or eight with Shakespearean titles: *Henry VI* (performed in 1592–1593, taken to be *Henry VI* Part 1), *Titus Andronicus* (1593–1594), and *The Taming of a Shrew* (1594) are usually taken to be Shakespeare's. Those which are thought to be by other authors include: *King Lear* performed in 1594, which is usually identified as the anonymous *King Leir* published in 1605; *The Mawe* (*Moor?*) in 1594–1595 (not usually identified as *Othello*), *Hamlet* (1594), *Henry V* (1595–1596), and *Troilus & Cressida* (1598). Henslowe's Diary reveals virtually nothing about Shakespeare.

The limited literary and theatrical records for Shakespeare leave many unanswered questions. First, it is not clear whether Shakespeare retained ownership of his plays and authorised their publication. The standard view that manuscript playbooks were owned by the company, under licence from the Master of the Revels, and that Shakespeare was indifferent to the printing of his plays has been called into question by Peter Blayney (1997) and Andrew Gurr (2009). Second, there is dispute over whether some anonymous plays were composed by Shakespeare, e.g. *The Taming of a Shrew* (1594). The majority view remains that these plays were by other playwrights and that Shakespeare revised them, but Lukas Erne has argued that the shorter versions were composed by Shakespeare for the stage and then revised into longer versions for publication and private study (*Shakespeare as a Literary Dramatist* 2003). Third, it is not known whether Shakespeare colluded over the pseudonymous use of his name on various title pages: *The Passionate Pilgrim* (1599); *Sir John Old-Castle* (anon in 1600; "by William Shakespeare" in 1619); *The London Prodigal* ("By W. Shakespeare" in 1605); *A Yorkshire Tragedy* ("by VV. Shakspeare" in 1608 and 1619); and *Troublesome Raigne of King John* (anon. in 1590; by W. Sh. In 1611; by "W. Shakespeare" in 1622).

A frequent assumption is that Shakespeare was the in-house playwright for the Chamberlain's Men and then for the King's Men. Against this view it should be noted that Shakespeare's plays are not particularly evident in public performances (as reported by Chambers 1930 and more fully by Andrew Gurr, *The Shakespeare Company* 2004). Only eight or nine of the plays in the First Folio are reported to have been acted at The Globe by the time of Shakespeare's death in 1616. The most famous performance was of *Richard II* in 1601.[14] In 1609, three plays which appeared in quarto stated on the title page that the play had been performed at the Globe: *Romeo & Juliet*, *Pericles*, and *Troilus & Cressida*. Three other plays were witnessed at The Globe in 1610/11 by Simon Forman as noted in his diary: *Macbeth*, *A Winter's Tale* and *Cymbeline*. There are also accounts that *Henry VIII* was in performance when The Globe burnt down in 1613.

Another concern is whether Shakespeare was writing for the general public at the Theatre and at the Globe, as is generally believed, or whether his plays were intended for the more sophisticated audience at court as argued by Alvin Kernan in *Shakespeare, the King's Playwright* (1995) and by Richard Dutton *Shakespeare, Court Dramatist* (2016), among others. Gurr notes that the main duty of the Chamberlain's / King's Men was to provide the royal court with dramatic entertainment. However, the records of performance at court are patchy. There is one record of a payment to three members of the company, Shakespeare, Burbage, and Kempe, on 15 March 1595 for two performances at court on 26 and 27 of December 1594 (*WS* ii. 319). In all, the Chamberlain's Men performed on 33 occasions at Court in the period 1594–1603. However, there is no clue as to the identity of any plays. When the players were incorporated as the King's Men, 28 plays performed between 1603 and 1616 have been named but less than half (12 or 13) can be identified with plays of Shakespeare. Although more of Shakespeare's plays are known to have been performed at court, the combined records (Revels' accounts, SR, title pages, Forman's diary, and witnesses to *Henry VIII* until 1616) mention performances of about 20 of the 36 plays from the First Folio, out of over 200 named plays, i.e. just 10% of the repertoire of the King's Men consisted of plays by Shakespeare.

Shakespeare's role as a sharer in the Globe from 1599 is more fully documented from legal records. The original deed of 1599 was amended in 1601, 1608, and 1615 (Gurr 2004). The court record of Ostler v Heminges (1615) records details about the sharers' interests in the Globe. According to the suit of Witter v Heminges and Condell (1619), Shakespeare was among the founders of the Blackfriars Theatre from its inception in 1608. This is the only record to suggest he was in London between 1604 and 1612. Because Shakespeare does not mention any shares in his will, it is assumed that he had sold them by 1610 (*WS* ii. 64–65), but there is no record. His income from the Globe has been estimated at £40 p.a. over a decade, and from the Blackfriars Theatre for two or three years at £80–£90 (Thomas 1964, 17). Andrew Gurr (2004) believes that in a good year when the London theatres were open, Shakespeare as a sharer stood to earn about £200 p.a.

No date of composition for any play of Shakespeare can be established with certainty from the extant sources. The surviving evidence is fragmentary and refers only to performance and publication. The Stationers' Register records the right of a stationer to publish a particular work, but there is no suggestion as to the time lapse between composition and publication: *Two Gentlemen of Verona* is usually dated to the early 1590s and was mentioned by Meres in 1598 but does not appear in the SR until 1623, a lapse of thirty years. Allusions to plays in performance offer no information as to date of composition. A further complication arises: mention of a play in performance does not guarantee which text was used, or sometimes even whether the play was Shakespeare's. There is a description in *Gesta Grayorum*, printed in 1688, of a performance of a play at Gray's Inn on Innocents' Day, 28 December 1594. Some find the description as an "unmistakeable" allusion to Shakespeare's *The Comedy of Errors* but the text used that evening may have been different from the text published in the First Folio nearly thirty years later. It is also possible that the "company of base and common fellows" who performed at Gray's Inn used another text by another playwright altogether.

The question of revision is another insoluble problem regarding Shakespeare's plays. We do not know if he revised them or to what extent. Chambers expressed the standard view that Shakespeare composed a 'once-and-for-all' version of each play. For example, Chambers takes Q2 *Hamlet* as the base text with some additions from F1, dismissing Q1 *Hamlet* as a "bad quarto" (*WS* i. 412). Chambers then dismisses references to a *Hamlet* play in 1589, 1594, and 1596 as a different play by another author (the Ur-*Hamlet* hypothesis). The single-text hypothesis was called into question by Wells & Taylor who were allowed by the Oxford University Press to present *King Lear* in two versions (one based on the 1608 Pied Bull quarto and the other on the somewhat different F1 text). Further challenges to the 'bad quarto' label have been made by Laurie Maguire (1996) and most recently about the validity of Q1 *Hamlet* by Margrethe Jolly (2014). Ann Thompson and Neil Taylor note in their Arden[3] edition of *Hamlet* (2006) the possibility that Shakespeare wrote an early version of *Hamlet* (c.1589) published as Q1, revised his own play into Q2 and again into the F1 version (2006, 44–46). If so, we should talk about nine dates for *Hamlet*, the three texts of *Hamlet* each capable of being dated separately for composition, first performance and publication.

Without any precise references, there is no possibility of a reliable chronology of the plays. Malone's *Attempt to Ascertain the Order* was only put forward (in 1778, 1790, and 1821) with considerable doubts, as we shall see in Section 4.1 below. The problem of chronology was then considered at length by Chambers with great caution (*WS* i. 243–275). However, his sequence was accepted without question by Schoenbaum (1975), and is followed by Wells & Taylor (1986) and by Wiggins (2012–5) as can be seen in Table 2.1. The structure posits that Shakespeare began writing in the early 1590s, publishing two narrative poems in 1593 and 1594. His plays were published from 1594 anonymously but from 1598 attributively. However, neither the date nor the title, not even the genre, of Shakespeare's earliest play is known. Against this 'late-starter theory' which suggests that Shakespeare did not begin writing plays until he was in his later twenties, an 'early-starter theory' dating the first plays to *c.* 1587–1588 has been argued in detail by Honigmann (1982, 88–90) and by Duncan-Jones (2001, 31–50). Both interpretations are feasible on the very limited records available. However, without firm dates it is impossible to trace the development of Shakespeare's dramatic art or to link any of the plays into his personal life. Any attempt such as Edward Dowden's *Shakespeare: A Critical Study of His Mind and Art* (1875) amounts merely to impressionistic criticism. It is therefore astonishing that Chambers, after his earlier caution, deals with the plays in his supposed order in which they were written (*WS* i. 275–499) and that Wells & Taylor should believe themselves able to determine their order of composition (1986).

The nature and extent of Shakespeare's collaboration with other playwrights is unclear. Following stylistic studies by Brian Vickers (2002), it is now generally accepted that two authors worked on different parts of a play such as *Henry VIII*. Their actual working practices remain unknown. With modern co-authors such as Antony Jay and Jonathan Lynn (*Yes, Minister*) or Richard Curtis and Ben Elton (*Blackadder goes forth*), etc., it is impossible for an outsider to determine which writer composed which parts: both sets of partners worked together. In the case of Shakespeare's co-authorship, however, it seems that whole sections of co-authored plays are sufficiently different to suggest that each part was composed separately. But whether the authors were working in different parts of the same room or in different places at the same time or even at different times is impossible to determine. It is plausible to argue that Shakespeare revised some shorter plays, e.g. a version of *Titus Andronicus* perhaps by George Peele, or that a short play of Shakespeare's, e.g. *Pericles*, was later expanded by another writer such as George Wilkins. For the moment, we do not know how co-authorship worked. (See Appendix D for possible scenarios.)

Another concern is with the reliability of information printed on title pages. The name of the playing company or companies is usually taken to indicate that the company mentioned had held ownership of a particular play but it might just be an indication that the play had been licensed for their performance by the Master of the Revels (Edmund Tilney from 1579 to 1610). Thus the mention of a playing company might be a fictitious claim by the stationer so as to circumvent licensing laws. Apart from the misattributions of *The London Prodigall* and *A Yorkshire Tragedy,* some title pages state that a play had been "newly corrected" which is occasionally correct: the title page of *Hamlet* (Q2, 1604–1605) states that it was "Newly imprinted and enlarged to almost as much againe as it was" which is correct when compared to the much shorter Q1 of 1603. However, "newly corrected" is used more often as an empty formula, frequently reprinted from a previous edition. Thus, the third edition of *Hamlet* (Q3, 1611) merely repeats the title page and the "newly corrected" formula when it has the same text as Q2. The Q5 edition in 1615 likewise repeats this claim without any changes to the text. In short, we have no idea about Shakespeare's working practices as a playwright. Such information would only come from personal papers by or about him, but these are missing.

From the issuing of cloth in 1604 until the Bellott-Mountjoy case in 1612, there is no record which actually locates Shakespeare in London, i.e. there is another period of lost years (Table 2.2).

A 1606 record of the Exchequer merely lists Shakespeare as a property holder in Stratford, while the Suit of John Witter v. Heminges and Condell (1619) refers to "Willelmo Shakespeare" as one of original shareholders of the Blackfriars Theatre, which from other documents

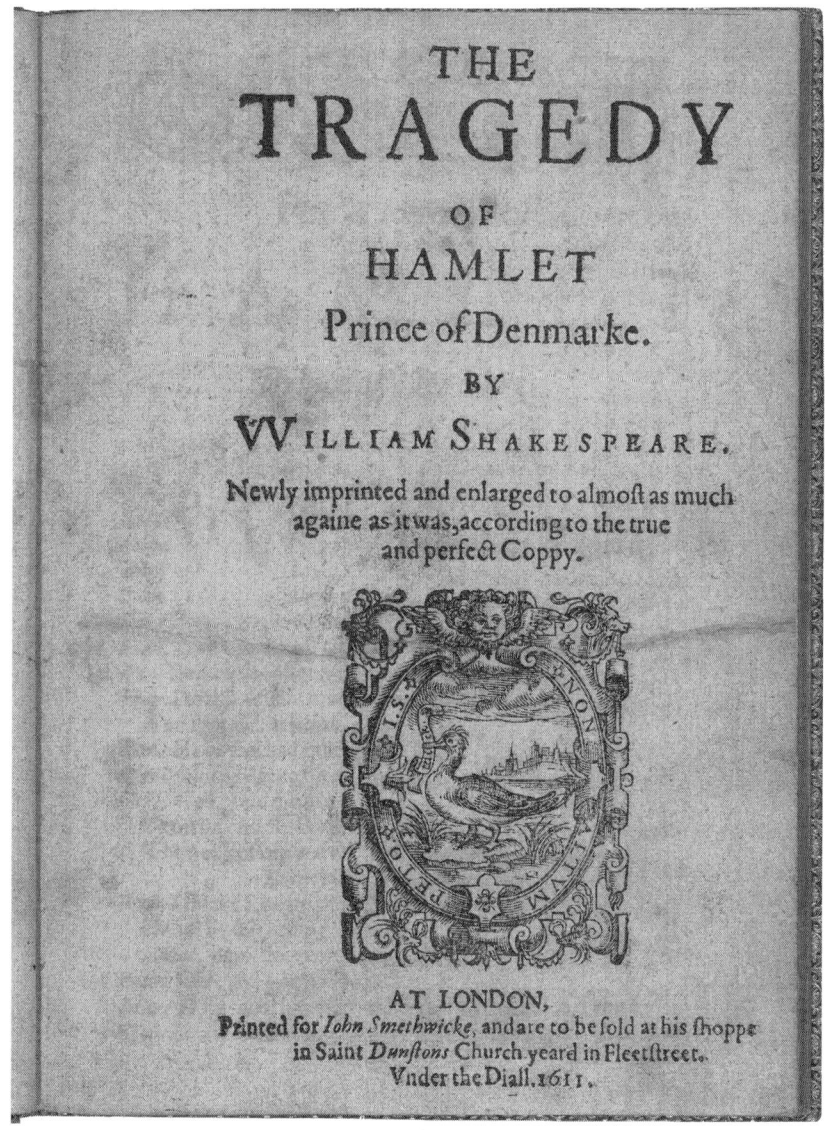

THE
TRAGEDY
OF
HAMLET
Prince of Denmarke.

BY

WILLIAM SHAKESPEARE.

Newly imprinted and enlarged to almoſt as much
againe as it was, according to the true
and perfect Coppy.

AT LONDON,
Printed for *Iohn Smethwicke*, and are to be ſold at his ſhoppe
in Saint *Dunſtons* Church yeard in Fleetſtreet.
Vnder the Diall. 1611.

Plate 2.6 The title page of *Hamlet* (1611) misleadingly claims that it is newly imprinted and enlarged to almost as much again. In fact, the text is identical to the 1604 edition (Q2).

can be dated to 1608. The court record does not confirm Shakespeare's actual presence in London. A 1610 record simply confirms his purchase of land from William and John Combe eight years earlier. During this period, Shakespeare is usually shown as at the peak of his powers and enjoying considerable success. There is no evidence for either of these contentions.

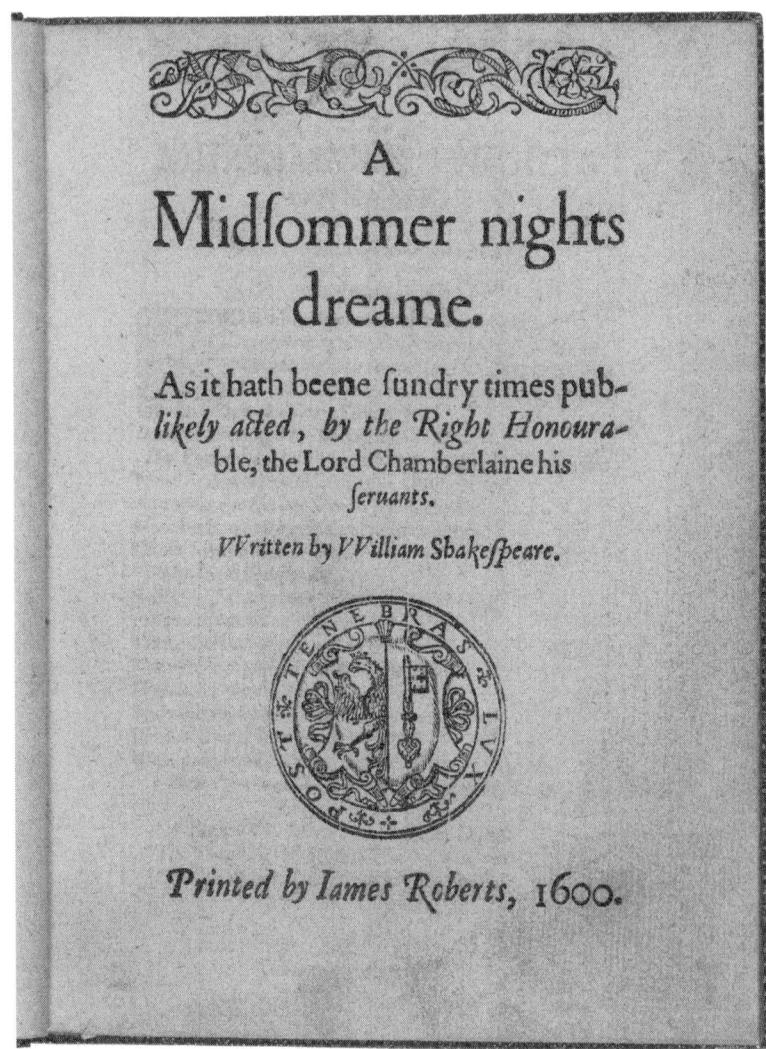

Plate 2.7 The title page to this edition of *A Midsummer Night's Dream* misleadingly states that it was printed in 1600, but it was in fact printed in 1619.

Recent 'Discoveries'

New 'discoveries' about Shakespeare are frequently claimed but have not added much to the biographical date for Shakespeare. In 2014, Martha Carlin drew attention to a manuscript by a traveller writing *c.* 1643

Table 2.2 Years when There Are Documented References to William Shakespeare in London 1564–1616

-	-	-	-	1604	-
-	-	-	1595	-	1615
-	-	-	1596	-	1616
-	-	-	1597	-	-
-	-	-	1598	-	-
-	-	1589?	1599	-	-
-	-	-	1600	-	-
-	-	-	-	-	-
-	-	1592?	1602	1612	-
-	-	-	1603	1613	-

(Edinburgh University Library MS La. II 422/211). The traveller notes in Southwark: "Ye Tabard I find to have been ye resort Mastere Will Shakspear Sir Sander Duncombe Lawrence Fletcher Richard Burbage Ben Jonson and ye rest of their roystering associates in King Jameses time as in ye lange room they have cut their names on ye Pannels." (*TLS* 24 September 2014). This gives the modern reader no more than a glimpse into Shakespeare's activities, *c.* 1603–1608. The roistering may have continued after the death of Lawrence Fletcher in 1608. It is not stated precisely who carved which name.

Amid all the celebrations for the anniversary of the National Poet were a number of new records which promised more than they delivered.[15] In April 2016, The National Archives announced the discovery of a new manuscript mentioning Shakespeare. The document, dated 17 May 1603, was found among the Warrants under the signet and privy seals for the issue of letters patent authorizing Shakespeare and his companions to perform plays throughout the realm under royal patronage. It thus represents an early stage in the issue of the extant letters patent which had been known since the eighteenth century. This 'discovery' says nothing new about Shakespeare.

A second 'new' document was announced at the end of June 2016 in the *New York Times,* which ran an article about a notebook describing coats of arms granted by William Dethick as York herald and Garter king of arms. This notebook was discovered by Heather Wolfe, of the Folger Shakespeare Library in Washington D.C., in the library of the College of Arms in London. It had however already been reproduced in an essay by Clive Cheesman in *Heralds and Heraldry in Shakespeare's England* (ed. Nigel Ramsay 2014) but gained little attention at the time. The notebook mentions the legend 'Shakespeare ye Player by Garter' which had been in the public domain since Alexander Pope described it in 1725. This 'discovery' therefore does not tell us anything new about Shakespeare.

A third 'discovery' was advanced by the Artistic Director of the RSC, Greg Doran. *The Times* (of London) reported on 8 October 2016 his claim that Shakespeare was inspired to compose *The Tempest* by events concerning HMS Prince Royal at Woolwich in 1610. Her launch was delayed by a storm which the master builder, Phineas Pett, apparently blamed on witchcraft. Doran overstates the problems. Pett made only an incidental mention of malignant forces. He described how spectators, including the King and the Prince Royal, gathered on the afternoon of 24 September 1610 in the expectation of watching the launch of the 55-gun ship of the line. However, the tide failed to lift the vessel sufficiently to clear the dock gates. So she had to be secured in place with cables. The shipbuilders then awaited the next tide in the early hours of the following morning. Pett sets the scene:

> … after midnight the weather was sore overcast and a very sore gust of rain thunder and lightning, which made me doubt [=fear] that there was some inderect workings amongst our enemies to dash our launching; this gust lasted about half an hour.…

There is only a little suggestion of witchcraft and no shipwreck. Pett continues:

> [High Water] no sooner entered but, the word being given to set all taut, the ship went away without any straining of crews or tackles.[16]

Thus the vessel launched easily, survived, and remained in service until (under her Commonwealth name 'Resolution') she was captured and destroyed by the Dutch in 1665. While it is true that in Shakespeare's play a storm is induced by magic, it serves only as a device to bring the antagonists together in one place and does not relate to the main plot of *The Tempest*. At no point did the crew of HMS Prince Royal land on a desert island where a dispossessed duke used magic powers to regain his lost dukedom. Overall, any 'new' evidence or research concerns only the history of the period and Shakespeare's assumed place in it.

Distribution of Records and Lost Years

Those who attempt a Life of Shakespeare acknowledge a period from 1585 to 1592 known as 'the lost years'. There are no records mentioning William between the baptism of 'Hamnet & Judeth' on 2 February 1585 and 1592, when he is apparently ridiculed by Robert Greene in *Groats-worth*. It is usual for biographers to include a chapter reviewing the speculation of others and presenting their own speculation regarding the 'lost years'. Among the more popular theories are: Shakespeare joined one or more touring companies such as the Queens' Men (Schoenbaum, Duncan-Jones), or Leicester's (Sidney Lee, A. F. Pollard), or Lord

Pembroke's Men (Acheson, J. Q. Adams), similar to the career paths of Thomas Heywood and Samuel Rowley, or Lord Strange's Men (Manley and MacLean).[17] Shakespeare worked as a legal attorney, according to Malone (1790, i. i. 307). It has also been said that Shakespeare was a 'schoolmaster in the country' (Aubrey) in Lancashire at a Catholic household (Honigmann),[18] at sea (Alexander Falconer, *Shakespeare and the Sea* 1964), and a soldier in the Low Countries, according to the wartime cabinet minister, Duff Cooper (*Sergeant Shakespeare* 1949). Claims as to what Shakespeare might or might not have been doing during the period 1585–1592 indicate the lack of evidence for the time span. However, the span of 'lost years' of 1585–1595 is in fact just one of three sets of 'lost years': childhood and youth (1564–1582), early adulthood (1585–1595), and middle age (1604–1612).

In contrast to the material for Shakespeare, the case of Ben Jonson proves most instructive. David Bevington compares the absence of personal material about Shakespeare with the extensive personal material for Jonson:

> A central problem is that Shakespeare wrote essentially nothing about himself. Unlike Ben Jonson, his younger contemporary, who loudly proclaimed in prologues, manifestos, essays and private conversations his opinions on the arts and writers from antiquity down to the Renaissance, and who has left us vivid testimonials of his feelings about the death of a son, about his wife ("a shrew, but honest"), about his conversion to Catholicism, and much more, Shakespeare has left us his plays and poems.
>
> Bevington, *Shakespeare and Biography* 2010, 3

A fair amount of Ben Jonson's correspondence has survived; Drummond kept a detailed journal of some of their conversations together which exists in a copy; Jonson published poems and prose which were personal. He wrote introductions in his own person to his published works. We know exact details about Jonson's patrons, his travels, his hosts, his library, and his personal grief 'On my Sonne' who died in 1603. Despite all this documentation, Jonson's most recent biographer, Ian Donaldson, states that biographical materials for Jonson's life "though comparatively well documented in relation to the lives of Shakespeare and other contemporaries" can only be known "imperfectly and in part." He adds that "Jonson's life is mainly a matter of gaps, interspersed by fragments of knowledge" (2011, 8–9).

Compared to the case of Jonson, Shakespeare's life is largely undocumented: it is less accurate to say that there are gaps in our knowledge of Shakespeare than to admit that there are "gaps in our ignorance" about him. Speculations, i.e. claims without foundation in contemporary records, have gradually accumulated during the seventeenth and eighteenth centuries in the treatment of Shakespeare's life. We will now consider how these specualtions have passed from mere myths to established "facts".

Notes

1 Richard Simpson. "Are there any extant MSS in Shakespeare's Handwriting? *Notes & Queries* 8 (1871) 1–3; A. W. Pollard, ed. *Shakespeare's Hand in the Play of Sir Thomas More. Shakespeare and Sir Thomas More.* Cambridge (1923). T. H. Howard-Hill, ed. *Shakespeare and "Sir Thomas More": Essays on the Play and Its Shakespearean Interest.* Cambridge (1991). John Jowett, ed. *Sir Thomas More.* London: Bloomsbury (Arden edn. 2011).

2 R. A. Hubler. 'On Looking over Shakespeare's Secretarie' in B. A. Jackson (ed.) *Stratford Papers on Shakespeare.* Toronto: Gage (1961, 52–70). Carol Chillington. 'Playwrights at Work: Henslowe's not Shakespeare's *Book of Sir Thomas More*' in *English Literary Renaissance* (1980, 439–79). Paul Wesrtine (2013) calls into question this and other opinions about Shakespeare's manuscripts. Diana Price. 'Hand D and Shakespeare's Unorthodox Literary Paper Trail' in *Journal of Early Modern Studies* 5 (2016, 329–52). Michael Hays also argues against the identification in "Shakespeare's Hand Unknown in *Sir Thomas More*: Thompson, Dawson, and the Futility of the Paleographic Argument. *Shakespeare Quarterly,* 67 (2016, 180–203).

3 See John Jowett "Johannes Factotum: Henry Chettle and Greene's Groatsworth of Wit" in *Papers of the Bibliographical Society of America* 87 (1993, 453–86). Lukas Erne "Biography and Mythography: Re-reading Chettle's Alleged Apology to Shakespeare" in *English Studies* 79 (1998, 430–40). Brian Vickers '"Upstart Crow"? The Myth of Shakespeare's Plagiarism' in *Review of English Studies* 68 (2017, 244–67).

4 Meres in *Palladis Tamia* (1598) simply names two groups of plays (six comedies balanced by six histories or tragedies) without any regard for sequence of composition or performance. De Grazia points out (1991, 175) that Meres does not mention any dates in his 333-page commonplace book, but gives "long heterogeneous inventories of classical authors and their British counter-parts, and contains many sententious and poetic passages freely transcribed from quotation books, epithet books and compendia of universal knowledge."

5 *Shakespeare in 100 Objects* by Janet Birkin (2014) and *Shakespeare's Restless World: An Unexpected History in Twenty Objects* by Neil MacGregor (2014) were issued by rival museums in London.

6 The Shakespeare Birthplace Trust was formed in 1847, after five homes and gardens in Stratford-upon-Avon were purchased as a national memorial to the Bard. The Shakespeare Birthplace Trust Act was passed in 1891 (amended 1930, and extended in 1961) with the intention "to promote in every part of the world the appreciation and study of the plays and works of William Shakespeare and to maintain and preserve the Shakespeare Birthplace properties for the benefit of the nation."

7 Levi Fox *In Honour of Shakespeare.* Norwich: Jarrold (1972, 17). There is a long terrace of medieval timber buildings in Chapel Street, now occupied by the Mercure Hotel.

8 The original drawing by Dugdale is preserved in the Dugdale library at Merevale Hall, Warwickshire. It was the subject of Diana Price's article "Reconsidering Shakespeare's Monument" in *Review of English Studies* 48 (1997, 168–82). There is some confusion of dates: in his notebook, Dugdale wrote "Stratford Sup[ra] Avon 9 July 1634" in the top left hand corner. The same page ends with a transcription of the epitaph of Susanna Hall, who died in 1649. It is reasonable to assume that Dugdale went to the church at least twice to record and verify the monuments.

9 C. C. Stopes *Shakespeare's Environment* (1914, 117–19). J. Bund in *The Civil War in Worcestershire, 1642–1646* reports that Royalist forces

plundered Stratford and the surrounding area in April 1645 (1905, 153–14). The plunder was later recovered.

10 Kate Bennett, 'Shakespeare's Monument at Stratford: A New Seventeenth-Century Account' in *Notes & Queries* 47 (2000, 464).

11 Mary Edmond "It was for gentle Shakespeare cut" in *Shakespeare Quarterly* 42.3 (1991, 339–44) argues that the portrait was by Martin Droeshout, the Elder, but this is rejected by June Schlueter ("Martin Droeshout Redivivus: Reassessing the Folio Engraving of Shakespeare" in *Shakespeare Survey* 60 (2007, 237–251).

12 There are difficulties in being precise: the parish register at Holy Trinity Church counts as one document but mentions William on four occasions. The final total depends on whether the "mr Shaxspere" who sold a "lod of ston" to the Corporation in 1598 was the father John, the son William or one of his brothers (*WS* ii. 96).

13 Tom Reedy. "William Dugdale on Shakespeare and his Monument" in *Shakespeare Quarterly* 66, (2015), 188–196). Also, Tom Reedy. "William Dugdale's Monumental Inaccuracies and Shakespeare's Stratford Monument" in *Shakespeare Survey* 69, (2016), 361–379).

14 The title page to the 1608 quarto of *Richard II* states that it had been acted at The Globe. The Examination of Sir Gilly Merrick before Lord Chief Justice Popham and Edward Fenner (17 February 1601) established: "The play was of King Henry the Fourth, and of the killing of Richard the Second, and played by the Lord Chamberlain's players" (*WS* ii, 324). Some commentators, e.g. Worden 2006, doubt that the play was Shakespeare's.

15 The Folger Library lounted an exhibition entitled 'Shakespeare: the life of an icon"; the following were listed as the 'highlights':
   – the only surviving copy of the first edition of the first Shakespeare play to be printed, *Titus Andronicus*
   – Shakespeare's copy of the bargain and sale for his purchase of a residence in Blackfriars near the winter theater of the King's Men
   – Shakespeare's copy of the final concord for his purchase of New Place in Stratford-upon-Avon
   – the draft "letters patent" authorizing a coat of arms for Shakespeare's father, and subsequently Shakespeare
   – a fragment of a bookseller's list which includes one of Shakespeare's "lost" plays, *Love's Labors Won*
   – a section of a play thought to be in Shakespeare's own handwriting
   – the only surviving letter written to Shakespeare the earliest references to Shakespeare as a playwright and a poet

16 Based on Harl. MSS. 6279 (British Library). William Gordon Perrin, ed. *The Autobiography of Phineas Pett*. London: Navy Records Society (1918) 83.

17 Lawrence Manley and Sally Beth MacLean *Lord Strange's Men and Their Plays*. Yale (2014, 280–320). The diverse possibilities have been summarised by Terence Schoone-Jongen *Shakespeare's Companies: William Shakespeare's Early Career and the Acting Companies, 1577–1594*. Farnham: Ashgate (2008).

18 The Lancastrian hypothesis received support in 2014 from the former Archbishop of Canterbury, Rowan Williams, who composed a play entitled *Shakeshafte* set in Lancashire in 1581. In notes to the play, it is claimed a will unearthed in 1851 shows that a Will Shakeshafte, on the recommendation of a former Stratford schoolmaster, John Cottam, was acting as a schoolmaster for a Catholic family in Houghton Tower, Lancashire. Apart from the doubtful identification of Shakeshafte as Shakespeare, it should be noted that there is no record anywhere of any recommendation by John Cottam; nor is there any record of 'Will Shakeshafte' ever acting as a schoolmaster to any family either in Lancashire or elsewhere.

3 Inventing the Myths
The Seventeenth and Eighteenth Centuries

I must confess my readiness to combat every unfounded supposition respecting the particular occurrences of his life.
—George Steevens, 1780,
reported by E. Malone, ed. 1780. *Supplement
to the Edition of Shakspeare's Plays*, ii. 653.

In this chapter we will see how writers added to the Shakespeare myths in
the seventeenth and eighteenth centuries. Modern scholars such as Gary
Taylor (*Reinventing Shakespeare* 1989) and Michael Dobson (*The Making of the National Poet* 1992) have shown Shakespeare's increasing importance as a cultural icon during this period. The plays, often adapted,
became very popular both on the Restoration stage and in print: the 36
original plays of F1 were augmented by seven others in the Third Folio
of 1663–1664. The publication of the Fourth Folio in 1685 was further
indication of the importance of the works. His reputation was enhanced
by John Dryden, who placed Shakespeare at the apex of English theatre:
"*Shakespeare* was the *Homer*, or Father of our Dramatick Poets" (*Essay
of Dramatick Poesie* 1668). His status was confirmed in the literary biographical dictionaries of Edward Phillips (1674), William Winstanley
(1687), and Gerard Langbaine (1691).

However, there was very little interest in the life of the author. Most
readers were prepared to accept Shakespeare as a born genius who
would "warble his native wood-notes wild," as John Milton had said
in 1631. Into the documentary vacuum, a few writers advanced claims
which remain unverifiable. By far the most influential of these was Nicholas Rowe, who introduced his 1709 edition with a short essay called
Some Account of the Life &c. of Mr. William Shakespear. The *Account*
appeared frequently for the next century and a half, and various claims
still persist, almost unchallenged, to present day. In this chapter, we can
consider the myths which arose after the Restoration, as well as the biographical insights offered by editors such as Lewis Theobald (1733),
Samuel Johnson (1765), and Edward Capell (1767).

3.1 Early Fictions

During the seventeenth century, anecdotes concerning Shakespeare were recorded by three writers: Dr Thomas Fuller (1608–1661), John Aubrey (1626–1697), and Rev. John Ward (1629–1681). Fuller's research, in which he reviewed famous people county by county, was published post-humously in *Worthies of England* (1662). In the section on Warwickshire, he spoke of Shakespeare in just three paragraphs. His final paragraph consists of a description of his apparent interaction with Jonson:

> Many were the wit-combates betwixt him and *Ben Johnson*, which two I behold like a *Spanish great Gallion* and an *English man of War*; Master *Johnson* (like the former) was built far higher in Learning; *Solid*, but *Slow* in his performances. *Shake-spear*, with the *English-man of War*, lesser in *bulk*, but lighter in *sailing*, could turn with all tides, tack about and take advantage of all winds, by the quickness of his Wit and Invention. He died *Anno Domini* 16… and was buried at *Stratford* upon *Avon*, the Town of his Nativity.
>
> (Fuller 1662, 126)

Fuller's work is a kind of early dictionary of national biography. The significance of his entry regarding Shakespeare lies not in any factual content but in the recognition that Shakespeare deserved to be remembered. Fuller justifies his inclusion of Shakespeare, comparing him favourably with classical poets (Martial, Ovid, and Plautus) and somewhat surprisingly with classical philosophers (Heraclitus and Democritus). The second noteworthy point of Fuller's entry is its brevity. Shakespeare is listed as just one among ten or so writers of distinction in Warwickshire since the Reformation (i.e. from 1530 until 1660). Fuller offers only three biographical facts about Shakespeare: that he was born in Stratford, that he died there, and that he had "wit-combates" with Ben Jonson. For this last point, Fuller advertises his use of conjecture both in using the phrase "I behold" and in the laboured comparison of the authors with ships. Fuller does not mention these wit-combates in the corresponding entry for Ben Jonson (under the section Westminster). Later, Malone would dismiss Fuller's comments as a "short quibbling account of our poet, furnishing very little information concerning him" (Boswell 1821, ii. 4). The linking of Shakespeare and Jonson became commonplace in the seventeenth century, with Shakespeare's reputation in the ascendancy from the Restoration onwards (Bentley 1945). Fuller's claim of rivalry between Jonson and Shakespeare seems to have been a Restoration fiction.

Another writer, Rev. John Ward, also made notes about Shakespeare in 1662, but these remained unpublished until 1839. Ward was vicar at

Stratford-upon-Avon from 1662 to 1681 and collected much information about other people in the town. When Charles Severn published Ward's diary in 1839, he described his excitement at the mention of Shakespeare, about whom "few, if any, undoubted particulars are known" (1839, x). Extracts from Ward's notebooks occupies pages 88–315. However, Ward's description of Shakespeare is confined to just one page in over 200 of printed text.[1] He mentions Shakespeare's daughters and grand-daughter in accord with the parish registers, to which as vicar he had direct access. However, he does not state his sources for the claims (not supported elsewhere) that Shakespeare provided two plays a year, or that he spent "att ye Rate of 1,000*l*. a year" (Severn 1839, 181). This amount is excessive: there is no evidence of Shakespeare receiving money at that rate while his outlay on property including tithes amounted to less than £1,000 in his lifetime. Similarly, there is no other source to suggest that "Shakespear, Drayton and Ben Jhonson, had a merry meeting, and itt seems drank too hard, for Shakespeare died of a feavour there contracted" (61). In fact, there is no document before his death in 1616 that Shakespeare ever met either of those two writers.[2] Overall, Ward added very little to the biographical material about Shakespeare.

However, biographers have tended to accept Ward's account of a "merry meeting" in the absence of any evidence to the contrary: Halliwell-Phillipps decided that the anecdote was a "late but apparently authentic tradition" without explaining why it was "apparently authentic" (1887, i. 267). Chambers sees "no reason to reject this report" (*WS* i. 89). Schoenbaum finds that the story of a drinking bout "does not stretch credulity" and even suggests an occasion for the event – Judith Shakespeare's marriage in February 1616 (1970, 120–121). No biographer of Jonson takes this anecdote seriously and there is no evidence that Jonson ever visited Stratford. In 1615–1616, Jonson was busy in London working on his edition of his *Works* with the publisher William Stansby (Donaldson 2011, 323–24). Anne Lake Prescott calls it implausible ("Michael Drayton" *ODNB* 2004).

A little more biographical material about Shakespeare was reported by John Aubrey (1626–1697), a small amount from a huge array of information collected during the Restoration period.[3] Aubrey clearly did not visit Stratford himself, as he refers the reader to the epitaph on Shakespeare's tomb in Dugdale's *Antiquities* (1656). Almost every biographical note about Shakespeare is either false or unverifiable. Fuller states that "His father was a Butcher, and I have been told heretofore by some of the neighbours, that when he was a boy he exercised his father's Trade, but when he kill'd a Calfe he would doe it in a high style, and make a Speech." Malone rejects the claim partly due to its vague attribution to "some of the neighbours," but also in noting that John Shakespeare was a glover not a butcher (1790, i. pt. ii. 166–70). The high-style butchery anecdote gained partial confirmation in a letter (dated 10 April

1693) by a lawyer named Dowdall, who described being shown around Holy Trinity Church at Stratford by a clerk "above eighty years old." Dowdall adds that "Shakespear was formerly in this Towne bound apprentice to a butcher, but that he Run from his master to London" (*WS* ii. 259; the letter is now in the Folger Shakespeare Library). Many commentators report the high-style butchery as an "early tradition" (*e.g.* Sidney Lee 1917, 25; *WS* i. 17). Schoenbaum is inclined to accept it as it was reported by the "earliest authorities" (1987, 74–75), even though this occurred about a century after it was supposed to have taken place. The phrase "early tradition" is ambiguous, suggesting that the tradition occurred soon after Shakespeare's death. However, "early" indicates no more than that Aubrey was the first to make this claim, there being none earlier.

Next, Aubrey speculates on the age when William came to London "I guesse about 18." He describes Shakespeare's appearance in such vague terms "handsome, well shap't man" as to suggest that no direct or indirect acquaintance. Nor is there any earlier authority for the assertion that Shakespeare only made one trip annually to Stratford. In a different part of his notes, Aubrey reported the suggestion that Sir William Davenant "seemed contented enough to be thought his Son. He would tell them the story as above, in which way his mother had a very light report, whereby she was called a Whore." Aubrey himself was doubtful about the claim as he reports only that Davenant "seemed contented enough" to be thought his son.[4] Schoenbaum linked the death of William's legitimate son, Hamnet (in 1596), to the birth of baby Davenant (in 1606) saying: "According to tradition, Shakespeare found solace at The Tavern in Oxford." Schoenbaum overlooks the discrepancy of a decade.

Aubrey's commented that Shakespeare spent time as a "schoolmaster in the countrey" without stating when or where. While this claim is dismissed by most commentators such as Malone, Schoenbaum, and Weis, it is accepted by others, including Sidney Lee and Chambers (*WS* i. 22). As to the location of this school, J. Dover Wilson placed it at Titchfield Abbey, Hampshire, claiming that Shakespeare worked as a tutor and as a master of revels for the Earl of Southampton (1932). E. A. J. Honigmann has Shakespeare travel north and argues that Shakespeare was a private tutor in Lancashire (1985, 2–3). Stephen Greenblatt, for whom "this particular item [of gossip] has more authority than most [other items of gossip]," accepts the schoolmaster in Lancashire interpretation (2004, 88) but does not explain the logic by which he came to this conclusion or how he evaluates the level of authority in different pieces of gossip. Overall, the totally divergent opinions about the "schoolmaster in the countrey" comment are only possible because of the absence of any contemporary record concerning Shakespeare during the second period of 'lost years' 1585–1592.

Aubrey claims that Shakespeare composed an extemporary epitaph for John Combe:

> Ten in the Hundred the Devill allowes,
> But Combes will have twelve he sweares and vowes:
> If anyone askes who lies in this Tombe,
> Hoh! quoth the Devill, 'Tis my John o' Combe.

Malone noted that two of the lines had previously appeared in 1608 and 1614 and that the entire epitaph about John Combe had been published by Richard Braithwaite in 1618 (1790, i, i. 120–122). Finally, another unlikely claim concerns the anecdote about the constable at Grendon as the inspiration for Dogberry in *A Midsummer Night's Dream* (who was actually presented in *Much Ado about Nothing*).

Aubrey's reliability was called into question by the writer who commissioned his investigations. For Anthony Wood, Aubrey was "a shiftless person, roving and magotie-headed, and sometimes little better than crased."[5] Malone was equally dismissive of Aubrey, calling him "a dupe to every wag who chose to practise on his credulity" (1790, i. pt. ii. 254). Altick dismisses Fuller's claims as "porous assertions" comparing them to other dubious claims that Francis Bacon died after contracting a cold while deep-freezing a fowl, and that Ben Jonson killed Marlowe on Bunhill "comeing from the Green-curtain play-house." Schoenbaum makes some use of Aubrey's anecdotes even though he states that they "belong not to the biographical record proper but to the mythos" (*Documentary Life* 1975, 72).

John Dryden had remained completely indifferent to any knowledge of Shakespeare's life. It is curious that while Shakespeare's plays were so frequently performed on stage, very little biographical information was circulating about the person who wrote them.

Within this biographical vacuum, a lesser playwright, John Dennis, was able to claim a royal connection in the preface to his 1702 adaptation of *The Merry Wives of Windsor*. Dennis stated that Elizabeth I had commanded Shakespeare to write another play about Falstaff in two weeks.[6] The claim, repeated by Rowe (1709, i. ix), is not mentioned in any earlier document. Two years later, Dennis enhanced the story saying that Elizabeth specified a ten-day period for the play's composition. Jonathan Bate and Eric Rasmussen are doubtful about any such royal command.[7] In her review of this anecdote, Helen Hackett notes the royal connections for *Merry Wives* with its performance at court in 1702 and setting near a royal castle. Hackett concludes:

> When Dennis in 1704 used the story of Elizabeth's commission for *The Merry Wives of Windsor* to expound upon the Queen's

encouragement of and pleasure in drama, he was making a polemical point about the contemporary neglect of playwrights by the Crown.

(2009, 25–26)

In other words, Dennis used the story in an attempt to secure royal patronage.

3.2 Nicholas Rowe's *Some Account of the Life &c.* (1709)

Early in the eighteenth century, the publisher Jacob Tonson acquired the rights to publish most of Shakespeare's plays. Tonson invited Nicholas Rowe to prepare an edition of the plays in six volumes, quarto. Subsequent editions of the plays were issued at regular intervals as the Act for the Encouragement of Learning (Statute of Anne 1710, 1/6) restricted copyright to a period of fourteen years. Nicholas Rowe was chosen to edit the plays because he was a prominent playwright: he had been enjoying his own success with plays such as *Tamerlane* (1702), *The Fair Penitent* (1703), and *Ulysses* (1706) and his name featured in the extended title. Rowe and Tonson made the following important additions to his new edition: he revised the text (which was based on Fourth Folio of 1685), gave a list of the *dramatis personae* for each play, and added stage directions, act/scene divisions, and illustrations based on contemporary stage performances of the plays. Thus Rowe can claim to have been the first critical editor of the plays of Shakespeare. The edition was immediately reissued (1709/10), and reissued in 1714 in duodecimo. Rowe introduced the first volume with two personal addresses: a dedication to the Duke of Somerset, Charles Seymour, and a preface entitled *Some Account of the Life &c. of Mr. William Shakespear*. The *Account* amounts to 40 pages in quarto at 28 lines per page, a little over 8,000 words in total. The rest of the first volume comprised the texts of the first seven comedies in sequence from F4.

Rowe himself is doubtful about the value of literary biography. At the outset of the *Account*, he dismisses any curiosity in literary biography as "trifling," (1709, i. 1).[8] A cursory reading of the *Account* shows that Rowe included very little biographical material about the poet's life. It is mostly a critical review of the works (more than seven-eighths of the essay) rather than a biography (less than one-eighth).[9] His purpose is to promote the plays and he mentions thirty-four by name and refers to almost forty named characters. While claiming "not to enter any Critical Controversie" (xxxiv), Rowe devotes most of the *Account* to answering adverse criticisms made by Thomas Rymer in *A Short View of Tragedy* (1693). Rowe asserts that the dramatist did not follow the classical unities in his plays as he did not know of them, having been forced to leave school early due to the "narrowness of his Circumstances, and the want of his assistance at Home" (II). He continues his discussion of Shakespeare's learning with the statement: "It is without Controversie, that he had no knowledge of the Writings of the Antient Poets" (III). Rowe is thus following Milton and anticipating Addison in viewing Shakespeare as a genius of nature. Rowe continues: "If he [Rymer] had a Pique against the Man, and wrote on purpose to ruin a Reputation so well establish'd, he has had the Mortification to fail altogether in his Attempt, and to see the World at least as fond of Shakespear as of his Critique" (XVI). Rowe quotes the "All the world's a stage" speech (XXI) as especially deserving of notice. He emphasises Shakespeare's poetic abilities: "His Images are indeed ev'ry where so lively, that the Thing he would represent stands full before you, and you possess ev'ry Part of it" (XXII). Overall, the *Account* is a disjointed collection of critical judgements interspersed with a little biographical material. Rowe's essay does not merit the title of "biography" because it is not a coherent narrative of the life of Shakespeare.

Rowe's biographical statements about Shakespeare amount to only one-eighth of the *Account,* as little as 1,000 words. A preface involving both biographical comments and critical appreciation was probably required by Jacob Tonson, the publisher. Tonson was republishing Dryden's edition of *Plutarch's Lives* in the early 1700s for which Dryden had written a substantial *Life of Plutarch* (1683 I, 1–126). To discover more about Shakespeare's life, Tonson advertised in the *London Gazette* and in the *Daily Courant* in March 1709 (Murphy 2003, 60). Little or nothing seems to have been forthcoming about Shakespeare's life from these advertisements. In the end, Rowe only mentions one authority, his friend the actor Thomas Betterton (1635–1710), who was by this time elderly. In line with his own inclination for a theatrical approach to Shakespeare, Rowe praises Betterton for his acting: "I cannot leave *Hamlet,* without taking notice of the Advantage with which we have seen this Masterpiece of *Shakespear* distinguish itself upon the Stage, by Mr. *Betterton's* fine Performance of that Part." (XXXIII–XXXIV). He adds that Betterton had contributed to the biographical record but is not specific:

> I must own a particular Obligation to him, for the most considerable part of the Passages relating to his Life, which I have here transmitted to the Public; his Veneration for the Memory of *Shakespear* having engaged him to make a Journey into *Warwickshire,* on purpose to gather up what Remains he could of a Name for which he had so great a Value.
>
> (1709, XXXIV)

As Rev. John Ward makes no mention of Betterton (or any other visitor to Stratford) enquiring about Shakespeare in the period 1662–1681, the date of Betterton's visit would seem to have occurred after 1681. Malone lamented Betterton's lack of rigour:

> Mr. Betterton was born in 1635, and had many opportunities of collecting information relative to Shakespeare, but unfortunately the age in which he lived was not an age of curiosity. Had either he or Dryden or Sir William Davenant taken the trouble to visit our poet's youngest daughter, who lived till 1662, or his grand-daughter, who did not die till 1670, many particulars might have been preserved which are now irrevocably lost.
>
> (1790, vol. i. pt. ii. n. 154)

However, there is doubt whether Betterton himself made the journey at all. According to Malone, William Oldys had left notes in which a member of Betterton's company, John Bowman, denied that Betterton had ever been to Stratford (1790, i. pt. ii. 157). No such visit was mentioned by his contemporary biographer, Charles Gildon (1710), or by his modern biographer, David Roberts (2010).[10] Nevertheless, somebody was able to provide information about Shakespeare from an inspection of the parish register at the Holy Trinity Church in Stratford.

Some of Rowe's biographical comments can be supported with reference to primary sources: the statements that William was born in Stratford in 1564; that he married a yeoman's daughter when he was young; and that he dedicated *Venus & Adonis* to Southampton. He notes the age of Shakespeare when he died, his place of burial and his three children. In addition, Rowe states that William obtained a coat of arms (the records show that it was his father who made the application).

A number of claims by Rowe cannot be verified and should be viewed with caution:

a   his father was a "considerable dealer in wool" (ii); although John Shakespeare was recorded as a glover by the authorities in Stratford, and Rowe may have been influenced by the illustration in Dugdale.

b   John Shakespeare kept William as an apprentice, and sent the young William to a "free-school" for some time (ii). There is no evidence as to where Shakespeare spent his childhood or that he ever attended school, either in Stratford or anywhere else. The suggestion by Arthur Gray (1926) that Shakespeare was brought up at an aristocratic household is tenable in the absence of evidence to the contrary.

c   He composed a ballad against Sir Thomas Lucy.

d   "the top of his Performance was the Ghost in his own *Hamlet*." This suggestion might well owe something to Dryden's adaptation of *Troilus and Cressida* in which the ghost of Shakespeare appears in the prologue to lend authority.

e   Shakespeare assisted Jonson early in his career, but Jonson later became envious. The apparent relationship between Shakespeare and Jonson is considered later, in Chapter 9.

Other claims about the life of Shakespeare were disproved long ago by Steevens and Malone.

f   Shakespeare was the eldest of ten children, whereas there were only eight; two older children seemed to have died in infancy (*WS* ii, 1–2).

g   William was caught deer-poaching and punished by the local magistrate, but there was no deer park at Charlecote in the sixteenth or seventeenth century and the punishments cited did not correlate with the legal sanctions at the time.

h   He was favour by the Queen; Rowe is echoing his friend John Dennis, perhaps in the hope of gaining royal support.

i   He was patronised by Southampton, who gave him £1,000. Rowe is himself skeptical saying he would not repeat the claim but for the fact that "the Story was handed down by Sir William Davenant, who was probably very well acquainted with his Affairs" (x). The amount cited exceeds the total cost of his property portfolio; perhaps Rowe was hinting to his dedicatee, the Duke of Somerset. The apparent relationship between Shakespeare and Southampton is considered later, in Chapter 8.

j   "The latter Part of his Life was spent, as all Men of good Sense will wish theirs may be, in Ease, Retirement, and the Conversation of his Friends" (xxxv), which is inconsistent with the purchase of the Blackfriars Gatehouse in 1613.

k   Shakespeare composed an epitaph for Mr Coombe, the only acquaintance at Stratford that Rowe mentions (xxxvi). George Steevens noted that the epitaph about John Combe had been published by Richard Braithwaite in 1618 without reference to Shakespeare. Moreover, he noted that two of the lines had previously appeared in other publications in 1608 and 1614 (Malone 1790, i. i. 120).

In short, Rowe did not write a biography. He wrote a critical appreciation of about 8,000 words which included some claims about the historical William Shakespeare. These biographical comments amount only to about 1,000 words in the essay (approximately 12% of the total) and are mainly unverifiable or simply wrong. Eighteenth-century editors accorded little value to Rowe's *Account* and never referred to it as a "biography". In their reviews of literary biography during this period, neither Stauffer (1941) nor Altick (1965) even mentions Rowe as a biographer of Shakespeare or indeed of anyone else. In the preliminary matter to his edition of Shakespeare, Dr Johnson prepared an essay of appreciation which is still widely acclaimed. He also included introductions by previous editors (Pope, Theobald, Hanmer, Warburton), only reluctantly adding Rowe's out of sequence at the end:

> As of the other editors I have preserved the prefaces, I have likewise borrowed the author's life from Rowe, though not written with much elegance or spirit; it relates however what is now to be known, and therefore deserves to pass through all succeeding publications.
>
> (Johnson 1765, i. sig. C8ʳ)

In his *Life of Nicholas Rowe* (1779), Johnson repeated this appraisal of Rowe's essay: "He prefixed a life of the author, such as tradition, then almost expiring, could supply, and a preface which cannot be said to discover much profundity or penetration. He at least contributed to the popularity of his author." Later still, Malone was even more dismissive of "Mr. Rowe's meagre and imperfect narrative" (1790, i. i. page lxiii) and gave copious notes to show that Rowe's biographical statements were largely mistaken, as noted by Samuel Monk in his introduction to the reprint:

> The biographical part of Rowe's *Account* assembled the few facts and most of the traditions still current about Shakespeare a century after his death. It would be easy for any undergraduate to distinguish fact from legend in Rowe's preface; and scholarship since Steevens and Malone has demonstrated the unreliability of most of the local traditions that Betterton reported from Warwickshire.
>
> (Monk 1948, 5)

While it is incorrect to cite Rowe as the "first biographer" of Shakespeare, Sidney Lee referred to Rowe's *Account* as "a more ambitious memoir than had yet been attempted" (1898, 1917). Lee's claim is extravagant: neither Rowe's nor any previous memoir of Shakespeare merit the description "ambitious". E. K. Chambers believes that Rowe made "the first attempt at a systematic biography of the poet" (*WS* i. 12). Like Lee, Chambers is going beyond the text in claiming that Rowe's preface was either "systematic" or a "biography." Samuel Schoenbaum makes the same mistake as Lee in stating that Rowe made the "first attempt at a connected biography of Shakespeare" (1970, 131), but the *Account* is no more connected than it is a biography. Gary Taylor calls it the "first substantial biography of Shakespeare ever published" (*Reinventing Shakespeare* 1989, 74). These adjectives – ambitious, systematic, connected, and substantial – afford far greater authority to Rowe's essay than it actually merits. Such claims however continue to be repeated in recent times by (among many others) Dobson (2001), Wells (2003), Ackroyd (2005), and Potter (2012). In this way, modern biographers of Shakespeare have attempted to present their own efforts at the end of a respectable tradition of Shakespearean biography stretching back to 1709, less than a hundred years after his death, and not to the Victorian period, almost three hundred years after Shakespeare's birth. The first recognisable biography of Shakespeare did not in fact appear until 1843 when Charles Knight included a narrative account of Shakespeare's life as volume VIII of his *Illustrated Edition of Shakespeare's Works*. Shortly afterwards, John Payne Collier wrote his own biography for his edition in 1844. Both are almost entirely fictional as will emerge in Chapter 5.

3.3 Reprints of Rowe's *Account of the Life &c.*

While there was little interest in Shakespeare's life before Malone began his biographical researches in the late 1770s, Shakespeare achieved iconic status. Quotations from his works were collected in commonplace books and were made "to give dignity and authority" to biographies of other people (Stauffer 1941, 16). An early critical monograph devoted entirely to a study of the text was published by John Dennis as *An Essay upon the Writings and Genius of Shakespeare* (1712). His plays were studied in secondary education, from 1728 at Westminster School. In the 1730s, a group of upper-class women formed the Shakespeare Ladies' Club and successfully lobbied for more productions of Shakespeare. A special monument was commissioned and Scheemakers's statue was set up in Westminster Abbey in 1740. David Garrick first performed a Shakespearean role, Richard III, in 1741 and further performances in Shakespeare plays astonished his audiences. In 1756, David Garrick had a neo-classical Temple constructed on the banks of the Thames upstream from Hampton Court to celebrate the genius of William Shakespeare. In the 1750s, William Hawkins became professor of poetry at Oxford University and began lecturing on Shakespeare. Such interest led large numbers to attend the belated Jubilee at Stratford in 1769. Shakespeare had by now fully achieved the status of National Poet, but with little or no interest in the actual events in his life.[11]

Mindful of the Act for the Encouragement of Learning (1710) which gave the printer exclusive licence to print works for fourteen years only, the Tonson family of publishers reissued the works of Shakespeare at regular intervals in the eighteenth century. In almost all of these, Rowe's *Account* was included as some kind of preface. Alexander Pope abridged and slightly rearranged Rowe's essay and this revised *Account* consists of just over 7,000 words, of which only about 1,000 words are biographical. Pope added the text of the document regarding John Shakespeare's Coat of Arms (taken from Rymer). Later editors simply added their own preface of appreciation to those of preceding editors. Thus Rowe's revised *Account* appeared without comment in the editions of Hammer (1743), Warburton (1747), Johnson (1765), and Johnson-Stevens (1773). At no point in the eighteenth or nineteenth centuries did anyone call it a

Plate 3.1 Garrick's Temple to Shakespeare: constructed in 1756 to a neo-classical design.

biography, even though the term was increasingly used as shown by over 150 titles in the eighteenth century in the ESTC. Malone was astonished that Rowe's *Account* remained the only attempt to offer biographical details about Shakespeare:

> That almost a century should have elapsed, from the time of his death, without a single attempt having been made to discover any circumstance which could throw a light on his private life, or literary career; that, when the attempt was made [by Rowe in 1709], it should have been so imperfectly executed by the ingenious and elegant dramatist who undertook the task; and that for a period of eighty years afterwards, during which this "god of our idolatry" ranked as high among us as any poet ever did in any country, all the editors of his works, and each successive biographer, should have been contented with Mr Rowe's meagre and imperfect narrative; are circumstances which cannot be contemplated without astonishment.
> (1821, ii. 10–11)

Like previous editors, Malone included Rowe's *Account of the Life &c.,* in his edition (1790, i. ii. 102–54) but "endeavoured, in some degree, to supply the defects of Mr. Rowe's short narrative, by adding to it copious annotations" (as reported in 1821, ii. n. 11). These notes are printed in a smaller font and are so extensive that some pages have no running text.

In fact, Rowe's *Account* was only included in Malone's edition "for the purpose of demolishing almost every statement [by Rowe] which it contained" (Boswell 1821, i. xix).

Alexander Pope's text was heavily criticised by Lewis Theobald (1688–1744) in *Shakespeare Restor'd* (1726), for cutting passages according to his own preference – a charge which applies equally to his treatment of Rowe's *Account*. Recognised as a superior editor by the younger Jacob Tonson, Theobald was invited to produce his own edition of the plays, published in 1733 and this edition was frequently reprinted. He replaced the prefaces of Rowe and Pope with his own preface, offering his own appreciation of the works (pages xv–lxix, about 53 of 68 pages). He began with an outline of Shakespeare's life, frequently citing Rowe (iv–xv), adding a few details, such as the family background described in the 1599 Grant of Arms (v), the charter for the licence awarded to the King's Men in 1603 (ix), the dates and ages of his wife and children (vi; xv), the 1614 fire at Stratford (xiv), the bequests of Hugh Clopton to the town (xii–xiii), and the fact that Queen Henrietta stayed at New Place in 1643 (xiv).[12]

Theobald is most useful in his admissions of ignorance as to the life of Shakespeare. He states that he is unable to answer certain questions: how long he continued in his father's business (v); how long his father lived (iv–v); when William left his native Stratford (v); or when he relinquished the Stage (ix). Theobald dismisses the suggestion of John Roberts (1729, 45) that Shakespeare's papers were burnt by an ignorant baker of Warwick or in the Great Fire of 1614 (xiv–xv). Nor is he convinced by the usual account of John Shakespeare, which he begins with "we are told" (iv) and ends with "Be this as it will" (v). Theobald omits any reference to Southampton or rivalry with Jonson. Theobald's incisive comments about the lack of biographical material for Shakespeare have been ignored by modern commentators. Schoenbaum (1970, 136–37) merely notes that Theobald added some details about New Place.

Shortly after Theobald's edition appeared, Peter Scheemakers's monument to Shakespeare was set up in Westminster Abbey in 1740. However, Theobald's insights into the life of Shakespeare were ignored when a separate 37-page pamphlet in duodecimo format of Rowe's *Account* was published anonymously under the title *The life of Mr. William Shakespear. Whose monument was lately erected in Westminster-Abbey, at the expence of the publick* (1743, London). The differently worded title was in keeping with the increased public interest in the life of Shakespeare and in biography generally. Schoenbaum dismisses this as "no more than a catchpenny attempt to capitalize on public interest in the Bard" (1970, 137). While it added nothing new to the existing material for the life of Shakespeare, it spread notions that Shakespeare attended school in Stratford, was caught deer-poaching and was patronised by Southampton. The next two major editors of Shakespeare, Sir Thomas

Hanmer (1744) and Dr William Warburton (1747), reprinted the prefaces of Rowe and Pope.

The second half of the eighteenth century witnessed the increase of biographical surveys and dictionaries, in which Shakespeare featured. Theophilus Cibber (1703–1758) in his four-volume *Lives of the Poets* (1753) was aware of interest in the lives of famous writers: "All men have discovered a curiosity to know the little stories and particularities of a great genius," but in the case of Shakespeare, he accepted "but few things known of this great man; few incidents of his life have descended to posterity" (i. 125). Cibber gave a significant account of Shakespeare in about 6,000 words, based on Rowe's *Account*. Cibber includes a new anecdote, being well aware of the tortuous route by which it was passed down:

> Here I cannot forbear relating a story which Sir William Davenant told Mr. Betterton, who communicated it to Mr. Rowe; Rowe told it Mr. Pope, and Mr. Pope told it to Dr. Newton, the late editor of Milton, and from a gentleman, who heard it from him, "tis here related.
>
> (1753, i. 130)

This explanation introduces the story about Shakespeare holding horses at the stage door:

> At that time coaches not being in use, and as gentlemen were accustomed to ride to the playhouse, Shakespear, driven to the last necessity, went to the playhouse door, and pick'd up a little money by taking care of the gentlemens horses who came to the play.
>
> (1753, i. 130)

This story, which was rejected by Malone, holds no value for Shakespeare's literary biography. The convoluted explanation of its provenance and the limited value of the anecdote serve to reinforce Cibber's original statement that there are "but few things known of this great man." One significant addition to the biographical data was the discovery of Shakespeare's will by Joseph Greene in 1747. The will, however, failed to give any insight into Shakespeare's literary career, mentioning no books and no contact with the theatre beyond the interlinear addition on the final page "to my ffellowes John Hemynges, Richard Burbage and Henry Cundell xxvis viijd A peece to buy them Ringes."

A less important anecdote, and one which has not attracted much attention, was recorded in 1762 by an anonymous contributor to the *British Magazine* who described how the landlord of the White Lion in Stratford told of Shakespeare's involvement in a competition with some "deep drinkers and merry fellows" at the nearby village of Bidford and was "forced to take up his lodgings" under a crab-tree for some hours

(*WS* ii. 286–87). The anecdote was embellished by John Jordan *c.* 1770 (*WS* ii. 291–92).

In the second half of the eighteenth century, critics were less concerned with the life and more with Shakespeare's greatness as an English or British poet. He was called: "the Glory of the British nation" in *Beauties of Biography* (1777, ii. 121); "the glory of his age and of his country" by Joseph Towers in *British Biography* (1766–1772, iv. 106); "The Prince of Dramatic Poets and the Glory of this Nation" in *Biographia Literaria* by John Berkenhout (1777, 397). George Sael in *Moral Biography* called him "the father of the English theatre, the great poet of nature, and the Glory of the British nation" (1798, 160); John Aitken in *General Biography* called him "the favourite of a whole enlightened nation" by (1799–1815, ix. 121). The similarity of sentiment and wording indicates the derivative nature of these biographical dictionaries, which added nothing new to the life.

With Shakespeare's growing popularity during the latter part of the eighteenth century, many people visited Stratford-upon-Avon in numbers in search of his birthplace and church monument, but little emerged that was new for the biographical materials concerning Shakespeare. Literary tourists took an interest grew in a mulberry tree which stood in the garden of New Place. The myth grew that Shakespeare had himself planted a mulberry tree in line with the recommendation of James I, who was said to have encouraged the planting of trees to help the silkworm industry. The story about James I and mulberries is hard to verify: and Shakespeare had already alluded to mulberries in *A Midsummer Night's Dream* (Q, 1600). The tree in the garden of New Place was not recorded before the 1740s: Altick (1965, 42–45) describes how the "poet-worship" accorded to Shakespeare resulted in the owner of New Place, a Rev. Gastrell, became so angry with the flood of visitors hoping for a souvenir that he had the tree removed in 1756 and demolished New Place itself in 1759 (Malone 1790, i. i. 117n-118n). Local craftsmen were selling holy relics apparently crafted from this tree for many years afterwards.

3.4 Dr Johnson's Unattempted Life of Shakespeare

Another edition of Shakespeare's works was commissioned by the Tonson family in the 1760s, this time from the great Dr Samuel Johnson, which appeared in 1765. The edition included a large amount of prefatory material written by previous editors (Rowe, Pope, Theobald, Hanmer, and Warburton). Johnson only "retained the authour's life [from Rowe] though not written with much elegance or spirit" (1765, i. sig. C8^r) as little or nothing about Shakespeare's life. He included the text of the will and the anecdote about holding horses. This edition was lauded for the great doctor's brilliant prefatory essay, but it produced little new either textually or biographically (Murphy 2003, 80–81).

It is remarkable that a writer such as Johnson who so promoted the genre of literary biography did not even attempt a biographical preface about Shakespeare. We have seen that Johnson had made many pertinent observations about the writing of biography in the 1750s and 1760s. He also knew and admired the works of Shakespeare well: he had quoted in over 1100 entries in his *Dictionary* of 1755. Furthermore, Johnson also came from the English midlands, Stratford being only slightly off the main route from London to Litchfield, Johnson's home town. During the time in which he was working on his edition in the early 1760s, Stratford was developing as a literary tourist attraction, mainly due to the success of Johnson's former pupil, David Garrick, the foremost Shakespearean actor of his age. Indeed, Garrick was planning the Stratford Jubilee from the mid-1760s, which further enhanced the value of Johnson's edition. Moreover, Johnson had previously been commissioned (almost certainly with a cash advance) to write such a life by the literary publisher Thomas Coxeter (1689–1747), according to Sir John Hawkins. Regarding criticism made in 1762 about his long-awaited edition of Shakespeare, Hawkins noted:

> [Johnson] confessed he was culpable, and promised from time to time to begin a course of such reading as was necessary to qualify him for the work [i.e. edition]: this was no more than he had formerly done in an engagement with Coxeter, to whom he had bound himself to write the life of Shakespeare, but he could never be prevailed on to begin it.[13]

Johnson's failure even to attempt a life of Shakespeare stands in stark contrast to his fifty-two biographical prefaces *Lives of the Most Eminent English Poets* (1779–1781). Dr Johnson's friend and biographer, James Boswell, reported a lament by Johnson about the loss of personal knowledge on Shakespeare and Dryden:

> How delighted should we have been if thus introduced into the company of Shakespeare and of Dryden, of whom we know scarcely anything but their admirable writings! What pleasure would it have given us to have known their petty habits, their characteristic manners, their modes of composition, and their genuine opinion of preceding writers and of their contemporaries! All these are now irrecoverably lost.
>
> (Boswell, *Journal of a Tour to the Hebrides*, 1785, 522–53)

Dr Johnson's inability to write a Life of Shakespeare simply derived from the lack of biographical material, which as he noted, tended to diminish with time:

History can be formed from permanent monuments and records; but Lives can only be written from personal knowledge, which is growing every day less, and in a short time is lost for ever. What is known can seldom be told; and when it might be told, it is no longer known.
(Johnson in 'Addison' *Prefaces, Biographical* 1781, v. 5, 71–72)

This observation seems to have had a profound impact on Boswell's friend, Edmund Malone, who was able through assiduous investigation to find enough material about Dryden for a biographical preface in *The Critical and Miscellaneous Prose Works of John Dryden* (1800), but not, as we shall see, for a life of Shakespeare.

In 1774, the House of Lords adjusted the fourteen-year rule in copyright when deciding the case of *Donaldson v Beckett*. The Lords ruled that copyright could be limited in its duration. One of the printers to benefit from this judgement was John Bell (1745–1831), who published an *Edition of Shakespeare's Plays* in 8 vols (1773–1774). To this, he added a ninth volume of poems, which was introduced with a "Life of Shakespeare" by Francis Gentleman (1774, ix. 5–36). This brief account, like Rowe's, contains mainly critical judgements, regarding both the genius of Shakespeare and the best readings, with few biographical comments. Gentleman was very inclined to make biographical inferences from the works: "As to his character, it must be fished out of his writings" (ix. 8). He is cautious about Shakespeare's religious views, suggesting that he followed the established church "though some strokes of popery appear in *Hamlet*" (ix. 28). He also finds a contradiction of Shakespeare apparently promulgating "the noblest ideas of general and particular liberty" in some plays while the English history plays promote the argument of "Divine right and passive obedience" (ix. 29). Paulina Kewes finds that these opinions anticipate historicist arguments about Shakespeare by two centuries (2002, 70), but offered nothing in the way of new research – just a few suggestions of Shakespeare's character "fished" from the plays. In his very limited way, Bell was slightly ahead of Malone.

3.5 Edward Capell's Neglected Insights (1767)

Not all editors simply reprinted Rowe's *Account of the Life*. Edward Capell eschewed the use of reprinting prefatory material altogether in his edition of 1767–1768 (10 vols, octavo). Capell had been working in isolation on the texts of Shakespeare from the late 1730s. After the dedication to Lord Grafton (then First Lord of the Treasury), Capell wrote his own introduction, offering a detailed analysis of the sources for each play. Capell gave a considerable amount of new information from the Stationers' Register and took note of *Palladis Tamia: Wits Treasury* by Francis Meres (1598) which had been discovered by Richard Farmer.[14] Like Dr Johnson, Capell lamented the lack of biographical material:

The truth is, the occurrences of this most interesting life (we mean, the private ones) are irrecoverably lost to us, the friendly office of registering them was overlook'd by those who alone had it in their power, and our enquiries about them now must prove vain and thrown away.

(1767, i. 71–72)

This insight has also been lost on many later biographers. Capell merely hopes that some kind of external biography might be written: "his publick [life] as a writer would have consequences more important" (i. 72). Capell realises that there are important questions for a literary biography of Shakespeare:

When he commenc'd a writer for the stage, and in which play; what the order of the rest of them, and (if that be discoverable) what the occasion; and, lastly, for which of the numerous theatres that were then subsisting they were severally written at first, are the particulars that should chiefly engage the attention of a writer of Shakespeare's Life, and be the principal subject of his enquiry.

(i. 72)

Capell encourages the biographer to include not just the texts of related documents but also "such anecdotes of common notoriety as the writer's judgment shall tell him are worth regard" (i. 73). Capell realised that Rowe's *Account* failed to give a coherent picture of Shakespeare's life as a dramatist. Capell's wish was that "the world of letters [would be] enrich'd by the happy acquisition, of a masterly Life of Shakespeare" (i. 73–74). Clearly, Capell, after forty years studying Shakespeare, found himself unequal to the task of writing a literary biography of Shakespeare.

During this period, another editor, George Steevens (1736–1800) had been comparing the readings in the First Folio with those in the extant quartos. The Tonsons published Steevens's text of the twenty known quarto versions in 1766 and invited him to assist Johnson with a new edition of the complete works which appeared in 1773 (sometimes known as *Johnson-Steevens* 1).[15] Like Johnson, Steevens reprinted the prefaces of most previous editors of Shakespeare including Rowe's *Account of the Life &c.* He mentions (1778, i. 203) the intention of William Oldys (who had died in 1761) to write "a regular life of our author" and reports some of Oldys's notes, e.g. that Shakespeare had played the part of Adam in *As You Like It* and that his younger brother visited London. Most importantly, Steevens included Malone's earliest attempt at a chronology (1778, i. 269–346), two years before Edward Capell's own brief effort to establish the sequence of plays (in *Notes and Various Readings of Shakespeare* (1779–1783, ii. ii. 183–86). Steevens then delegated to Malone the task of editing several apocryphal plays, the narrative poems, and the sonnets, which was published as a two-volume supplement in 1780.

Overall, there were so few documented references to Shakespeare's life known by 1780 that George Steevens, the most respected editor of his day, was able to declare that scarcely anything was known for sure about Shakespeare:

> All that is known with any degree of certainty concerning Shakespeare is –that he was born in Stratford upon Avon, –married and had children there, went to London, where he commenced actor, and wrote poems and plays, –returned to Stratford, made his will, died and was buried. I must confess my readiness to combat every unfounded supposition respecting the particular occurrences of his life. STEEVENS.
>
> (Malone, Edmond, ed. 1780. *Supplement to the Edition of Shakspeare's Plays*, ii. 653)

This note is buried in the commentary to Sonnet 93. The name "STEEVENS" occurs in upper case according to the customary practice at the time of indicating the author of such a note. The first part of Steevens's statement has been quoted frequently, often by those who wish to counterclaim that much information is known. The second part – to combat every unfounded supposition – has invariably been ignored. Most of the large mass of biographical data regarding the life of Shakespeare was anecdotal and speculative, with no basis in contemporary documents.

In their own ways, both Edward Capell and George Steevens issued a challenge about the writing of a biography of Shakespeare: Capell gave guidelines as to how an impersonal or external biography could be constructed; Steevens believed that no biography was possible. Malone took up these challenges and followed Capell's recommendations. How Malone hoped to meet this challenge through extensive investigations and why he ultimately failed will be considered in the next chapter.

Notes

1 Severn's volume (1839) is slim, with about 22 lines per page averaging about seven words per line. Scott McCrea has studied the manuscript and asked if Severn was confused about references to Shakespeare's daughter. 'Mrs. Queeny, RIP: A New Examination of Rev. John Ward's Notebooks' in *Notes and Queries* 59.2 (2012, 182–85).

2 The earliest document linking Shakespeare and Jonson was the list of actors in Jonson's *Works* in 1616. Michael Drayton mentions Shakespeare only once: in an elegy of 1627. Shakespeare did not refer to any writers anywhere by name.

3 John Aubrey's manuscripts were deposited with the Ashmolean Museum in Oxford in 1693 and at the instigation of Malone they were in part published in 1813 as *Brief Lives* (ed. T. Hearne). They were transferred to the Bodleian Library, Oxford, in 1860 and are now classed as Bodl. Aubrey MSS. The manuscripts were published in part in 1898 (2 vols. ed. Andrew Clark). The thorough modern edition *John Aubrey: Brief Lives with An Apparatus for the Lives of our English Mathematical Writers* was edited by Kate Bennet (Oxford University Press, 2015).

4 John Aubrey's note occurs in Bodl. Aubrey MS. 6, f. 46 in the section on Davenant (*Brief Lives* 1813, i. 204). It was ignored by Wood and by Rowe. Charles Gildon wondered whether Shakespeare's visits to Oxford were "for the beautiful mistress of the house or the good wine" in his continuation of Langbaine's *Account of the English Dramatick Poets* (1698, 32).

5 Anthony Wood (1632–1695) was seeking information for his great biographical register *Athenae Oxonienses*: 4 vols (1691–1692) London: Bennet. The first volume, covering the period 1500–1640, only mentions Shakespeare as a contemporary of Marlowe. Freeman and Gager. Wood's opinion of Aubrey was reported in *The Life of Anthony à Wood* ed. Thomas Hearne (1772).

6 John Dennis *The Comical Gallant*. London: A. Baldwin (1702) sig A2r. "This comedy [*Merry Wives*] was written at her command, and by her direction, and she was so eager to see it acted that she commanded it to be finished in fourteen days; and was afterwards, as tradition tells us, very well pleased at the representation" (*WS* ii. 263).

7 Jonathan Bate & Eric Rasmussen, eds. 2011. *Merry Wives of Windsor*. (Arden3).

8 In the following quotations from Rowe, roman numerals (III) refer to the original pagination of the 1709 edition, Volume I.

9 See Appendix B for the biographical comments of Rowe's *Account*. That Rowe offered a critical introduction to the plays has recently been mentioned by Brian Cummings in "Last Words: The Biographemes of Shakespeare" *SQ* 2014.

10 Charles Gildon. *The Life of Mr. Thomas Betterton, the late eminent tragedian*. London: R. Gosling (1710). David Roberts *Thomas Betterton: the Greatest Actor of the Restoration Stage*. Cambridge: Cambridge University Press (2010). A text purportedly from 1715 entitled "Some Further Account of the Life &c. of Mr. William Shakespeare" with reports of Betterton's conversations at Stratford has been dismissed as a forgery by Holderness (2009).

11 Christian Deelman, *The Great Shakespeare Jubilee*. London: Michael Joseph (1964). Alan Kendall, *David Garrick: A Biography*. New York: St. Martin's Press (1985).

12 Theobald states that King Charles the First's queen stayed three weeks at New Place, but Halliwell-Phillips established that the sojourn lasted only three days from 11 to 13 July 1643 (*Outlines* 1886, ii. 108).

13 Sir John Hawkins, *The Life of Samuel Johnson, LL.D.* London: Chambers, (1787, 440). I am indebted to Dr Paul Tankard of the University of Otago for bringing this allusion to my attention.

14 Richard Farmer. *An Essay on the Learning of Shakespeare: Addressed to Joseph Cradock, Esq.* 1767. Farmer's expanded essay was included in Steevens's 1793 edition (*Johnson-Steevens* 4) and in later editions.

15 Revised editions were published in 1778 (*Johnson-Steevens* 2), 1785 (*Johnson-Steevens* 3), 1793 (*Johnson-Steevens* 4), 1803 (the first variorum edition or *Johnson-Steevens* 5), and 1813 (the second variorum edition or *Johnson-Steevens* 6). All of these editions contained Rowe's *Account*.

4 Doubting the Myths

Malone's Unwritten Life of Shakespeare

Despite the most diligent inquiries, very few particulars have been recovered, respecting Shakespeare's private life or literary history.
—Edmund Malone (1790)

In the mid-eighteenth century, the Scottish philosopher David Hume
had asserted that "Nothing is more dangerous to reason than the flights
of the imagination." Later Hume added: "A wise man, therefore, pro-
portions his belief to the evidence."[1] His skepticism regarding belief and
evidence was not highly regarded at first but became fundamental to the
outlook of the Enlightenment later in the eighteenth century. Hume's
caution can be seen in the careful note struck by Shakespearean editors
such as Edward Capell and George Steevens, and especially in the work
of Edmund Malone (1744–1812). Malone's wide-ranging research, his
even-handed discussion, and his publications have gained high regard
among modern scholars. Schoenbaum refers to him as "perhaps the
greatest of all Shakespearian scholars" (1970, ix). Similarly, Wells and
Taylor describe him as "the most talented and influential of all scholars
to have dedicated his energies to the explication of Shakespeare's life
and work" (1987, 55). Marcus Walsh pays a more detailed tribute to
Malone's "brilliant contextualizing scholarship" (2010, 160):

> To the existing body of known and reproduced documents asso-
> ciated with the bard, Malone added a number of deeds and sev-
> eral wills, including a new and accurate text of Shakespeare's own
> will, and transcripts, from the Prerogative Court of Canterbury,
> of the wills of John Hall, husband of Susannah Shakespeare, the
> playwright's daughter, and of Thomas Nashe, husband of his grand-
> daughter Elizabeth.
>
> (Walsh 2010, 185)

Malone spent forty years establishing what was known about Shakespeare and where it was documented. He also instigated the search
for chronological development in Shakespeare's biography and set the

broader context by establishing periods in history of the English theatre. He intended to take up the challenges of Capell and Steevens by
constructing a life of Shakespeare in "one uniform and connected narrative," but his hope remained unfulfilled by the time of his death in 1812.
He conceded that the known materials were not sufficient for a coherent
narrative and doubted that such materials would ever be recoverable.
Many contemporary documents published by the time of Malone relate
to contextual matters: Shakespeare's family, general life in Stratford and
Warwickshire, and the history of the theatre in English; few records
appertain directly to Shakespeare's life. Malone's attempt at a chronology of the plays, an essential prerequisite for any literary biography,
remained in his own estimation conjectural. His vast array of materials
relating to Shakespeare's life and times were published posthumously by
his friend and literary executor, James Boswell Jr., in the edition of 1821,
which became known as the 'third variorum.'

4.1 Attempt at a Chronology of the Works

Malone's earliest contribution to the biographical study of Shakespeare
was his *Attempt to Ascertain the Order in Which the Plays Attributed
to Shakspeare Were Written,* which was published in *Johnson-Steevens*
2 (1778, i. 269–346) when Malone was part of Steevens's editorial team.
Malone revised and expanded the *Attempt to Ascertain* for his own
edition (1790 volume I, part I, 261–386) with a further expanded version that was published in the posthumous edition (1821, ii. 288–468).
Previous editors of Shakespeare had shown little interest in dating the
plays; Rowe had vaguely wondered which plays of Shakespeare were
among his earliest (1709, i. vii; 4). Pope suggested that "the works of
his riper years are manifestly raised above those of his former" (1725, i.
51) without detailing which plays he means or how he knows when they
were composed. Dr Johnson noted in his preface: "By what gradations
of improvement he proceeded, is not easily known; for the chronology of
his works is yet unsettled" (1765, i. sig. C3ᵛ). Capell had emphasised this
same point in his preface but was aware that the chronology might not
be "discoverable" (1767, 71–72).

Malone accepted this challenge both for his chronology of
Shakespeare's works and for his *Rise and Progress of the English Stage*
(1790, i. i.). In a note on *Cymbeline* (1790, i. i. 357), he reported with
sadness that Heminges and Condell "manifestly paid no attention to
chronological arrangement" when compiling the First Folio according
to genre rather than in the chronological sequence of performance preferred by Jonson (1616). Malone outlines his own method "to collect
into one view, from his several dramas, and from the ancient tracts
in which they are mentioned, or alluded to, all the circumstances that
can throw any light on this new and curious enquiry" (1778, i. 272;

repeated verbatim 1790, i. ii. 264; 1821, ii. 292). He also read other critics carefully and made much use of Thomas Tyrwhitt's *Observations and Conjectures* (1766) and Richard Farmer's *Essay on the Learning of Shakespeare* (1767). Malone inferred that Shakespeare did not start writing plays before 1591 (1778, i. 276–77) as his name was absent from the reviews of William Webbe (*A Discourse of Poetrie* 1586), George Puttenham (*The Arte of English Poesie* 1589), and Sir John Harington ("Brief Apologie of Poetrie" 1590–1591):[2]

> If even *Love's Labour's Lost* had then appeared, which was probably his first dramatick composition, is it imaginable, that Harrington should have mentioned the Cambridge Pedantius, and *The Play of Cards* (which last he tells us was a *London* comedy) and have passed by, unnoticed, the new prodigy of the dramatick world?
>
> (1778, i. 278)

Malone thus placed Shakespeare's earliest play in 1591, immediately after Harington published his essay. Malone accepted Tyrwhitt's identification of Shakespeare with the "upstart crow" in *Groatsworth of Wit* (1592) soon after Shakespeare began his career as a professional writer. Malone considers the limited evidence for each play in turn, noting which plays were mentioned by Meres in 1598, and whether they were published in quarto or recorded in performance. After reviewing such evidence as was available, Malone felt able to offer a table of dates for the plays, ranging from 1591 to 1614. The chronologies of Chambers (1930) and Wells and Taylor (1987) accept Malone's starting point and generally follow his sequence and dating.

However, Malone was aware of the difficulties from the outset: the title of his essay, *An Attempt to Ascertain the Order*, indicated his own caution: "However, after the most diligent enquiries, very few particulars have been recovered, respecting his private life, or literary history" (1778, i. 270). Therefore, Malone concedes, "probability alone is pretended to."

Malone originally suggested that *Love's Labour's Lost* was the earliest play due to the "frequent rhymes," "its artless and desultory dialogue, and the irregularity of the composition" (1778, i. 280–81). Then he gave a later date for the play to 1594, even though his view of the play remained unchanged (1790, i. 294; and again in 1821, ii. 327 with expanded footnote). In his revised essay (1790, ii. 296), Malone changed his criteria for dating the earliest play, stating that *Love's Labour's Lost* must have come after *Comedy of Errors* and *A Midsummer Night's Dream* as there is "more attempt at delineation of character" than in other comedies. None of these criteria (incidence of rhyme, desultoriness of dialogue, or extent of characterisation) are established indicators of time of composition.

Malone places *Romeo and Juliet* in 1595, ignoring Tyrwhitt's suggestion that the Nurse ("'Tis since the earthquake now eleven years", *Romeo & Juliet*, 1. 3. 23) was referring to the earthquake of April 1580, which would date the play eleven years later to 1591. Malone believes that Shakespeare in the Nurse's speech is simply portraying "the characteristic traits, which distinguish old people of the lower class" (1778, i. 290–92). His initial date for *Hamlet* was 1596 (1778, i. 292), based on the allusion by Thomas Lodge to "the ghost which cried so miserably at the theatre, like an oyster-wife, Hamlet, revenge!" After the discovery of another allusion to a play about Hamlet, which had been made by Thomas Nashe in his preface to Robert Greene's *Menaphon* (1589), Malone postulated another play about Hamlet by another author. Malone later revised his preferred date for *Hamlet* to 1600 by assuming that the reference in Lodge was to the assumed earlier play on the same subject (1821, ii. 373).[3]

He presents other tenuous criteria for dating plays. After noting no reference to either *Timon of Athens* or *Coriolanus* before their inclusion in the First Folio of 1623, Malone assigns these plays to 1609 and 1610, "a period, to which we are not led by any particular circumstance to attribute any other of his works" (1778, i. 337). Malone dates *Macbeth* to 1606 mainly by linking it with the welcome given by three weird sisters to King James upon his arrival in Oxford; it is possible that the two events were not connected or that *Macbeth* was earlier. As with *Coriolanus*, Malone arbitrarily assigned a date of 1607 to *Julius Caesar*, shortly after William Alexander's play of the same name had been performed and published: "This, I imagine, was prior to our author's performance." Malone's use of the phrase "I imagine" signals his own conjecture (1778, i. 332).

Malone expanded his *Attempt to Ascertain* from 77 to 126 pages for his 1790 edition. From the original essay, Malone makes only two significant changes: he brought forward the date of *The Taming of the Shrew* from 1606 to 1594; and he put back *The Winter's Tale* from 1594 to 1604. In the preface, he mentions one further change:

> Some information, however, which has been obtained since that essay was printed in its present form, inclines me to think, that one of the two plays which I allude to, *The Winter's Tale*, was a still later production than I have supposed; for I now have good reason to believe, that it was first exhibited in the year 1613; and that consequently it must have been one of our poet's latest works.
>
> (1790, i. i. lxi–lxii)

Malone's uncertainty is evident in the phrase "inclines me to think." Malone saw an allusion to *A Winter's Tale* in Jonson's *Bartholomew Fair* (1614) and he associates a first performance with recent composition.

Malone also finds a reference in Henry Herbert's *Account Book of the Revels* which states that *A Winter's Tale* had been licenced by Sir George Buc, who did not start licencing plays before 1610 (according to Malone's researches). Malone is making certain assumptions which cannot be verified: an alternative is that the play was written earlier, but not performed in public until 1610.

A further, expanded version of the *Attempt to Ascertain the Order* was published by Boswell Jr. in volume II of the 1821 edition of the works pages 288–468, where it follows the incomplete "Life of Shakespeare" (considered later in this chapter). At 179 pages, this version is almost half as long again as the second version published in 1790. He retained his note of pessimism:

> The period at which Shakespeare began to write for the stage will, I fear, never be precisely ascertained, unless some manuscript or printed document, relating to him, which has hitherto eluded all our researches, shall fortunately be hereafter discovered.
>
> (1821, ii. 167)

He adjusted the dates of seventeen plays slightly; only the dates of three plays have been radically revised by subsequent scholars. Malone (1821, ii. 388–401) dates *Henry VIII* to 1603, discarding Sir Henry Wotton's description of the play as "new" in his description of the fire at the Globe in 1613. Malone is aware of Wotton's letter but considers that the performance in 1613 was a revival. Malone's position is tenable. Second, Malone originally dated *Twelfth Night* to 1614 but revised this to 1607 (1821, ii. 441–45) due to Maria's reference to "the new map with the augmentation of the Indies" – which he took as allusion to *Eastward Ho!* (performed in 1604; published in 1607), Dekker's *Westward Ho!* (published 1607),[4] and Marston's *What You Will*. Malone was unaware of Manningham's Diary which records a performance of the play (or at least of a similar play) at the Middle Temple on 2 February 1602. Third, Malone revised his original date for *Othello* from 1611 to 1604 after he claimed to have found a reference to a performance in that year; Boswell was "unable to discover upon what evidence he knew this important and decisive fact" (1821, ii. n. 404).[5] Malone continued to date *Julius Caesar* to 1607, arguing that Shakespeare composed it shortly before *Antony & Cleopatra*, which was listed in the Stationers' Register in 1608, noting that neither play was published until 1623.[6]

Although Malone made exceptional efforts in the search for contemporary records, the documentary gaps were so large that his chronology remained conjectural. Thus in his edition he retained the sequence of plays in the First Folio (Comedies, then Histories, then Tragedies) in line with most previous editors. At the end of the first version of his essay, Malone confirms that he is only making an attempt:

If the dates here assigned to our author's plays should not in every instance, bring with them conviction of their propriety, let it be remembered that this is a subject on which conviction cannot at this day be obtained; and that the observations now submitted to the publick, do not pretend to any higher title than that of "An AT-TEMPT to ascertain the chronology of the dramas of Shakspeare".

(Original emphasis; 1778, i. 346)

Malone was aware that to some readers the "inquiry will appear a tedious and barren speculation" (1821, ii. 468). Despite these shortcomings and Malone's own cautionary words, most modern editors accept that an outline is possible and follow his approach to dating the plays.

Malone realised that a chronology of the works was an essential prerequisite for a literary biography of Shakespeare. His approach and his findings have been very influential on subsequent commentators such as Dowden (1875) and editors such as Chambers (1930) and Wells and Taylor (1987). However, the following general criticisms can be made not only against Malone but also against these editors:

i   Malone's starting date of 1590–1591 depends on Harington's omission of Shakespeare's name or plays from his "Brief Apologie of Poetrie" (1590–1591). Malone's assumption is that Shakespeare must always have been such an outstanding playwright that he would have attracted the attention of these writers. This assumption is open to question on a number of points. First, most of Harington's tract engages with Philip Sidney's *Defense of Poesie,* both of which were written in rural seclusion. Malone may not have been aware that Harington was banished from court for much of the 1580s at the queen's command, not to return until he had completed his translation of Ariosto's *Orlando Furioso*. His tract was written during his period of rustication. Thus Harington, absent from London until 1591, was not a reliable authority for recent performances of plays at court or in the London theatres. Second, Harington, Puttenham, and Webbe might have seen some plays of Shakespeare in performance but not mentioned him as they were dealing not with dramatists, but with poets. Third, Shakespeare may have been writing plays during the so-called 'lost years' 1585–1592 without any of them being performed (Honigmann 1982). Fourth, it is also possible that Shakespeare was a member of a playing company such as the Queen's Men, who performed plays without any attribution of the playwright's name (McMillan and MacLean 1998, 84–93).

ii Acceptance of the assumption by editors from the eighteenth to the twentieth centuries that the texts in many quartos were "surreptitiously and lamely Printed in his Life-time" (Rowe 1709, i. x; Steevens 1766; Pollard 1909; Chambers 1930). More recently, many quartos have been accepted as early versions by Shakespeare (Maguire, *Shakespeare's Suspect Texts* 1996; Erne *Shakespeare as a Literary Dramatist* 2003; Jolly, *The First Two Quartos of Hamlet* 2014).

iii   Malone assumed that Shakespeare composed only one version of a play and that any variations were due to outside interference. However, it is possible that Shakespeare produced different versions of the same play, with revision possibly years apart, as Wells and Taylor concluded for *King Lear* (*Works* 1987).

iv   Shakespeare confined himself to working on one or two plays at a time; it is possible that Shakespeare would have a number of plays in preparation at the same time; or that he would have ceased working on one play mid-composition only to resume it at a later stage.

v   Malone assumed that plays were performed shortly after composition: "it is improbable that he should have suffered it [his earliest attempt at a play] to lie in his closet, without endeavouring to derive some profit by it" (1821, ii. 308). It remains a possibility that Shakespeare completed a play for which there remains no mention of its performance (if any): there are no references whatsover to *Coriolanus, Timon of Athens*, and *All's Well* before their first publication in the First Folio of 1623.

iv   Inconsistent application of the word "date" as referring to original composition, first performance, or first publication; these distinctions were made by Thompson and Taylor who imply that there could be as many as nine dates for *Hamlet* – three each for Q1, Q2 and F1 (Arden3, 2006, 44).

v   Assumption that Shakespeare began by revising the works of others (generally discarded) and unaware or unwilling to accept co-authorship or collaboration, as was established by Vickers (2002) and is now accepted by one biographer, Lois Potter (2012).

vi   Subjective criteria used for accepting some contemporary allusions, e.g. to Essex in the phrase "the general of our gracious empress" (*Henry V*, Chorus to Act V) or rejecting others, e.g. to the possible allusion to the 1580 earthquake in *Romeo and Juliet* which he dismissed in 1778, but later found "not so improbable" (1821, ii. 350).

vii   The conjecture that more rhyme in a play is an indication of earlier composition. *Love's Labour's Lost,* which has most rhyme,[7] is now placed in the mid-1590s. While rhyme is no longer accepted as an indication of date, other stylistic variations are now taken as evidence of change in the author's style (i.e. not as a conscious control over his style).

viii   Over-reliance on Meres for negative evidence that Shakespeare had not composed *Hamlet* by 1598 as he made no mention it. In fact, Meres did not refer to any play called *Hamlet* (whether Shakespeare's or by anyone else) even though there were references to a play about Hamlet in 1589, 1594, and 1596. The play might have been composed by Shakespeare before then but remained unknown to the public. Malone suspected that Meres was not a particularly reliable authority, noting Meres's omission of *The Taming of the Shrew* was not sufficient to prove that Shakespeare had not written his version by 1598 (1790, i. i. 293). Malone also observed that Meres "enumerates Jonson among the writers of *tragedy*, though no tragedy of his writing, of so early a date [by 1598], is now extant" (1790, i. i. 399).

ix The possibility that some dateable items in the plays were later additions, e.g. the reference in *Henry V* to the return of "the general of our gracious empress," which is usually associated with Essex in Ireland in 1599 or the reference to the Porter's speech in *Macbeth* to the "farmer that hanged himself on the expectation of plenty" which is usually taken to refer to food shortages in 1605–1606. Even if these references are contemporary with the composition of the play, they do not specifically allude to these events and might refer to another general or another food shortage.

In addition, some of Malone's approaches have been discarded:

x Malone asserts the "strong probability" that unpublished works were late. One play, mentioned by Meres, *Two Gentlemen of Verona*, was not published until 1623 but is usually placed in the early 1590s.

ix Malone makes judgements about anonymous quartos, as Shakespearean or not, despite the lack of evidence as to their attribution, e.g. *The Taming of a Shrew* (1594).

Like Malone, E. K. Chambers in his chapter "The Problem of Chronology" (*WS* i. 243–74) offers his chronology only with an extreme caution that later commentators ignore. Wells and Taylor ("The Canon and Chronology of Shakespeare's Plays" in *Textual Companion* 1987, 69–144) are much more assured in determining their preferred sequence of composition and assigning dates. The result is the assumption made by most modern commentators that the chronology is well established and "in its final form".

A few modern scholars, however, have proposed a radical change to the Malone / Chambers starting point, thus undermining the entire dating scheme. E. A. J. Honigmann argues that Shakespeare began writing plays in the late 1580s when he was staying in Lancashire with the Hesketh family (*Shakespeare's Impact* 1982). His "early starter theory" (but not the Lancastrian hypothesis) has been accepted and developed by Katherine Duncan-Jones, who imagines how Shakespeare joined the Queen's Men in the mid-1580s and began writing plays for them *c.* 1588 (*Ungentle Shakespeare* 2001). This theory, which brings the dates of the composition of most plays earlier than is usually accepted, and is tenable, despite the criticisms of Wells and Taylor (1987). However, neither the early-starter, nor the late-starter theory can be verified as there are no contemporary records as to the date of composition of <u>any</u> play by Shakespeare. On present evidence, therefore, any chronology of the works appears to be only a little more than "tedious and barren speculation."

4.2 Use of the Poems for Biographical Inference

Malone was also the first editor to offer any biographical interpretation of the Poems in the first (of his two) volume supplement (1780) to the *Johnson-Steevens* 2 edition. He revised and expanded his extensive commentary on, and biographical inferences from, Shakespeare's poems in the 1790 edition volume X, and again in 1821, volume XXI. Whereas Francis Gentleman had made biographical inferences from the plays ("Life of Shakespeare" 1774, ix), Malone made his inferences from the poems. The narrative poems and the sonnets had been excluded by Rowe in his 1709 edition, but were published in an additional volume by Charles Gildon (1710, 1714), using the 1640 Benson text.[8] Although Steevens reprinted the sonnets in his 1766 edition of the early quartos, he felt uneasy as to their literary merit. Regarding the phrase "master-mistress of my passion" (Sonnet 20.2), Steevens stated: "It is impossible to read this fulsome panegyrick, addressed to a male object, without an equal mixture of disgust and indignation" (Malone 1780, i. 596). When Steevens brought out subsequent editions of Shakespeare, he refused to include the sonnets and other poems, claiming that "the strongest Act of Parliament that could be framed, would fail to compel readers into their service," and that Malone's "instruments of criticism" had been disgraced by being applied to the poems (1793, i. vii; repeated verbatim 1803, i. 31; and again 1813, i. 30–31).

Despite Steevens's opposition, Malone remained keen on the poems throughout his life: he included the sonnets with the other poems in the tenth and final volume of his 1790 edition with extensive notes. Boswell published the poems in Volume XX (of 21 volumes) in the third variorum (1821). Margreta de Grazia points out that, unlike previous editors, Malone began his editing career with the sonnets which may have encouraged his view of them as autobiographical (1991, 205). From the beginning, Malone restored the 1609 sequence and the text, which he saw as significant, claiming that 1–126 were addressed to a male friend and the remaining twenty-eight sonnets to a mistress. The 1609 sequence is thus a crucial basis for Malone's narrative interpretation. In addition, Malone argued that the 'rival poet' in Sonnets 78–80 was a real person identifying him as Edmund Spenser. Other poets have been confidently identified as the 'rival poet' by various scholars e.g. George Chapman (by Acheson 1913), Francis Davison (by Duncan-Jones 1997, 64, but not in 2001), and Christopher Marlowe (by Bate 1998). From the time of Malone, most biographers have sought to reveal not only the 'rival poet' but also the 'dark lady' and the 'fair youth'. Some of these identifications are considered in Chapter 9. Malone made another biographical connection in response to the phrase "As an unperfect actor" in Sonnet 23: while Shakespeare may have witnessed performances by visiting acting companies in Stratford (e.g. by the Earl of Warwick's Men in 1574), Malone suggests that perhaps he composed this sonnet only after his own first performances in London. On this, as on other inferences, Malone was very cautious: "Whether the lines before us were founded on experience, or observation, cannot now be ascertained. What I have advanced is merely conjectural" (Malone 1790, x, 210–11).

Malone wrote a lengthy note on Sonnet 93 (1778, i. 653–57; repeated verbatim 1790, x, 265–69; and 1821, xx, 305–9) contrasting his own interpretation with Steevens's. Malone formed the opinion that on the subject of jealousy, Shakespeare was writing from personal experience. Steevens rejected this line of interpretation:

> That Shakespeare has written with the utmost power on the subject of jealousy, is no proof that he ever felt it. Because he has, with equal vigour, expressed the varied aversions of Apemantus and Timon to the world, does it follow that he himself was a Cynic or a wretch deserted by his friends? STEEVENS.
>
> (1778, i. 656)

George Steevens thus rejected the idea that Shakespeare's first-person poetry could constitute biographical evidence. Biographers, however, have often treated the sonnets as literal. They not only accept but also claim to identify a 'rival poet', but also a 'dark lady', and a 'fair youth'. They accept that the sonnets were placed in the 1609 sequence by Shakespeare and believe that all of the first 126 are to a friend or lover who is male. A few commentators have rejected any autobiographical interpretation, saying that the poems are part of a tradition of courtly poetry in a line involving poets such as Petrarch, Ronsard, and Sidney. James Schiffer has conducted a thorough review of the different biographical claims and the various counterclaims (in his Introduction to *Shakespeare's Sonnets* 2000, 3–71).

All of the positions are tenable, but none can be verified. Edmondson and Wells agree, concluding that without external corroborating evidence, such attempts at identifying personas in the poems with historical figures are futile (2004, 22–27).

4.3 Ambition for a Life of Shakespeare

When Malone published his edition of the Works of Shakespeare in 1790, he included so much prefatory material that the first volume, which was printed last, had to be divided into two: part 1, approximately 500 pages, contained previous prefatory material and Malone's expanded *Attempt to Ascertain the Order*. Part II contains approximately 600 pages, beginning with his new essay, *The Rise and Progress of the English Stage*, and the text of many documents. He realised that the diffuse material needed to be brought together and he announced his ambition to collect the biographical material into a "Life of Shakespeare": "At some future time I hope to weave the whole into one uniform and connected narrative" (1790, i. i. lxiii). At this time he was cautious about the biographical value of the existing material, conceding that despite "the most diligent inquiries, very few particulars have been recovered, respecting his private life or literary history" (1790, i. i. 262). Much of the material related to the historical, social, or literary period, not to the man himself.

Malone made diligent enquiries, and in 1780 discovered Edward Alleyn's *Diary*,[9] and *Henslowe's Diary* in 1789 at Dulwich College. From these, he made extensive notes and a transcript of thirty-eight pages for his inclusion in his treatise on *Rise and Progress of the English Stage*. He added his own research about each of the actors (1790, i. ii. 204–18), and a five page review of the life of Henry Wriothesley, third earl of Southampton, placed in the same volume as the poems (1790, x). He included some prefaces of previous editors (Rowe, Pope, and Johnson) but omitted the prefaces of Theobald, Hanmer, and Warburton "because they appeared to me to throw no light on our author or his works" (1790, i. i. lxiii). He included Rowe's *Account of the Life &c.* but dismissed it as "meagre and imperfect" (1790, i. i. 102–54) and added his own extensive commentary, Malone discusses every additional anecdote reported by Oldys, Farmer, and other scholars (1790, i. i. 155–70).

Malone also devoted much effort to the exposure of forged texts. The late eighteenth century saw growing interest in Shakespeare, with a large number of assertions, documents, and souvenirs of the great poet, many of them of dubious origin. Malone sought to distinguish what was based on documentary evidence from what was hearsay or forgery:

> From iconography, to forgeries, to Shakespearean relics, to unreliable Stratford legends disseminated by self-appointed local historians, to bitter editorial rivalries, the country was awash with erroneous, unreliable, or misleading information. One of the tasks Malone took upon himself from the beginning was to stem the flow, or at least to purify it with facts.
>
> (Martin 1995, 28)

In 1796, Malone responded promptly to William Henry Ireland, who claimed to have discovered letters written by Shakespeare, Southampton, and Elizabeth. In this tract, Malone demonstrated his scholarly approach when carefully explaining why they were forgeries.

All of these activities – reviews of previous writers, new research and exposure of forgeries – were essential prerequisites for his proposed "Life of Shakespeare". In addition, Malone's interest in biography was heightened by his close friendship with two authors of pioneering biographical works: Samuel Johnson, who published his *Lives of the Most Eminent English Poets* in 1779–1781 and James Boswell, who published his *Life of Samuel Johnson* in 1791. Malone had known Boswell from their time at the Inner Temple together in 1763 and knew Dr Johnson from 1764 (Martin 1995, 5–6). When Malone was invited to join the Literary Club in 1782, he had become a close friend of Johnson, Boswell, and many other literary figures. However, their attempts at biography were different from Malone's proposed "Life of Shakespeare". Boswell had known Johnson well for over twenty years and had recorded many of the great doctor's *bons mots:* his *Life of Samuel Johnson* was a personal memoir expanded with comments and anecdotes from other friends and acquaintances, not least Malone himself.[10]

Malone wanted to take nothing on trust, but to consider the subject as wholly new. He thus began his search for contemporary records. At Stratford Corporation, he found the letter dated 1598, by Richard Quiney asking Shakespeare for a loan, expressing the hope in a letter to Boswell on 1 September 1793,[11] that he would find Shakespeare's reply and more correspondence. No further letter was found. From the parish register at the Holy Trinity Church, he reported details about Shakespeare's family and corrected various errors including the name of Shakespeare's son from Samuel to Hamnet. He discovered much material in Stratford, but nothing useful about Shakespeare's actual life. Like Rowe, Malone issued an advertisement in 1795 for any documents relating to Malone's proposed "Life of Shakespeare", which was "now nearly ready for the Press." Malone wished to expand his proposed "Life of Shakespeare" "by drawing from some hitherto unexplored Repository papers of a very different complexion from the miserable trash [the Ireland forgeries] we have now been examining." This advertisement was unsuccessful. Malone's new "Life of Shakespeare", which was "now nearly ready for the Press" in 1796, remained unfinished when he died in 1812.

Next, Malone tried to find relevant material from identified three people who might have kept papers relating to Shakespeare: Lady Barnard, the poet's grand-daughter; Ralph Hubaud, a business associate from Stratford; and John Heminges, the theatre manager; but no documents from these sources were forthcoming. Malone consulted various archives at Chancery, the Stamp Office, the Tower of London, the Exchequer, the office of the Lord Chamberlain, and the Diocese of Worcester. He discovered the Office Book of Sir Henry Herbert, Master of the Revels (1623–1642), and made extensive transcripts. The original had disappeared by 1849 when Edward Rimbault advertised for any information about the manuscript in *Notes & Queries* December 1849, 130.[12]

Malone wrote to his friend Thomas Warton in Oxford, asking him to consult John Aubrey's manuscript in the Bodleian Library, and send transcriptions of various passages about Jonson and Shakespeare, much of which was previously unknown (Martin 1995, 132–33). Malone was also in touch with people in Stratford.[13] A wheelwright named John Jordan sent him various accounts of Shakespeare and his family, including a Spiritual Testament purporting to be a Catholic will of John Shakespeare. Some labourers, it was claimed, had found the testament in the rafters of the 'birthplace' in 1757 and someone wrote a six-page copy in 1784. Malone gave an account of its provenance and at first declared that it was probably genuine (1790, i. ii. 161–65), but later changed his mind, which he intended to explain in the forthcoming Life (1796, 198–99). However, Boswell made only a brief reference to Malone's dismissal of this document (1821, ii. 517). The spiritual testament has become a topic of controversy.

The original document has disappeared and for a long time it was considered a forgery (Lee 1915, 646). Chambers believes that, if genuine, the document could only pertain to John Shakespeare for a brief period of his earlier life (*WS* ii. 383). Schoenbaum was more sympathetic and printed a facsimile of the Folger copy of a similar document (1975, 43–46). Robert Bearman has reviewed the controversy, concluding that a freestanding copy of the printed testament was genuinely discovered as Jordan recounted, but that John Shakespeare's name was added later (2003). The spiritual testament is accepted by biographers who propose that William followed his father in adhering to the old religion, e.g. Michael Wood, who accepts it as "unquestionably" genuine (2003, 83), and Stephen Greenblatt, who is slightly less confident (2004, 101). This controversy arises from the lack of any reliable evidence as to what Shakespeare's religious views were. Even if the document is accepted as genuine for the father's affiliations, it does not afford evidence as to what the son believed.

During the 1790s, Malone often wrote to his friend Thomas Percy, (Bishop of Dromore in Co. Down, Ireland) about his ambition to write "the Life of Shakespeare, on which I am now employed" (21 September 1793).[14] A year later, Malone wrote: "I have got through half his life and hope to finish it this summer" (3 June 1794). Almost a decade after that, he seems to have regressed: "I have above half the life of Shakespeare to write" and says he has been delayed by "so many discoveries with respect to the plays" (3 January 1803). Little changed in the next four years: "my favourite object is the Life; of which about a third part remains to be written" (6 June 1807). Another two years later, Malone had become desperate: "I still cherish a hope that I shall live to finish the 'Life of

Shakespeare', about two thirds of which are done" (21 March 1809). He continued work on his second edition of Shakespeare's works, which he had held back pending the new, definitive life. In the meantime other editions were published: *Johnson-Steevens* 4 in 1793, *Johnson-Steevens* 5, the first variorum in 1803, Chalmers's nine-volume edition of the works with illustrations by Fuseli, and a facsimile of the First Folio in 1807. Sadly for Malone, twenty years after announcing his ambition to write a "Life of Shakespeare", it remained unfulfilled at his death in 1812. He appointed his godson, James Boswell Jr. (1778–1822) as his literary executor. Boswell struggled to manage the mass of disorganised papers left by Malone.

Boswell published the new edition of the works from Malone's papers in 1821, nine years after Malone died. This edition, known as the third variorum, became the scholarly standard in the nineteenth century until the publication of the Cambridge edition of 1863–1866 (Murphy 2003, 280). Whereas previous editors had generally followed the sequence of the Folio, this edition presented plays to some extent in Malone's supposed order of composition. There were three volumes of preliminary material: the first began with the usual reprints of earlier prefaces. Boswell included Rowe's *Account* but omitted Malone's excessive notes. Instead, Boswell Jr. incorporated these points into "Mr. Malone's more extensive and correct work on the same subject" (1821, i. xix). In volume III, Boswell included Malone's expanded *History of the English Stage* (now at 294 pages) and the text of many other documents.

Malone's unfinished account of Shakespeare's life appeared in Volume II, divided into four sections: he began with Malone's narrative account of Shakespeare's early life, mistakenly entitled "The Life of Shakespeare," which presented an outline life of Shakespeare as far as 1592 (in 287 pages). Next, Boswell placed Malone's expanded version of *Attempt to Ascertain*, now in 179 pages (1821, ii. 288–467). Then, Boswell placed Malone's discrete discussions on topics in Shakespeare's life and family (1821, ii. 469–524). Finally, Boswell placed (1821, ii. 525–697) transcriptions of documents with Malone's notes which contextualised Shakespeare's life but did not mention him directly: including John Shakespeare's Bill of Complaint against John Lambert; Robert Arden's will; the Grant of Arms to John Shakespeare; the Grants to Robert Arden; a Genealogical Table of Robert Arden; a list of bailiffs at Stratford; and the Incorporation of Stratford. At the start of volume II, Malone sets out an ideal situation for any biographer:

> Of all the accounts of literary men which have been given to the world, the history of the life of Shakespeare would be the most curious and instructive, if we were acquainted with the minute circumstances of his fortunes, the course and extent of his studies, and the means and gradations whereby he acquired that consummate

knowledge of mankind, which, for two centuries, has rendered him the delight and boast of his countrymen.

(1821, ii. 1–3)

Malone was however well aware that neither his own investigations nor his appeal to other researchers had found much of relevance:

[B]ut many of the materials for such a biographical detail being now unattainable, we must content ourselves with such particulars as accident has preserved, or the most sedulous industry has been able to collect.

(1821, ii. 3–5)

Malone recorded the large number of writers who might have written about Shakespeare's life but did not. Previous researchers missed the opportunity to interview surviving relatives of Shakespeare: "our poet's grand-daughter, Lady Barnard, who did not die till 1670. His sister, Joan Hart, was living in 1646; his eldest daughter, Susanna Hall, in 1649; and his second daughter, Judith Queeny, in 1662" (1821, ii. 7). Among those writers who might have enquired further was Sir William Dugdale,

whose Antiquities of Warwickshire appeared in 1656, only thirty [sic] years after the death of our poet, we might reasonably have expected some curious memorials of his illustrious countryman: but he has not given us a single particular of his private life; content-ing himself with a very slight mention of him in his account of the church and tombs of Stratford upon Avon.

(1821, ii. 4)

Thomas Fuller in *Worthies of England* (1662) only gives "a short quib-bling account of our poet, furnishing very little information concern-ing him" (1821, ii. 4). That Anthony Wood "should not have collected any anecdotes of Shakespeare, has always appeared to me extraor-dinary" (1821, ii. 5). Malone next considers two contemporaries of Shakespeare, who did not publish their projected surveys of English poets: Thomas Heywood (*c.* 1573–1641) mentioned "a work which he appears to have long had in contemplation... a general, though sum-mary, description of all the poets."[15] William Browne (*c.* 1590–1645), the pastoral poet, "had a similar intention of writing the *Lives of the English Poets*; which, however, he never executed" (1821, ii. 6). Malone then regrets the omission of Izaac Walton, who wrote lives of Hooker, Donne, Wotton, and Herbert (1679) but did not write his "Life of Shakespeare". Similarly,

[N]either the booksellers, who republished our author's plays in 1664 and 1665, employed any person to write the Life of Shakespeare; nor did Dryden, though a warm admirer of his productions, or any other poet, collect any materials for such a work, till Mr. Rowe, about the year 1707, undertook an edition of his plays.

(1821, ii. 6–7)

Malone lists many others who might have researched Shakespeare's life and is astonished that "almost a century should have elapsed, from the time of his death [in 1616], without a single attempt having been made to discover any circumstance which could throw a light on the history of his private life, or literary career" (10–11).

Overall, Malone fell well short of the intention, which he stated in 1790, of providing "one uniform and connected narrative" of the "Life of Shakespeare". Volume II of the 1821 edition is unreadable from start to finish; it only provides a series of discussions on different topics. Malone cannot be blamed for any lack of effort on his own part – he was a prolific researcher and writer throughout his life. He was prevented from writing his intended coherent "Life of Shakespeare" by a lack of suitable biographical materials, due to the deficiencies and omissions of previous writers and researchers. Almost half of volume II (pages 1–287) deals with Shakespeare's early life. Much of this involves a lengthy and tedious refutation in 113 pages that Spenser was alluding to Shakespeare in *Tears of the Muses* (1821, i. 167–279). For Shakespeare's early life, Malone quotes only three contemporary documents which name him: his own baptism and that of his children. The vast majority of the text and discussion of Malone's "Life of Shakespeare" is concerned with family background, everyday life in Stratford, description of legal documents, and his discussion of posthumous anecdotes. He rejects the deer poaching story, which he traces to the unpublished material of William Fulman (1632–1688), a fellow of Corpus Christ College, Oxford. Malone shows that every version refers to a deer park and park gates, but Charlecote did not have a deer park during this period (1821, ii. 118–48). He also rejects the anecdote about horse-holding, first, noting that the originator of the anecdote was unreliable, second by questioning the tortuous manner by which it was passed down from Davenant to Cibber (1821, ii. 157–66). Despite his general skepticism, Malone took for granted some myths which had been prompted by Rowe: that Shakespeare spent his childhood in Stratford and attended the school there, that he was patronised by Southampton, and that he retired to Stratford. Malone's 1821 "Life of Shakespeare" is actually a series of discrete discussions about a wide range of topics mainly about Shakespeare's family and times. It neither offers a full life, nor a continuous narrative, nor a coherent view of Shakespeare as a person.

Margreta de Grazia (*Shakespeare Verbatim* 1991), has criticised Malone as over-reliant on external documentary evidence and ignored what had been established by "consensus and authority" which she defines as the "contributions which had been passed down over the generations linking his period to Shakespeare's" (1991, 50–51). She defends Rowe's use of the deer poaching anecdote as concerned not with "recording facts" but with "a significant occasion" when Shakespeare had to leave Stratford and seek his fortune in London. For de Grazia, the deer poaching story "dramatized the critical juncture of his life" (1991, 107). In this, she displays a greater interest in following the narrative paradigm suggested by Joseph Campbell in *Hero of a Thousand Faces* (1949) than in historical accuracy, an approach consistent with many modern biographers of Shakespeare.

Edmond Malone merits the greatest respect for having placed so much emphasis on obtaining, recording, and publishing biographical material about Shakespeare. He was a scrupulous researcher who questioned many claims about Shakespeare and traced their origins, revealing that myths such as the deer poaching story was unlikely. He undertook the difficult task of establishing a chronology of the plays on limited and patchy evidence and he remained cautious about his outline. However, Malone was unable to meet the challenge of Edward Capell and George Steevens in writing a biography of Shakespeare due to a lack of biographical material. The next chapter will show that Malone's skepticism was respected and quoted by most commentators during the nineteenth and twentieth centuries when presenting the information known about Shakespeare's life.

Notes

1 The quotations are taken from *A Treatise of Human Nature* (1739) and *An Enquiry concerning Human Understanding* (1748). David Hume (1711–1776) spent some of his later life in London where he had opportunities to meet Dr Johnson and George Steevens. When he retired to Edinburgh, he was visited by James Boswell. It seems unlikely that Malone was personally acquainted with Hume.

2 Sir John Harington (1561–1612) published "Preface, or rather a Briefe Apologie of Poetrie" prefixed to his translation of Ariosto's *Orlando Furioso* (1591).

3 The notion of an earlier play, referred to as the *Ur-Hamlet*, has generally found acceptance among scholars but the latest Arden editors of the play conclude their discussion by stating that a version of Shakespeare's play might date back to 1589 (Thompson, Ann and Neil Taylor. eds. 2006. *Hamlet*. Arden3).

4 *Twelfth Night* 3.2.74-75 was taken by Henry Hallam in 1839 to refer to Edward Wright's 'A Chart of the World on Mercator's Projection' in *The Principall Navigations, Voiages, Traffiques and Discoveries of the English Nation* (1598–1600), ed Richard Hakluyt.

5 Malone may have had access to the Revels Accounts of 1604–1605, where *The Moor of Venis* is recorded as one of seven Shakespeare plays performed "by the

King's Maiesties plaiers" before the King at the Banqueting Hall, Whitehall in November and December 1604. The Revels Accounts were not published until 1842 by Peter Cunningham. They are accepted as genuine by Chambers, who reviews the controversy surrounding their publication (*ES* iv, 135–41).

6 Malone was unaware of the 1599 diary entry by Thomas Platter, who mentions witnessing a performance of a play about the Emperor Caesar. Platter's account was first published in 1899 by Gustav Binz 'Londoner Theater und Schauspiele im Jahr 1599' in *Anglia* 22 (456–64). Chambers (1930, i. 397) and Wells and Taylor (1987, 121) believe that Platter was referring to an early performance of Shakespeare's play. Ernest Schanzer (1956) argues that Platter was referring to a different play ('Thomas Platter's Observations on the Elizabethan Stage' *Notes and Queries* 201, 466–67). Doubt remains as to whether Platter saw Shakespeare's play or whether it was composed in 1599.

7 Chambers's Table II 'Rhyme' puts the incidence of rhyming lines in *Love's Labour's Lost* at 62% of the total lines in verse; second is *Midsummer Night's Dream* at 43% with three other plays at 19% (*WS* ii. 399)

8 Benson made many changes from the 1609 text, including various masculine pronouns to a feminine form. He also made changes to the sequence and omitted eight sonnets altogether (18, 19, 43, 56, 75, 76, 96, and 126).

9 Edward Alleyn (MS IX at Dulwich College) documented his life on a daily basis from September 1617 to October 1622.

10 Adam Sisman (2001) describes how Malone assisted James Boswell Sr. in preparing the second edition of his *Life of Johnson* (1791). After the death of Boswell Sr. in 1795, Malone took responsibility for later editions between 1799 and 1811.

11 James Boswell. *The Correspondence of James Boswell with David Garrick, Edmund Burke and Edmond Malone* (ed. By P. S. Baker *et al.*) New Haven, CT: Yale University Press (1986, iv. 427).

12 George Chalmers (1742–1825) also made selective transcriptions. J. Q. Adams collected the transcriptions and published them in *The Dramatic Records of Sir Henry Herbert: Master of the Revels 1623–1673* (1917), Yale: Yale University Press.

13 Neither Malone nor Chalmers mentions the Rev. James Wilmot, who may have been making enquiries in Warwicks about Shakespeare during the 1780s. A manuscript, now in the University of London purports to give Wilmot's negative findings. It is now thought to be a forgery by K. E. Attar: 'The Cowell manuscript or the First Baconian: MS 294 at the University of London' in *Shakespeare Survey* 65 (2012, 323–36).

14 Quotations of Malone's letters are taken from Arthur Tillotson, ed. *The Percy Letters, volume 1: The correspondence of Thomas Percy & Edmond Malone*. Baton Rouge: Louisiana State University Press (1944).

15 Thomas Heywood. *Hierarchie of the Blessed Angels*. 9 vols. (1635) London: Adam Islip. Heywood briefly mentions his proposed "Liues of all the Poets, Forreine and Moderne, from the first before *Homer*, to the *Novissimi* and last, of what Nation or Language soeuer" (i. 245); and within the poem echoes Meres when briefly referring to "Mellifluous Shakespeare, whose inchanting Quill / Commanded Mirth or Passion, was but Will" (iv. 206).

5 Filling in the Gaps
Constructing a Life of Shakespeare: 1805–1975

Nothing could be more highly gratifying than an account of the early studies of this wonderful man, the progress of his pen, his moral and social qualities, his friendships and failings, and whatever else constitutes personal history. But on all these topics, his contemporaries and his immediate successors have been equally silent.

—Alexander Chalmers (1805)

Like Steevens and Malone, Alexander Chalmers held serious doubts about the possibility of writing a biography of Shakespeare. This caution remained dominant during the nineteenth and twentieth centuries despite increasing pressure to write exemplary biographies, especially of literary figures. Such skepticism was often repeated in the nineteenth century by literary historians and by editors. The first real attempt at a biography of Shakespeare – a continuous narrative account of his life published as a separate monograph – did not appear until after Carlyle gave his famous lecture on Shakespeare in "Hero as Poet" in 1840. Charles Knight in his *Pictorial Life* (1843) created a highly fictionalised picture of the dramatist for the Victorian reading public. After Knight, other biographies of a similar nature, combining contextual description with inference and speculation, began to appear. Shakespeare, the greatest writer in English, was presented as "a respectable citizen, a successful businessman, and a moral paragon" (Kewes 2002, 78). Perhaps the most important Shakespearean researchers of the Victorian period, James Halliwell(-Phillipps),[1] abandoned the idea at writing a biography and concentrated on researching, transcribing, and assessing documents (*Outlines*, seven editions, 1881–1887). At the end of the nineteenth century, Sidney Lee prepared an entry for the *Dictionary of National Biography* (*DNB*) (1897), which was subsequently reprinted as a monograph. However, as the study of English Literature developed at universities in the twentieth century, scholars remained cautious about the possibility of any biography of Shakespeare, or whether it should play any part in the appreciation of the works. Another distinguished researcher of Shakespeare's life and theatre during this period, Sir Edmund Chambers, also eschewed traditional biography (1930). Some new documents naming Shakespeare have been discovered since the time of Malone, but these had not contributed to the revelation of Shakespeare's character or to the understanding of his literary career. Summing up his great review, Samuel Schoenbaum wondered whether it was possible to write any biography of Shakespeare at all (*Shakespeare's Lives* 1970, 767).

5.1 Skepticism in the Nineteenth Century

In the first half of the nineteenth century, three important literary historians, Alexander Chalmers, John Payne Collier, and Henry Hallam, recognised that it was not possible to write a biography of Shakespeare. Alexander Chalmers (1759–1834) edited the works of Shakespeare in 1805, for which he drew together the known biographical facts and anecdotes in a *Sketch of the Life of Shakespeare* covering birth to retirement in 13 pages (i–xiii) adding posthumous material in 33 further pages (xiii–xlvi). Chalmers offered this apology about the thinness of the account: "Our readers will perceive that less is known of Shakespeare than of almost any writer who has been considered as an object of laudable curiosity" (1805 i. xxii). As a biographer who revised the *General Biographical Dictionary* in 32 volumes (1812–1817) and published *The British Essayists: With Prefaces Historical and Biographical* in 45 volumes (1817), Chalmers was in a very good position to compare what was known about the life of Shakespeare with the biographical material available for other writers. The *Sketch* was reprinted with *The Works* many times in the nineteenth century. Schoenbaum dismissed Chalmers's *Sketch* because it added nothing new to the existing material (1970, 248), ignoring Chalmers's insights on the lack of material for a life of Shakespeare.

Another major literary figure of the nineteenth century who recognised the paucity of material available for the life of Shakespeare was John Payne Collier (1789–1883), more famous for his later forgeries. Collier began his career as a very successful critic, publishing his three-volume *History of English Dramatic Poetry* in 1831. Regarding Shakespeare, he noted: "On looking back to the life of Shakespeare, the first observation that must be made is, that so few *facts* are extant regarding him: nearly everything interesting is derived from tradition, or depends upon conjecture" (1831 i. 329). Collier's own investigations at the British Library had revealed the diary of John Manningham, with two interesting references: the entry for 2 February 1601–1602 described a performance of *Twelfth Night*, second. the entry for 13 March 1601–1602 gives the anecdote about Shakespeare enjoying the delights of a young lady before Burbage could arrive. Manningham was not particularly interested in the theatre: within the diary, there is only one notice of a play and only one mention of Ben Jonson.[2]

Another literary historian, Henry Hallam (1777–1859), made the same point about the small extent of knowledge concerning Shakespeare, but in a way that was more relevant to literary biography. Whereas Collier noted that "nearly everything interesting is derived from tradition, or depends upon conjecture," Hallam states in his *Introduction to the Literature of Europe* (1837–1839) that "we scarcely know anything" about William Shakespeare. He continues:

> All that insatiable curiosity and unwearied diligence have hitherto detected about Shakespeare serves rather to disappoint and perplex us than to furnish the slightest illustration of his character. It is not the register of his baptism, or the draft of his will, or the orthography of his name that we seek. No letter of his written, no record of his conversation, no character of him drawn with any fulness by a contemporary has been produced.
>
> (1837 ii. 237–38)

Three editors repeated this view in their biographical prefaces to the *Works*: Samuel Weller Singer in 1826 (i. 4; repeated in 1856), Alexander Dyce in 1827 (repeated in 1857, i. xvi), and Henry Bohn who commented on the "dearth of information" about Shakespeare's life (1863, 2–4). Singer added the cryptic allusions in Robert Greene's *Groatsworth of Wit* and Henry Chettle's *Kind Hart's Dream* (1592).

Another scholar, James Halliwell-Phillipps, devoted most of his adult life to researching and publishing material regarding the life of Shakespeare. He lamented the fact that recent biographers of Shakespeare had resorted to conjecture and imagination in constructing a biography, "each one bitterly complaining of the paucity of facts, but making ample amends by conjectures of their own" (1848, vi). As a result of his disenchantment at the deceptions by his one-time friend, Collier, he concentrated on primary research, transcribing many documents about Shakespeare. He published his results in *Outlines of the Life of Shakespeare*, first issued in 1881 in a restricted format, but successively expanded.[3] The seventh edition of 1887 appeared in two volumes with over 550 pages of supportive material (transcriptions of documents and illustrative notes). The index is rather poor and the documents and notes are in no particular order.

Despite all his efforts, Halliwell-Phillipps only added two new documents about Shakespeare: the 1594 payment "to William Kempe, William Shakespeare and Richard Burbage" for court performances (1887, i. 121); and the Great Wardrobe list of 15 March 1604 with its allotment to "diverse persons" of red cloth for the Coronation Procession (i. 212). He also published transcriptions of newly discovered documents, such as the Shakespeare marriage license from the Worcester Diocesan Register (ii. 55–56) with his own extensive discussion (i. 61–67). He further reported other documents of less significance: that William had a grandfather called Richard and an uncle called Henry

(ii. 207–9); that John Shakespeare sold some property in 1597 (ii. 13); that Anne Hathaway was named as Agnes in the 1581 will of her father (ii. 195); that Shakespeare sued Philip Rogers in 1604 for a petty mount (ii. 29); and that "one q*uart* of sack and one q*uart* of clarrett winne geven to a precher at the newe place" in 1614, although Shakespeare is not mentioned and might not have been present to entertain the minister (ii. 244). These documents offer very limited interest to the biographer or to the literary biographer. Like Malone, he came to accept that a biography of Shakespeare was not possible. Overall, Halliwell-Phillipps achievement lies in the collective publication and evaluation of all the texts relevant to the biography of Shakespeare, however disorganised they were presented.

5.2 Emergence of Romantic Biography

Despite these cautious statements made by distinguished scholars and editors of the day, publishers continued to print something about the life of Shakespeare. Alongside Chalmers's *Sketch*, they continued to issue Rowe's "meagre and imperfect" *Account* despite awareness that it contained few accurate statements about Shakespeare's life and many unsupportable anecdotes. It was published as a preface as late as 1859 for George Routledge's reprint of *Johnson-Steevens* 6. This publisher even issued Rowe's *Account* as a separate pamphlet in 1848, 1854, and 1856. Rowe's *Account* also served as the basis for numerous publications during the nineteenth century such as encyclopaedias, magazine articles, compilations, travel writing, and even guidebooks to Stratford. Rowe's Account was expanded by John Severn who was the first to publish the Diary of John Ward in 1839. Severn elaborated Ward's brief allusion to the "merry meeting" with Jonson and Drayton (183) by describing Shakespeare's death in very moving terms:

> Shakspeare was sick, and they came to cheer, to sooth and to sym-
> pathize with his sufferings. Animated and excited by their long-tried
> and much-loved society, as the sound of the trumpet rouses the spirit
> of the dying war-horse, their presence and voices made him forget
> the weakness that even then was bowing him to the very dust.
>
> (65)

None of these details are contained either in Ward's account or in any other source material. Further speculation emerged in Thomas de Quincey's entry about Shakespeare, which was written in 1838 for the *Encyclopaedia Britannica* (7th edn., 1842) and issued as a monograph in 1864. De Quincey's life contained many more conjectures than might be expected in an encyclopaedia. On Shakespeare's appearance, he offered the unfounded claims: "We believe ourselves warranted in assuming

that William Shakespeare was a handsome and even noble looking boy"
(1864, 58) About the retirement, he states:

> The four or five latter years of his life Shakespeare passed in digni-
> fied ease, in profound meditation, we may be sure, and in universal
> respect, at his native town of Stratford; and there he died, on the 23d
> of April, 1616.
>
> (1864, 68)

Many writers expressed doubt at the content of this entry, including
intellectuals such as Matthew Arnold: "its approbation weeps hysterical
tears and its disapprobation foams at the mouth."[4]

During the Romantic period, there was a significant change in attitude towards the sonnets. George Steevens had taken the view that the
sonnets were poor poetry and offered no biographical insights (1793
i. 103) and Malone was very cautious as to whether the sonnets might
be taken as a source of biographical understanding. Biographical study
was becoming an increasingly important part of literary criticism in the
early part of the nineteenth century, writers and poets were delighted
to discover Shakespeare's own feelings and experiences everywhere in
his poetry, interpreting the sonnets as confessional biography. In 1796,
August Wilhelm Schlegel claimed that the sonnets are "valuable primarily because they seem to be inspired by a love and friendship that were
not imaginary." After translated the works into German (1797–1810),
von Schlegel, expanded his approach saying that the sonnets "paint most
unequivocally the actual situation and sentiments of the poet; they make
us acquainted with the passions of the man."[5] George Chalmers deftly
dismissed the possible homoerotic interpretations of the sonnets while
still asserting their claim to autobiography by stating that the "sugr'd
sonnets were addressed by Shakspeare to [Queen] Elizabeth" (1797, 53)
and that the printer simply made a mistake in printing the pronouns
'he' for 'she.' In 1808, William Wordsworth agreed that "Shakespeare
expresses his own feelings in his own person" and emphasised the value
of the sonnets in constructing the life:

> *Scorn not the sonnet. Critic, you have frowned,*
> *Mindless of its just honours; with this key*
> *Shakespeare unlocked his heart.*[6]

Anna Jameson in 1829 avoided any suggestion of a love triangle or homoerotic overtones by claiming that only some of the poems were addressed
to Southampton but that most of the others were addressed "in Southampton's name to that beautiful Elizabeth Vernon."[7] In 1832, William
Hazlitt called them "interesting as they relate to the personal feelings of
the author." In the same year, James Boaden labelled a persona in the

sonnets as the 'fair youth' identified as William Herbert (1580–1630, who became the third earl of Pembroke in 1601).[8] In 1833, Samuel Taylor Coleridge stated that Shakespeare showed his "love towards a male object – an affection beyond friendship, and wholly aloof from appetite."[9] The approach of supplying the deficiency of documented records by referring to the works was well understood by D. L. Richardson:

> A regret has often been expressed that we have little beyond a collection of barren dates in what is called the life of Shakespeare. Now I conceive and in this opinion I do not stand alone, that if any new light be thrown on Shakespeare's life and character, it must result from a careful and profound study of these sonnets.
>
> *(Gentleman's Magazine,* 1835)[10]

Richardson reviews previous historical identifications of personas in the sonnets and offers his own opinions as to the intended recipients (mainly Elizabeth Vernon on behalf of Southampton). In 1835–1836, an anonymous writer published 'The Confessions of William Shakespeare' which expanded a literal interpretation to the sonnets into a continuous account of Shakespeare's own thoughts and feelings.[11] In 1838, Charles Armitage Brown, a close friend of John Keats, attempted to reconstruct Shakespeare's adult life in *Shakespeare's Autobiographical Poems,* based on his own extended interpretation of the sonnets.

A different approach towards satisfying the Victorian appetite for information about Shakespeare was to describe the context in detail. Robert Bell Wheler published newly discovered documents relating to the Shakespeare family (1806), a guide to Stratford-upon-Avon, reporting Shakespeare's purchase of the Stratford tithes, and papers relating to the proposed enclosure of Welcombe (1814). Wheler showed commendable caution when considering such traditions as the features of Shakespeare's face on the Monument were taken directly from a face-mask:

> How far we are to rely on such a Tradition is to be considered for I know not to what source it can be traced; yes we should remember how many traditions there are, more wild and improbable than this, upon which great confidence is placed.[12]

Wheler later discovered the marriage licence bond from the archives of the Consistorial Court of Worcester (1836). Wheler's contextual approach was taken further by Nathan Drake (1766–1836) in his two-volume *Shakespeare and His Times* (1817). Drake's study was scarcely a biography as it consisted mainly of contextual description with the figure of Shakespeare acting as "the medium for a comprehensive and connected view of the Times in which he lived" (1817 i. iii). Drake's subtitle "A History of the Manners, Customs and Amusements,

Superstitions, Poetry and Elegant Literature of his Age" indicates its main emphasis on describing the historical context (1817 i. v). The two-volume study is derivative, collecting together all the material separately published by the main eighteenth century editors of Shakespeare (Rowe, Pope, Theobald, Harmer, Warburton, Johnson, Steevens, Reed, and Malone), as well as other researchers such as Tyrwhitt, Farmer, Oldys, and Ritson, loosely organised around Stratford in volume I and London in volume II. For Drake, tradition was sufficient authority for many assertions. His excess of contextual information becomes a substitute for a literary portrait of the subject. One anonymous reviewer wrote in *The Gentleman's Magazine* that "with indefatigable diligence, the Author has illustrated every possible point that has the smallest reference to his subject" (1818, no. 88, 242). Drake's study was imitated by Augustine Skottowe's two-volume *Life of Shakespeare* in 1824, which offered no new material.

Four years after Malone's third variorum edition appeared, Rev. William Harness published his edition of *The Works* (eight volumes) in which he included a biographical preface in 74 pages (1825, volume I, i–lxxiv). Harness scorned biographical inferences from the works (e.g. regarding the Shakespeare marriage) but was fully inclined towards accepting the posthumous anecdotes, e.g. that Shakespeare would kill "a calf in high style." In 1838, Thomas Campbell edited a two-volume edition of Shakespeare's plays, to which he prefixed his own narrative memoir entitled "Remarks on the Life and Writings of William Shakespeare" in about 56 pages (1838 i. ix–xlv). Campbell begins with the standard admission: "It is justly regretted by the present age that so little has come down to us respecting the personal history of Shakespeare." Campbell made many inferences from the works, being the first to claim that Prospero's abjuration of magic was also Shakespeare's farewell to the stage: "Here Shakespeare himself is Prospero, or rather the superior genius who commands both Prospero and Ariel. But the time was approaching when the potent sorcerer was to break his staff" (1838 i. lxiv). The identification of Prospero with a retiring Shakespeare has remained part of both the critical and the biographical traditions. Like Rowe's *Account,* most of Campbell's introduction is far more a critique than a biography.

5.3 Exemplary Life and National Biography

Following James Stanfield's demand that biographers to express "national heroism and national genius," Thomas Carlyle accorded the highest praise to Shakespeare in his lecture *On Heroes, Hero-Worship, and The Heroic in History*:

> This King Shakespeare, does not he shine, in crowned sovereignty, over us all, as the noblest, gentlest, yet strongest of rallying-signs;

indestructible; really more valuable in that point of view than any other means or appliance whatsoever?

(published 1841, 184)

In the same year as Carlyle's lectures, The Shakspere Society was founded by Charles Knight, John Payne Collier, Alexander Dyce, and James Halliwell-Phillipps (among others). Each of these co-founders not only went on to edit their own edition of the works, but also published a biography of Shakespeare. As Carlyle undertook to praise Shakespeare's genius in the most lavish terms, Knight determined to write a narrative account of Shakespeare's life suitable to a National hero: *William Shakspere, a Biography* (1843) was the final volume to his *Pictorial Edition of the Works* (1838–1841) and included over 200 illustrations in almost 550 pages. Knight, however, included many fictional elements in his narrative, such as the description of the joy attendant upon his baptism at the Holy Trinity Church. He imagined the domestic bliss enjoyed by the youthful William:

> The happy days of Shakespeare's boyhood are nearly over. William Shakespeare no longer looks for that close of day when, in that humble chamber in Henley Street, his father shall hear something of his school progress, and read with him some English book of history or travel – volumes which the active presses of London had sent cheaply among the people.
>
> (1843, viii. 110–1)

This is simply speculation as there is no record of Shakespeare's youth or of active presses sending books cheaply among the people (as Knight himself had done with the *Penny Cyclopædia* throughout the preceding fifteen years. Knight accepts without comment the suggestion that William witnessed the Princely Pleasures at Kenilworth in 1575, and describes them as if Shakespeare had attended (76–89), a myth which remains current (e.g. Greenblatt 2004, 46).[13] This Knight further aims to present an idealised life by introducing the scene of a betrothal to Anne Hathaway a year before marriage, for which there is no record. Knight uses the material published by John Payne Collier in 1835, but had to delete these points from later editions when some of Collier's materials were shown to be forgeries. He accepted John Ward's recently published account (Severn 1839) of Shakespeare's death from fever after "a merry meeting" with Jonson and Drayton. However, he dismissed the idea of excessive drinking as the cause of the fever, imagining instead Shakespeare's Christian piety in the final moments. In a further attempt to redeem Shakespeare, Knight argued Shakespeare did not need to mention his wife in his will as she would automatically receive one-third dower arrangements (1843 viii. 530). Subsequent commentators have argued over this point ever since. It is not clear whether a widow in Stratford would be entitled to the same right of dower as in London (Greer 2007, 320–2).

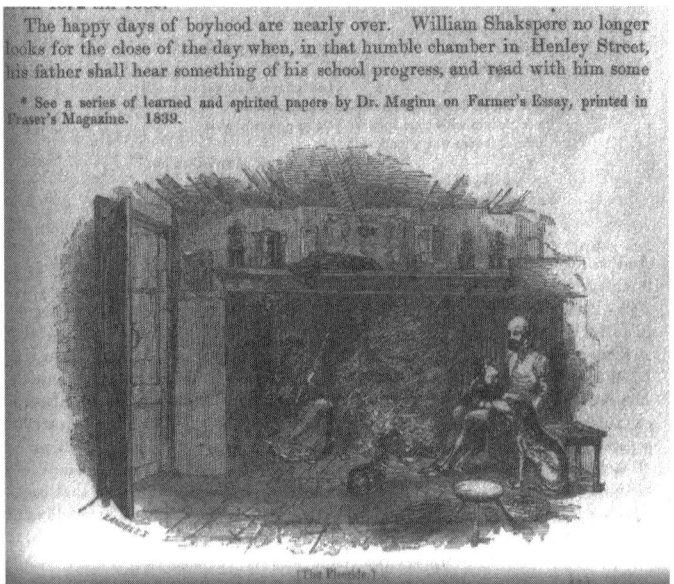

The happy days of boyhood are nearly over. William Shakspere no longer looks for the close of the day when, in that humble chamber in Henley Street, his father shall hear something of his school progress, and read with him some

* See a series of learned and spirited papers by Dr. Maginn on Farmer's Essay, printed in Fraser's Magazine. 1839.

Plate 5.1 Knight's idealised view of Shakespeare's childhood.

That Knight was indulging his imagination was immediately recognised by a reviewer in *The Athenaeum* (2 March 1844), who criticised his building "hypothesis upon hypothesis," wishing he would "confine his fancy within the bounds." Another critic in *The Spectator* of 2 September 1843 made the same point about Knight's "descriptive reverie", using "upwards of five hundred pages, where five pages would contain all the known facts." For the 1850 and 1867 editions, Knight reduced his *Biography*, but it remained largely fictional as recognised by J. Parker Norris:

> In this work [Knight's *Biography of Shakespeare,* 1867], which is very well known, the author did not tie himself down to bare facts, but gave free rein to his imagination. As a chronicle of what might have happened to the poet and what he probably did, the people he was likely to have met, etc., this is not surpassed by anything which has been written on the subject. But those who wish to ascertain what we really know of Shakespeare must consult other books. [14]

Knight's biography of Shakespeare, however, was widely read and remained in print until at least 1900 (by Peter Collier of New York).

While Knight, de Quincey, and various other writers simply speculated about Shakespeare's life, a few went further and forged documents to support their views of Shakespeare. The forgeries of William Henry Ireland (1775–1835) who had claimed to possess letters and other texts, including Shakespeare's love letters to his wife, were exposed by Edmond Malone (1796).[15] The most infamous fabricator, however, was originally an eminent Shakespeare scholar. John Payne Collier discovered and published new documents concerning Shakespeare, which are now accepted. In addition to Manningham's diary, from which he had published excerpts in 1831, he noted that Shakespeare was listed as hoarding ten bushels of corn in February 1598 (1844, i. clxiv), he found a suit in Chancery regarding Shakespeare's non-payment of tithes (1844, i. ccxl), and made use of the Revels Accounts recently discovered by Peter Cunningham (1844, i. 3).[16] He was the first writer to link an allusion in *Willobie His Avisa* with Shakespeare (1858, i. 115n) and to publish the examinations of Sir Gilly Meyrick (i. 153–54) and of Augustine Phillips (iii. 214), following Essex's "desperate affair." These last documents were significant contributions to the political and theatrical history of 1601.

To these documents, Collier claimed other discoveries in the Duke of Devonshire's Library at Bridgewater House in London, published in *New Facts Regarding the Life of Shakespeare* (1835). Collier stated that Shakespeare was a member of the Blackfriars company in 1589 and that Southampton wrote a letter of support in 1608. For his own edition of the works, he included a *Life of Shakespeare* in about 200 pages (1844, i. pp. lxix–cclxvi; revised in 1858, i. 39–235). By now, he had changed his opinion as to the lack of documentary evidence. In this preface, Collier stated:

> I have been anxious to include the most minute particles of information, whether of tradition or discovery. This information is now <u>hardly as scanty as it was formerly represented</u>, and by the favour of friends and my own research, I have been able to add to it some particulars entirely new, and of no little importance.
>
> (emphasis added, 1844, i. viii; 1858, i. xli)

Eventually many textual emendations and documentary discoveries were exposed as fabrications by (among others) Clement Ingleby, who collected all the criticisms into one publication in 1861 (Freeman & Freeman 2004, ii. 882).[17]

Overall, the major significance of forgers such as John Payne Collier lies in demonstrating the paucity of relevant literary documentation in the biographical material concerning Shakespeare. Three further points of significance emerge from the case of Collier's forgeries, regarding the public, the publishers, and the scholars. First, the reading public then and now are so avid for information about Shakespeare that many accept these forgeries as uncritically as they accept unfounded myths.

Second, publishers are clearly interested in the Shakespeare industry from a financial point of view, without regard to the authenticity or reliability of documents quoted: despite suspicions surrounding Collier, Joseph Whitaker published editions by Collier in 1853 and 1858 without eliminating his textual emendations based on the Perkins Folio. Third, the verdicts of writers such as Sidney Lee, who lists the forgeries (1898, 367–369), and Samuel Schoenbaum, who gives a detailed account of his exposure (1970, 348–361), have become part of the dominant narrative of Shakespearean biography, overlooking the significance of Collier's authentic findings. Nevertheless, Lee and Schoenbaum might well be considered as culpable as Collier in failing to question their own assumptions, e.g. that Shakespeare spent his childhood in Stratford, where he was educated, or that he enjoyed the patronage of the Earl of Southampton. These myths are presented as established fact in almost every modern account of Shakespeare's life.

The process of national celebration of Shakespeare through biography was most effectively realised when Sidney Lee in 1897 came to publish the entry for him in the *DNB*. Shakespeare's cultural status gained the longest entry in the *DNB* at 49 double-columned pages (about 63,000 words). This was later exceeded only once, by the entry for the one person deemed to have greater importance, Queen Victoria.[18] Lee's *Life of William Shakespeare* was then issued as a monograph in 1898.[19] The significance of Lee's study rests not so much on his views of "critical points" in the life of Shakespeare but the fact that he attempted a coherent narrative at all – against the admissions by many nineteenth century biographers from Chalmers to Halliwell-Phillipps. Echoing Collier's revised statement that the biographical material for Shakespeare was "hardly as scanty as it was formerly represented" (Collier *Works* 1844 i. viii), Lee makes the following claim:

> The scantiness of contemporary records of Shakespeare's career has been much exaggerated. An investigation extending over two centuries has brought together a mass of detail which far exceeds that accessible in the case of any other contemporary professional writer.
> (*DNB* 1897, li. 395; repeated verbatim 1899, 361)

Lee is prepared to make a concession that there are gaps, but he believes that these gaps are not so large as to render the attempt at a biography impossible:

> Nevertheless, some important links are missing, and at some points appeal to conjecture is inevitable. But the fully ascertained facts are numerous enough to define sharply the general direction that Shakespeare's career followed. Although the clues are in some places faint, the trail never eludes the patient investigator.
> (*DNB* 1897, li. 395; repeated verbatim 1899, 361)

Whereas in the earlier editions, he noted that "<u>some important</u> links are missing," by 1915 he had downgraded the omissions to just "<u>a few</u> links" (1915, 637). Lee's claim that there is sufficient material for a coherent narrative account of Shakespeare's life was not repeated by any serious scholar in the twentieth century until Schoenbaum (1975).

In some ways, Lee's *Life* was an important counter to tendencies among Victorian bardolaters. His study was far better organised than Halliwell-Phillipps's *Outlines* and very well indexed. He wanted "an exhaustive and well-arranged statement of the facts of Shakespeare's career, achievement, and reputation," reducing "conjecture to the smallest dimensions consistent with coherence" (1899, vi). He gives a linear account of Shakespeare's life in seventeen chapters (about 60% of the work, pp 1–283), with fourteen additional chapters dealing with specific issues (1899, 284–446). Lee allotted some space to each play, indicating the main sources, early performances, earliest known publication, and assumed dates of composition. Unlike other commentators, he generally avoids making inferences from the plays, e.g. observing that in Prospero "traces have been sought without much reason of the lineaments of the dramatist himself" (257). He takes the sonnets to be mainly "literary exercises" in contrast to critics who believe that "Shakespeare avows the experiences of his own heart." Although he had previously identified Mary Fitton as the 'dark lady' in the earlier *DNB* entries for Mary Sidney and William Herbert, he later rejected close identification of historical figures with assumed personas in the sonnets.

Despite this statement of approach, Lee frequently makes conjectures. He asserts that Shakespeare was forced into marriage by Anne Hathaway's kinsmen, who "<u>doubtless</u> secured the deed [marriage licence] on their own initiative." He solves the problem of the name Anne Whateley by stating with confidence: "The husband of Anne Whateley cannot reasonably be identified with the poet. He was doubtless another of the numerous William Shakespeares who abounded in the diocese of Worcester" (1899, 24). Lee states that Nicholas Rowe was "Shakespeare's first adequate biographer" (126) despite the fact that only a small fraction of what Rowe offered in *Some Account of the Life &c* was biographical. Lee maintains the myths initiated by Rowe that Shakespeare spent his childhood in Stratford, where he attended the local school (1899, 13–15), that he was caught stealing deer and punished, which he accepts as "a credible tradition" (27–29); that Shakespeare had "no patron but one" based on the "trustworthy tradition" of the Davenant anecdote that Southampton gave Shakespeare a thousand pounds (125–27). Lee does not clarify why any of these anecdotes should be considered trustworthy. He further accepts that Shakespeare inspired envy in Jonson (176) and that he retired to Stratford (264).

Lee issued an expanded edition of *A Life of William Shakespeare* in 1915 and mentioned the findings by the Wallaces of twenty-six documents relating to the Bellott-Mountjoy lawsuit (1612), which had been discovered in 1909 and published in the *Nebraska University Studies* (1910). Lee found it hard to attribute any significance to these papers which merely stated that Shakespeare had lodged with the Mountjoy family in Silver Street *c*. 1604. Most of his discussion is confined to a long footnote (1915, 276–277). The Wallaces also published details of other lawsuits: Keysar v. Burbage (1610), Ostler v. Heminges (1615), and Witter v. Heminges and Condell (1619). These cases added to the material for the history of the King's Men and of the Globe, but only referenced Shakespeare indirectly.

Overall, Sidney Lee's *Life of William Shakespeare* uses speculation and the testimony of later anecdotes to expand the extant material, confining biographical inference to the sonnets. Notwithstanding these defects, it was frequently reprinted and remained the most respected narrative account of Shakespeare's life for the next seventy-five years.

5.4 Dowden and the Adoption of a Chronology

During the Victorian period, scholars addressed Dr Johnson's desire to know "by what gradations of improvement he proceeded," and began to promote an intellectual or spiritual biography of Shakespeare. Such an approach is not possible due to lack of reliability in any chronology of the works. At a public lecture in Dublin in 1863, John Kells Ingram issued a challenge to establish the chronological order of Shakespeare's works so as to trace the poet's development.[20] Ingram's lecture seems to have had a profound influence on Edward Dowden. A decade later, F. J. Furnivall asserted (1874, xxii) that Shakespeare's works "must be studied in chronological order" listing the plays in a table which was "merely tentative, and open to modifications for any good reasons" (1875, xliv). Furnivall made minor adjustments to Malone's final attempt at dating the plays. His chronology was apparently supported by the verse tables of F. G. Fleay, which were later shown by Chambers to be unreliable. Nevertheless, statistical analysis of various stylistic features Shakespeare's language has enjoyed a vogue ever since. Wells and Taylor compiled statistical tables of style, which they claim helps to date the composition of the works (1987, 93–108). They refer to undefinable categories such as colloquialisms and rare words, which they use in a very subjective manner to reinforce their own chronology. Brian Vickers accepts that stylistic or linguistic features are of "secondary value" and can only "play a part in confirming or questioning a date established on other grounds" (2002, 126). Since neither the dates nor the sequence of Shakespeare's plays can be established, there is no hard base to such styles of language and meter. Two assumptions are open to doubt: that Shakespeare's writing evolved gradually and unconsciously, without retrograde; and that Shakespeare exercised no control over them.

Another member of the New Shakespere Society was working on his own study of Shakespeare's development. Unlike Furnivall and Fleay who claimed to follow a scientific approach, Edward Dowden followed his own instincts for Shakespeare's supposed development in *Shakespere: A Critical Study of his Mind and Art* in 1874. This study proved very influential and was frequently repeated: its twelfth edition was published in 1901. Dowden confidently delineated the playwright's development of "intellect and character from youth to full maturity" (1875, xiii). He assumed that the chronology was "sufficiently ascertained" so as to enable the study the development of Shakespeare as an artist and as a man. He accepts Malone's chronology without comment (1875, 5). He felt able to group the plays into four phases, which he believed corresponded to phases in Shakespeare's life: (a) in the workshop (b) in the world (c) out of the depths (d) on the heights. Dowden proposed that characters such as Romeo, Hamlet, and Prospero reflect Shakespeare's personality at different stages of his career. He postulated links between the genre of plays and Shakespeare's emotional state. Dowden's "third period" which he claimed arose out of some terrible emotional upset, has been welcomed so as to explain the impulse behind the great tragedies and the problem comedies:

> From 1604 to 1610 a show of tragic figures, like the kings who passed before Macbeth, filled the vision of Shakspere; until at last the desperate image of Timon rose before him; when, as though unable to endure or to conceive a more lamentable ruin of man, he turned for relief to the pastoral loves of Prince Florizel and Perdita; and as soon as the tone of his mind was restored, gave expression to its ultimate mood of grave serenity in *The Tempest*: and so ended.
>
> (1874, 223)

Although Dowden's psychological approach to Shakespeare predates Freud, his subjective extrapolation of Shakespeare's inner feelings from the plays proved very influential on subsequent scholars. His division of the plays into four phases and assignment of dates within these phases has remained established. E. K. Chambers refers to the "admirable treatment of Professor Dowden" which greatly influenced his own sequencing and dating of the plays (1930, i. 251). Dowden's four phases were also adopted by Peter Alexander (*Shakespeare's Life and Art* 1939). Dowden's study was still being issued as recently as 1967 by Routledge.

Other scholars criticised Dowden's phases and his attempts at a psychological approach to the plays. An anonymous reviewer in *The*

Examiner (6 March, 1875, 272–274) disparaged Dowden for purporting to uncover "central principles" about Shakespeare, which are "too relative for precise explanation" and then putting them into "dogmatic propositions." The reviewer notes that Dowden's theory is not borne out by the surviving "slender facts" of Shakespeare's life. In 1909, Sidney Lee rejected the "personal theory" that Shakespeare composed plays according to variations of private sensation and personal experience, a point emphasised by C. J. Sisson in his lecture on "the mythical sorrows of Shakespeare" (1934, 8). Sisson remained highly skeptical about Dowden's four phases "which prevails invulnerable to criticism as orthodox faith" (1950, 1).

Furthermore, Dowden completely ignores Shakespeare's activity in the theatres, mentioning neither the Globe nor the Blackfriars. Perhaps the important criticism of Dowden concerns the chronology, which he believes is generally well-established. Dowden is unaware that there is no hard evidence to the date of composition of any of Shakespeare's plays, that Shakespeare may have revised some, many, all or none of his works, and that Shakespeare's texts may have interpolations from other people. Finally, there is no evidence that Shakespeare composed plays consecutively, rather than working on two or more texts at the same time, or that for a time he left unfinished one play while working on others. Overall, Dowden's critical study offers an interesting and thought-provoking theory about Shakespeare's apparent development which cannot be verified.

5.5 Rejection of Bardolatry in the Twentieth Century

Victorian writers held Shakespeare in such great reverence that in 1901 Bernard Shaw coined the term 'bardolatry' to dismiss the indiscriminate eulogies of the National Poet. In 1903, the novelist Henry James wrote a satirical short story called *The Birthplace* mocking it as "the most sacred known to the steps of men, the early home of the supreme poet, the Mecca of the English-speaking race." A few years later, Shaw reviewed the stage adaptation of Frank Harris's *The Man Shakespeare and His Tragic Life-Story*, observing: "Everything we know about Shakespeare can be put into a half-hour sketch."[21] Shaw was speaking on behalf of many writers in saying that the picture of Shakespeare's life was over-blown. Reviewers of Sidney Lee's *Life* were similarly unimpressed. An anonymous critic in *The Times* on 2 December 1915 stated that the material for Shakespeare's life has "been twisted by a master artificer into the cunning semblance of a biography." A similar view was taken by another reviewer, Thomas Seccombe, in *The Observer* (12 Dec. 1915): "No data exist for personal interpretation." In *The Daily Telegraph* (15 Dec. 1915), the reviewer states: "There is so little to say about Shakespeare the man. It would all go into one or two chapters of direct narrative, and it is all a record of external events. . . [Lee's descriptions] are not the exhibition of a human soul, not biography, not Shakespeare."

These acknowledgements of the lack of sufficient materials for a life of Shakespeare were echoed by many academics throughout the twentieth century. In 1920, Arthur Acheson gave robust warnings about how repeated speculations can become accepted as fact: "These assumptions [about the 'lost years'], which were advanced tentatively by former scholars and merely as working hypotheses, have now, by repetition and the dogmatic dicta of biographical compilers, come to be accepted by the uncritical as ascertained facts" (*Shakespeare's Lost Years in London 1920*, 7). In 1921, George Saintsbury reviewed the knowledge about Shakespeare and decided that almost the whole matter is "a great Perhaps."[22] In 1934, the British Academy invited C. J. Sisson to deliver its prestigious Shakespeare Lecture, in which he attacked Shakespearean biographers for their imaginary reconstructions of the life. In 'The Mythical Sorrows of Shakespeare' Sisson stated that "the dramatizing of Shakespeare the man has gone too far" and showed that there was no evidence to a portrait of "a man shaken by personal passion, moving from mood to mood, from optimism to pessimism and back again to resigned imperturbability" (1934, 10). Sisson points out the inconsistency of interpretation:

> It appears that in 1607 Shakespeare's brother Edmund died, an event which helped to infuriate him. Fortunately, in 1608 his mother died, an event which restored him to a kindlier mood. So various are the effects of deaths in the family upon a great poet.
>
> (Sisson 1934, 15)

A similar verdict was made in a review of "Shakespeare's Life and Times" which until 2004 used to appear annually in *Shakespeare Survey*. In 1949, D. J. Gordon noted that there "is no end to the exploration of the age in which Shakespeare lived out his life" adding that no serious biographer would attempt the life itself: "to write of this life itself or of the 'personality' of Shakespeare is now it seems reserved for the bold, the crazy, or the amateur" (*Shakespeare Survey* 2, 1949, 144). One such bold biographer, Ivor Brown, defended the attempt: "all excursions in discovery of Shakespeare are essays in conjecture and any one may compete" (1949, 29).

Perhaps the most heartfelt complaint when reviewing biographies about Shakespeare was expressed by Ernest Brennecke of Columbia University:

> A short time ago the Editor of [*Shakespeare*] *Quarterly*, in what
> must have been a particularly sadistic mood, asked me to read a
> dozen or so of the latest Shakespeare biographies.
>
> (*Shakespeare Quarterly*, 1950)[23]

In 1953, the Merton Professor of English Literature at Oxford University
F. P. Wilson spoke for many scholars: "We *know* we cannot write a biography of Shakespeare; we *think* we can write one of Marlowe."[24] The
lack of biographical material continues to be the case with Shakespeare.
The literary theorist, Meyer Abrams, who presented a broad appreciation of literary criticism in the early nineteenth century, noted that
life-writing about Shakespeare contains "the largest mass of conjectural
biography under which any author has ever staggered on his way to im-
mortality" (1953, 249). The same point has been made by another historian of literary criticism, Richard Altick, who states that it is not possible
to write a biography of Shakespeare (or of most authors before Swift) because "not enough revelatory personal documents survive" (1965, 353).
One modern philosopher, Ray Monk, considers that lengthy biographies
of Shakespeare depend on "supposition, speculation, and plain guess-
work." He continues:

> The "truths which transmit personality" [as described by Virginia
> Woolf] are simply not available to the biographer of Shakespeare;
> there are no letters, no recorded conversations, no diaries, no auto-
> biography and no vivid recollection of his personal foibles from his
> closest friends.[25]

In the absence of such personal papers, fictions in the form of inferences
and speculations accumulate.

Documentary Collection

In the twentieth century, by far the most influential review of documents relating to Shakespeare was conducted by Sir Edmund Chambers
(1866–1954). Chambers devoted a large part of his long life towards
elucidating the biography of Shakespeare. His research and collations
of previous periods resulted in the two-volume *Mediaeval Stage* (1903)
and the four-volume *Elizabethan Stage* in 1923. Finally in 1930, he
published his two volume study on *William Shakespeare*. The subtitle
of his findings about Shakespeare *A Study of Facts and Problems* indicates his reluctance to write the biography as he had originally envisaged. He merely states his purpose: "I collect the scanty biographical
data from records and tradition, and endeavour to submit them to the
tests of a reasonable analysis" (1930 i. ix). Chambers's study of the

"facts" has been accepted as accurate in its transcriptions of documents relating to Shakespeare, his works and the context. His discussion of the "problems" has also been widely lauded as "dispassionate, aloof from bardolatry, meticulous, totally informed" (Schoenbaum 1970, 711–12). Chambers found the narrative biographies of Sir Sidney Lee and J. Q. Adams inadequate as they "do not represent the sources with precision" and that "some of the subjective inferences are too confident" (1946, 7). These criticisms are valid for any narrative biography. Chambers's study of facts and problems work has remained the handbook for scholars ever since despite later documentary collections, notably by Roland Lewis, who adds considerable discussion (1940), and Catherine Loomis (2002).

Chambers admits to making his own conjectures, e.g. that unevenness in stage directions and character naming "is not inconsistent with what we may suspect of Shakespeare's temperament" (1930, i. 203). According to this view, everything counts as "not inconsistent" as we have no record of what Shakespeare's temperament was like. Chambers accepted the prevailing opinion as to which text of *Hamlet* was authoritative:

> Q2 substantially represents the original text of the play, as written once and for all by Shakespeare, and that F1, Q1, and *Der bestrafte Brudermord* (B. B.) are all in various ways based upon derivatives from that test.
>
> (*WS*, i. 412)

All of these conjectures seem plausible, but they also indicate that Chambers's presentation of the "facts" is made with a certain amount of editorialising intervention. Elsewhere, he is prepared to accept a state of ignorance on critical points, such as the 'lost years':

> The main fact in his earlier career is still that unexplored hiatus, and who shall say what adventures, material and spiritual, six or eight crowded Elizabethan years may have brought him. It is no use guessing. As in so many other historical investigations, after all the careful scrutiny of clues and all the patient balancing of possibilities, the last word for a self-respecting, scholarship can only be that of nescience.
>
> (1930, i. 26)

Apart from the documentary collections of Lewis (1940) and Loomis (2002), there have also been various encyclopaedias (Halliday 1952; revised 1964; O. J. Campbell and Quinn 1964; Dobson and Wells 2001). This approach to Shakespeare is an entirely acceptable alternative to an attempt at a narrative life.

5.6 Persistence of Bardolatry in the Twentieth Century (to 1975)

"Creative biographies" was the derogatory phrase used by the skeptical C. J. Sisson in his review of studies of Shakespeare's life written in the first half of the twentieth century (in *Shakespeare Survey* 1950). Sisson's only exceptions were the *Life* by Sidney Lee (revised 1925) and *A Life of William Shakespeare* (1923) by J. Q. Adams. As the first Director of the Folger Shakespeare Library, Joseph Quincy Adams (1880–1946) was a respected scholar. His *Life* is characterised by admissions of uncertainty and many linguistic hedges: Regarding the Shakespeare marriage, Adams offered his opinion that there is "<u>no reason</u> to suppose that the marriage was not one of true love" and that there are "<u>no grounds</u> for the theory that Anne failed to make a good wife," claiming that "he <u>seems</u> to have had her with him in London" (1923, 76). The hedges, 'no reason', no grounds', and 'seems' indicates the lack of evidence either way. Adams makes an appeal to norms as to patronage, stating that just as Spenser was patronised by Sir Philip Sidney and Daniel by the Countess of Pembroke, so Shakespeare must have enjoyed the patronage of Southampton after the youthful earl came in to "control of his fortune and was just beginning a career of extravagance" (1923, 150–151). While none of these claims can be disproved, they can all be called into question and in effect Adams is merely giving his opinion on a series of gaps in the biographical record for Shakespeare.

The biographical tradition from Malone onwards presented Shakespeare as a firm protestant and a member of the Church of England. However, some commentators from the early twentieth century had found evidence suggesting Shakespeare was in secret a Catholic. Herbert Thurston had considered the Catholic connection suggestion but concluded that "the number of Shakespearean utterances expressive of a fundamental doubt in the Divine economy of the world seems to go beyond the requirements of his dramatic purpose" (*Catholic Encyclopedia* 1912, xiii 749–751). The Catholic interpretation was developed by J. Dover Wilson in *The Essential Shakespeare: A Biographical Adventure* (1932). Accepting the lack of biographical material, he acknowledges that his account is "largely conjectural." He announces in the preface: "Here, in a nutshell, is the kind of man I believe Shakespeare to have been." He believes that John Shakespeare was "almost certainly" an ardent Catholic, who refused to allow his son to be educated by a Protestant minister and there is "not a tittle of evidence" that William ever attended the Stratford Free School (40–41). Wilson asserts that the attack on him as "an upstart crow" (45–47) resulted from Shakespeare's early career as a reviser of other people's works, an argument popular among Victorians but now often discredited. He claims that Shakespeare enjoyed close friendships with various nobles, including Lord

Strange (61–62), Essex and Southampton, for whom he apparently provided dramatic entertainment at Southampton's country house in Titchfield, Hampshire (64–65). He assumes that Shakespeare was a member of the Essex circle, luckily avoided implication in the 1601 uprising and went into mourning for two years after Essex's execution (107). As a result of this bitter experience (and not of his son's death in 1596), according to Wilson, Shakespeare changed his interest and began composing problem comedies and tragedies (119). Wilson's study drew sharp criticism from Charles Sisson in 1932, who distinguished facts, such as the execution of Essex in 1601, from speculation about Shakespeare's supposed reaction to this event. Sisson dismisses Wilson's Life as "a theory deduced from a series of conjectures which, once made, are assumed to be facts" (1932, 475–476).

Another biographer to offer a greater challenge to the dominant narrative was Sir Arthur Gray (1926), who speculated how Shakespeare had been brought up with Michael Drayton at Polesworth Hall, near Coventry. Gray, Master of Jesus College, Cambridge, suggested that Shakespeare served as a page to Sir Henry Goodere. His theory has been dismissed by subsequent biographers but has the merit of explaining Shakespeare's access to a wide range of literature during his youth. Gray's account cannot be ruled out because there is no evidence as to where William actually spent his childhood.

The twentieth century also saw further psychobiographies of Shakespeare. Psychobiographers use and evaluate the subject's own testimony, such as diaries, journals, letters, and accounts from trustworthy witnesses so as to establish the subject's personality with the intention of explaining his or her motives and decisions. However, in the case of Shakespeare, such personal materials are simply lacking. Those who attempt a psychobiography of Shakespeare have to select passages from the works on the assumption that they have autobiographical relevance. Some writers have followed the claim made by Karl Elze (1857, xxii) that the death of Hamnet in 1596 influenced Shakespeare's revision of *Hamlet*. In *The Interpretation of Dreams* (1900),[26] Sigmund Freud developed the connection: "it can only be the poet's own psychology with which we are confronted in *Hamlet*." In his 1910 essay on *Hamlet and Oedipus*, Ernest Jones (1949, 108) developed the apparent link between the death of Hamnet and the writing of *Hamlet*.[27] Jones also claimed that Hamlet had an Oedipal complex (i.e. Jones treated the character 'Hamlet' as a real person), which is apparently "an echo of a similar one in Shakspere." Laurence Olivier portrayed Hamlet in such a Freudian manner in the 1948 film, with Gertrude, played by Eileen Herlie (b. 1918) who was actually ten years younger than Olivier (b. 1907). Greenblatt is the only modern biographer to offer a psychobiography of Shakespeare (2004). Philip Armstrong (*Shakespeare in Psychoanalysis* 2001) has shown that the works of Shakespeare have been used very successfully to illustrate psychoanalytic theories. However, they do not constitute any trustworthy witnesses to Shakespeare's own experiences or feelings, a biographical fallacy previously exposed by Wimsatt and Beardsley (1946).

Notes

1 James Orchard Halliwell (1820–1889) added his wife's surname 'Phillipps' in 1873 so as to take over management of her property (*DNB* xxiv, 119).
2 Manningham's Diary (BL Harl. MS 5353) was mentioned by John Payne Collier (1831 i. 327–333). The Diary was published as volume 99 in the Camden Old Series, ed. Bruce, *Diary of John Manningham, of the Middle Temple, and of Bradbourne, Kent, Barrister-At-Law, 1602–1603* (1868). Sydney Race rejected the Diary as a forgery in 'Manningham's Diary: The Case for Re-Examination'. *Notes and Queries* (1954, 380–383).
3 Halliwell-Phillipps, James O. *Outlines of the Life of Shakespeare*. London: Longmans, Green and Co. 1st edn. 1881. Each later edition was expanded: 2nd edn., 1882; 3rd edn., 1883; 4th edn., 1884; 5th edn. 1885. 6th edn. 2 vols, 1886; 7th edn., vol. I: 416pp.; vol. II: 432 pp; in 1887. There were posthumous reprints: an Eighth Edition (1889), a Ninth Edition (1890), and a Tenth Edition (1898).
4 The publishers, Adam and Charles Black, issued de Quincey's entry as a short monograph entitled *Shakespeare, a Biography* in time for the ter-centenary of Shakespeare's birth. Matthew Arnold's criticisms were published in "The Literary Influence of Academies" *Cornhill Magazine* 10 (1864, 154–72) and reprinted in *Essays in Criticism: First Series*, London: Macmillan (1865, 66).
5 Abrams (1953, 246) quotes von Schlegel's essay in Schiller's *Horen* (1796). A. W. von Schlegel. *A Course of Lectures on Dramatic Art and Literature* (1808. trans. John Black and A. J. W. Morrison. London: Henry G. Bohn 1846, 352).
6 William Wordsworth. "Essay, Supplementary to the Preface (1815)." In *The Prose Works of William Wordsworth*. 3 vols. Owen, W. J. B. and Jane Worthington Smyser, eds. Oxford: Clarendon Press (1974) iii. 69.
7 Anna Jameson. *Loves of the Poets: The Romance of Biography; or Memoirs of Women Loved and Celebrated by Poets, from the Days of the Troubadours to the Present Age*. London: Colburn, (1829) i. 240.
8 Boaden's essay "On the Sonnets of Shakespeare" first appeared in *The Gentleman's Magazine* (1832) and was published separately in 1837. It has been reprinted in Boaden and Wivell (2013).
9 Carl Woodring, ed. *The Collected Works of Samuel Taylor Coleridge* volume 14. *Table Talk*, (1990) 377–78.
10 D. L. Richardson. "On Shakespeare's Sonnets, their Poetical Merits, and on the question to whom they are addressed" in *The Gentleman's Magazine* (1835) 250–6; 361–370.
11 This was published anonymously in four instalments in 1835–1836: "The Confessions of William Shakespeare" in the *New Monthly Magazine*. London: Henry Colburn; volume 43, 1–9 & 306–312; volume 44, 319–336; volume 45, 47–69.
12 R. B. Wheler letter to John Britton, 1814 (Shakespeare Centre Library and Archive ER1/34/3).
13 Hackett (2009, 54–70) has traced the Kenilworth myth to Bishop Thomas Percy ("Essay on the Origin of the English Stage" in *Reliques of Ancient*

English Poetry, 4th edn.1794). Malone had accepted the idea in his *Inquiry into the authenticity* (1796) but it was not included in the third variorum (Boswell 1821). Walter Scott (*Kenilworth* 1821) developed the myth by imagining an encounter between Elizabeth and an adult William who was already an established playwright.

14 J. Parker Norris. "The Editors of Shakespeare." in *Shakespeariana: a critical and contemporary review of Shakespearian Literature* 5, January 1888, 72–75.

15 There are two detailed accounts of Ireland's forgeries: Bernard Grebanier. *The Great Shakespeare Forgery: A New Look at the Career of William Henry Ireland.* New York: W. W. Norton (1865). Patricia Pierce. *The Great Shakespeare Fraud. The Strange, True Story of William-Henry Ireland.* Stroud: Sutton Press (2004).

16 Peter Cunningham. *Revels at Court, being Extracts from the Accounts of the Revels at Court in the time of Queen Elizabeth and James I.* London: Shakspere Society, (1842) 203–217. Because Cunningham was something of a protégé of Collier, the Revels at Court was a suspect text during the nineteenth century and rejected as forged by Sidney Lee (1898, 368–9) and by S. A. Tannebaum, *Shakspere Forgeries in the Revels Accounts.* (New York: Columbia University Press (1928). Freeman & Freeman trace the suspicions about Cunningham (2004 i. 403–7).

17 Nicholas Hamilton. *An Inquiry into the Genuineness of the Manuscript Corrections in Mr. J. Payne Collier's Annotated Shakspere, Folio, 1632: and of Certain Shaksperian* Documents *Likewise Published by Mr. Collier.* London: R. Bentley (1860). Ingleby, C. M. *A Complete View of the Shakspere Controversy.* London: Nattali (1861).

18 Peter Holland gives some figures (2006, 139–140). The entry for Queen Victoria appeared in a supplement in 1901. According to the *ODNB* website, the entry for Shakespeare remains the joint longest (with Churchill's and Elizabeth I's) in the 2004 edition at about 35,000 words.

19 Sidney Lee. *A Life of William Shakespeare.* London: Smith, Elder & Co. (1898). 4th edn. 1899; 5th edn. 1905. The original edition amounted to just under 500 pages. The edition of 1915 was expanded to 776 pages. It has been reissued since.

20 John Kells Ingram. *A paper on the chronological order of Shakespeare's plays.* Dublin: Trinity College Library, Ms. I. 6. 34. This was published as 'Shakespeare' in *The Afternoon Lectures on English Literature.* London: Bell & Daldy, (1863, 95–131). The significance of Ingram's part in the biographical tradition was overlooked by Schoenbaum (1970) and Taylor (*Reinventing Shakespeare* 1989) but has been described by Andrew Murphy. "Shakespeare and Chronology: Edward Dowden's Biographical Readings" in *Forum for Modern Language Studies* 46 (2010, 130–7).

21 G. B. Shaw *Three Plays for Puritans.* London: Richards, intro. page xxxi (1901). Bernard Shaw. Review of Frank Harris's play (*Shakespeare and his Love,* 1910) in the *Nation* 8, 24 December 1910; repr. in *Bernard Shaw's Book Reviews,* ed. Brian Tyson (Philadelphia, PA: University of Pennsylvania Press, 1996 ii., 240–54).

22 George Sainstbury. "The Character of our Knowledge about Shakespeare." In *The Cambridge History of English and American Literature.* 18 Vols. Volume V. *The Drama to 1642: Part 1.* Cambridge: Cambridge University Press (1921).

23 Ernest Brennecke. "All kinds of Shakespeare – factual, fantastic, fictional." *Shakespeare Quarterly* 1, (1950, 272–80).

24 F. P. Wilson. *Marlowe and the Early Shakespeare*. Oxford: Clarendon Press, (1953, 1).

25 Ray Monk. "This Fictitious Life: Virginia Woolf on Biography, Reality, and Character." *Philosophy and Literature* 31 (2007, 32).

26 Sigmund Freud. *Die Traumdeutung*. Leipzig und Wien: Franz Deuticke (1900. Tr. A. A. Brill. 1913. *The Interpretation of Dreams: the Material and Sources of Dreams*. London, Macmillan.). Freud's comments come in a note to his lengthy section on 'Typical Dreams'. See Marinelli, Lydia & Andreas Mayer. *Dreaming by the Book: Freud's 'The Interpretation of Dreams' and the History of the Psychoanalytic Movement*. New York: Other Press (2003).

27 Emrys Jones studied under Freud in Vienna and in 1920 published "The Oedipus-Complex as An Explanation of Hamlet's Mystery: A Study in Motive" in *The American Journal of Psychology*. This paper was expanded in 1923 (*Essays in Applied Psycho-Analysis*. London: International Psycho-Analytical Press) and published as a monograph in 1949 as *Hamlet and Oedipus*. London: V. Gollancz.

6   Re-Imagining the Life

Samuel Schoenbaum

> I quickly learned the truth of the observation that biography tends towards oblique self-portraiture. How much this must be so with respect to Shakespeare, where the sublimity of the subject ensures empathy and the impersonality of the life record teases speculation!
> —Samuel Schoenbaum (1970)

For the first three-quarters of the twentieth century, study of Shakespeare's life and times remained comparatively neglected among scholars. Academics attached to University English Departments remained New Critics, concerned mainly with close analysis of texts. Against this prevailing trend, Samuel Schoenbaum's monumental review of *Shakespeare's Lives* published in 1970, fostered interest in the historical William Shakespeare, even though its conclusion was pessimistic about the possibility of writing a life of Shakespeare. However, new perspectives on literature emerged in the 1970s and 1980s: the advent of Marxist and New Historicist approach to literary renewed interest in the author by seeking meaningful connections between the text, its production, and its cultural background. Such new perspectives coincided with the publication of Schoenbaum's *William Shakespeare: A Documentary Life* (1975). Just five years after expressing his doubt as to whether any biography could be written at all, Schoenbaum took a different view about the "meagre store" of biographical material, deciding instead that there are enough records to enable a biography based on contemporary records. Modern Shakespearean biographies not only follow Schoenbaum in accepting this claim, they also follow his narrative structure from birth to death.

6.1 Shakespeare's Lives (1970)

In 1970, Schoenbaum published his monumental review of Shakespeare's biography – *Shakespeare's Lives*. The study involves dismissing all previous various attempts at a life of Shakespeare (72–768) for one reason or another: perhaps due to their reliance on uncorroborated posthumous anecdotes; maybe for their excessive description of the context; or most seriously for their biographical inferences from selected passages in the works or their use of intuition. Throughout, Schoenbaum refers to various studies as 'biographies' when they were something else. First, he claims that Rowe's 1709 *Acount of the Life &c.* was the "first full-dress biography of Shakespeare" (1970, 76), rather than a critical appreciation of Shakespeare with a few doubtful biographical statements included. Second, he repeatedly refers to Malone's posthumous "Life of Shakespeare" (1970, 236–48), whereas the first three volumes of the Boswell edition of 1821 contains many essays and illustrative notes, not a continuous, coherent narrative. The outcome is that Schoenbaum invents a much longer tradition of Shakespearean biography than actually exists, affording it some kind of pedigree which it does not deserve. By so doing, he can locate his own biography of Shakespeare (1975) as the culmination of a tradition which never really existed. Schoenbaum was particularly disparaging of biographies in the twentieth century – by reputable scholars and by popular writers – for being too speculative. He uses the term 'Shakespeare Industry' to refer not just to the commercialisation of Stratford but also to the plethora of studies of Shakespeare's life and times (1970, 754). He observes that biographers discovered no new documents but used the existing framework to include their own subjective interpretations and insights (1970, 754–55).[1]

S. Schoenbaum *Shakespeare's Lives* ('Materials for a Life', 1970, 3).

I Death and Burial

He died in rainy April. That was on the 23rd, according to tradition, the day he entered upon his fifty-third year. About the circumstances of his passing, there would afterwards be conjecture. Two days later (so the registers of Holy Trinity Church tell us) he was buried – "full seventeen foot deep, deep enough to secure him"* according to the unlikely testimony of William Hall, rector of Acton in Middlesex and prebendary of St. Paul's, who journeyed to Stratford in 1694, there to visit "the ashes of the great Shakespear."[1] His remains lie beneath the floor of the chancel next to the north wall. Only those who had made their mark in the world were interred in this way; ordinary folk lie beneath the moss-green headstones in the churchyard on either side of the long avenue, lined with lime trees that leads to the entrance. In the churchyard, his mother and father had been laid to rest despite the fact that John Shakespeare had held high civic office. In time, the poet's younger daughter would join them there.

* A grave that deep is unlikely with the river so close by.
[1] Letter of William Hall to Edward Thwaites, Bodl. MS Rawlinson D. 377, f. 90; printed by E. K. Chambers, *William Shakespeare: A study of Facts and Problems* (Oxford: Clarendon Press, 1930) II, 260.

In the opening section, "Materials for a Life" (3–71), Schoenbaum reviews the biographical material for the life of Shakespeare and clearly commits the same transgressions which he castigates in others.

The following shortcomings of the historical review are immediately apparent:

- "He died in rainy April." It is rather odd to begin a factual review of evidence with a novelesque opening pronoun. It is also strange to begin with news of his death, which apart from a brief entry in the parish register and the will gaining probate, passed unnoticed. There were no laments or eulogies about Shakespeare published at the time. Finally, the mention of rain seems may be a literary reference to Chaucer or T. S. Eliot, but is not only irrelevant to a historical review. There is no suggestion that wet weather contributed to his death. In fact, there is no record of the weather for April 1616 and the Met Office climate charts for the nearest weather station, Wellesbourne, six miles to the east of Stratford for the period 1981–2010, indicate that April is on average the third driest month.
- "That was on the 23rd, according to tradition." So from the opening line Schoenbaum shows that he is not concerned so much with facts as with traditions. The term 'tradition' is quite emotive: usually we wish to respect and preserve our traditions. However, in writing any biography, the word 'tradition' frequently means that it has been repeated without regard to any contemporary document. The earliest reference by a commentator on Shakespeare's death as occurring on the 23rd was by Malone, reported in Steevens's edition (1778, I, 181), about 250 years after the event. However, Dugdale had recorded the epitaph on which Shakespeare's death was dated 23 April 1616 in *Antiquities* (1656, 520).
- "Two days later (so the registers of Holy Trinity Church tell us) he was buried." This is somewhat misleading as the register simply states "Deaths: 1616. April 25. Will Shakspere gent." It does not say 'two days later' or 'two days after his death'. Schoenbaum seems to use this phrase to corroborate the tradition that he died on 23rd April.
- "he was buried full seventeen foot deep." This is impossible as the base of the hole would have been below the water table and hence under water when dug. The church is located close to the River Avon and the surrounding water table is quite high, as Schoenbaum mentions in a footnote. Such a note would have been added late in the process of compiling the printed page, indicating that he had preferred to report a tradition until he became aware of a common sense observation.
- "unlikely testimony of William Hall, rector of Acton in Middlesex and prebendary of St. Paul's." It seems very strange that Schoenbaum should mention any person whose testimony was 'unlikely' only to follow with William Hall's titles which would rather serve to establish his authority. Hall's testimony does indicate the poet's growing reputation but does not merit a citation in a historical review of Shakespeare's life.
- "Only those who had made their mark in the world were interred in this way." It is possible, perhaps, likely that Shakespeare was buried within the church because he was one of the tithe-holders.

Plate 6.1 Richard Greeene's Drawing in 1762 of the Holy Trinity Church. The charnel house on the right was demolished in 1800. The wooden spire was rebuilt in stone in 1763. [Folger].

Regarding the monument in Holy Trinity Church, he notes the discrepancy between the Hollar drawing (Plate 2.3, page 31) and its present appearance (Plate 2.5, page 33). However, he states, somewhat high-handedly: "The best, and safest, explanation is that this illustration, like others in the volume [Dugdale's *Antiquities*], misrepresents the object, in keeping with the freedom exercised by seventeenth-century engravers." However, it is not at all clear why this should be the best explanation or in what sense it can be considered the "safest". However, Schoenbaum shows no doubt when summing up: "For better or worse, the image in the monument is authentic" 1970, 8).

Schoenbaum then reviews the materials for the life. Although he notes the "meagre store" of the documentary record, he does not give even a brief list of these records. The entire list would take about eight pages in the near 800-page edition of *Shakespeare's Lives* (see Appendix A for an outline list of records mentioning Shakespeare). The handwritten records which mention Shakespeare by name (or one of many variants) number about eighty, mainly held in Stratford by the Birthplace Trust or in the National Archives at Kew. Shakespeare is cited as the author on about 46 publications (about half of which are republications) before 1616. There are only 18 references to William Shakespeare by name in print before 1616, all of them too brief to afford any insight into Shakespeare as a person or as an author.

The main part of *Shakespeare's Lives* consists of reviews of previous attempts at a biography. He states his mission to "distinguish between the probable, the possible, and the preposterous" (1970, 76). That is to say, his intention is to assess different levels of likelihood. However, we have already seen how he misrepresents the essays of Rowe and Malone as a "Life of Shakespeare". Furthermore he ignores the admissions by Johnson, Steevens, Chalmers, Hallam, and many others that no biography is possible. He repeatedly claims that biographers of Shakespeare are simply describing themselves (see page 154–5 for detailed consideration of biographical displacement).

Schoenbaum rightly devotes a large section of *Shakespeare's Lives* (1970, 506–526) to a detailed consideration of Sidney Lee's *Life of Shakespeare* (first published in 1897 in the DNB, and in various editions as a monograph subsequently). He notes that Lee's biography dominated the study of Shakespeare's life for three-quarters of a century "amounting almost to a monopoly" (524). He explains that Lee assembled "much useful information in a unified and readable narrative" and, perhaps most importantly for Schoenbaum, he demonstrated "the feasibility of Shakespearean biography on the large scale."

While Schoenbaum is quite gentle in pointing out the deficiencies of other biographies, he seems uncharacteristically vituperative about Lee's *Life* (525–526), stating poetically that Lee's "monument of erudition has survived less well that that other, shattered, monument which Ozymandias commissioned for his own vainglory." The tenor of the comparison suggests that Lee was mainly interested in his own reputation which is an opinion not borne out by Lee's enormous, yet largely anonymous, contributions to the *DNB* and his decade of teaching literature at the East London College. Moreover, Schoenbaum uses derogatory terms - "the muddle-headedness, the imprecisions, the unwarranted assumptions and certainties" – to describe Lee's work, implying it was entirely without merit. Finally, he states rather grandly that at the close of the nineteenth century, "the moment would seem to have been in hand for a grand summary of Shakespearean biography" but that Lee was found wanting. Despite these negative criticisms, Lee's *Life of Shakespeare* has remained a very reliable *Life* far more so than those of subsequent academics such as J. Q Adams (1923) and J. D. Wilson (1932). Perhaps Schoenbaum was simply trying to justify the need for his own attempt at *A Documentary Life* (1975).

Rather surprisingly, Schoenbaum consistently refers to Rowe's *Account* (1709) as a biography, although it only contains a few biographical claims, most of which are either wrong or unevidenced. He similarly refers to Malone's "Life of Shakespeare" (1821), even though it is a series of discrete discussions. The effect of this is to indicate a tradition of Shakespearean biography going back to 1709, and not beginning with Knight's highly fictionalised account in 1843.

Schoenbaum's concluding remarks strike a pessimistic note about the feasibility of such an undertaking: "Perhaps we should despair of ever bridging the vertiginous expanse between the sublimity of the subject and the mundane inconsequence of the documentary record" (1970, 767). *Shakespeare's Lives* was very positively received as a "major contribution to biographiography" and has been held high esteem by Shakespeare scholars ever since.[2]

6.2 William Shakespeare: A Documentary Life (1975)

Five years after the publication of Shakespeare's Lives, Schoenbaum triumphantly changed his pessimistic view of Shakespearean biography with *William Shakespeare: A Documentary Life*. In this, Schoenbaum claims to combine "a straightforward account of Shakespeare's life" with facsimiles of "records and documents" (1975, ix).[3] In the original preface, he observes that few original records survive and there are no personal papers of Shakespeare detailing his thoughts and feelings. He thus concedes that "it would be idle to deny some legitimate basis to skepticism regarding the whole enterprise of Shakespearian biography" (ix). By this convoluted sentence, he allows doubt as to whether a biography of Shakespeare is possible, without drawing too much attention to the concession. Nevertheless, in line with J. Payne Collier and Sidney Lee, he insists that "the records themselves are more numerous that is popularly supposed" (ix) and he proceeds on the assumption that these are sufficient to write a narrative account of Shakespeare's life based on contemporary records. He wishes to distinguish his own work from "most of the innumerable popular biographies of Shakespeare that augment the facts with speculation or imaginative reconstructions or interpretative criticism of the plays and poems" (x).

Schoenbaum's *Documentary Life* was enthusiastically reviewed by many academics not only for its reproductions of documents, but also for its narrative account. It has been highly acclaimed since. According to Nina Bawcutt in *Shakespeare Survey*:

> Pride of place in this year's review must undoubtedly go to Samuel Schoenbaum's *William Shakespeare: A Documentary Life*. . . . nothing is included simply because it is picturesque or typical of the age. . . . As a biography, it deals scrupulously with the facts of Shakespeare's everyday life, making no attempt to explore his inner development. The legends that grew up after his death are affectionately dismissed.
> (1976, 168)

Bawcutt made some criticisms of the original publication as bulky and lacking transcriptions. However, neither she nor any other reviewer has ever challenged Schoenbaum's framework for Shakespeare's life. Susan Snyder was also very impressed, calling it "a splendid life." David Bevington praised its "factual and lucid account of Shakespeare's life" amounting to a "sound and expert summary of our knowledge about Shakespeare the man."[4] When the book was issued with a small number of revisions in a more compact form in 1977, reviewers tended to concentrate their praise on the narrative account of Shakespeare's life in equally generous terms. Kenneth Muir states that the value of the *Compact* version "lies in the fact that, while it never deviates into fiction, it actually gives us a more interesting account of Shakespeare's life than do those biographers who let their imaginations work overtime."[5] Stanley Wells stated that "with this book, Dr. Schoenbaum joins the ranks of the heroes of Shakespearean scholarship" and that no writer before "had ever so comprehensively studied attempts to discover the facts about Shakespeare's life and to assemble them into biographical narratives" (1996, 15). Gary Taylor calls it the "most respected biography of Shakespeare in the second half of the twentieth century" (*Reinventing Shakespeare* 1989, 332).

These reviewers, however, did not notice the weaknesses as outlined in the previous chapter: that very few documents mention William Shakespeare in his childhood, youth, or early adulthood; that there is very limited evidence for Southampton as Shakespeare's patron; that there is no evidence as to when Shakespeare began to write plays, whether he ever revised his own plays or those of others, whether he was ever paid for any play, or whether he ever collaborated with any other writer. Nonetheless, academics now felt they had a framework of Shakespeare's entire life, within which they could offer their own interpretations but outside which they could rarely stray.

Despite the title, most of *A Documentary Life* is contextual or speculative. Only a quarter of the documents presented in facsimile are of contemporary records citing Shakespeare (56 out of a total of 218). Ten images cite events prior to 1564 (including births of older siblings), 60 are contemporary but do not mention Shakespeare; and 92 were created after his death in 1616. Furthermore, Schoenbaum fails to acknowledge that for more than the first half of Shakespeare's life (from his birth until the 1592 allusion in *Groatsworth* when Shakespeare was 28), there exist just five contemporary documents alluding to Shakespeare. One mention, the records of the King's Bench in Bill of Complaint about Estate at Wilmcote 1588–1589, merely indicated that William was alive and heir to the plaintiffs.

To overcome this lack of direct reference, Schoenbaum resorts to contextual inference based on his own assumptions and prejudices in the following chapters:

Table 6.1 Schoenbaum's use of records

No.	Chapter Headings	Records Mentioning William Shakespeare
1	Stratford Town and Stratford Church	(None)
2	The Shakespeares	(None)
3	Offspring	One record: baptism
4	Rise and Fall	Mention in court record of King's Bench
5	John Shakespeare's Spiritual Testament	(None)
6	Faith and Knowledge	(None)
7	Early Employment and Marriage	Three records: marriage license; birth of children
8	The Lost Years	(None)
9	London and the Theatres	(None)

In *A Documentary Life*, these events are described in 108 pages (1987, 3–110) out of a total of 262 pages of total text. In the next chapter ('The Upstart Crow'), there is a nine page discussion concerning one allusion in *Groatsworth*. However, the allusion is ambiguous and might not refer to Shakespeare. Lukas Erne argues against the interpretation that either Green or Chettle were referring to Shakespeare: "The cumulative effect of the evidence against Shakespeare [as the recipient of the Chettle apology] is such that it partakes of mythology, rather than biography, to keep drawing inferences about Shakespeare's early years in London from Chettle's apology" (1998, 440). In the next chapter, Schoenbaum devotes seventeen pages to 'Plays, Politics and a Patron' in which he can only cite Shakespeare in the dedications to *Venus* and *Lucrece*. Thus 26 more pages are based on just three allusions. The first 134 pages, more than half of the entire study, expand just seven allusions to Shakespeare.

Schoenbaum describes the family and hometown context in about a third of his study (1987 3–95). He dismisses the suggestion of Richard Davies (*c.* 1690) that Shakespeare 'dyed a papist' (55). He perpetuates Rowe's unevidenced assumption that Shakespeare spent his childhood in Stratford, where he attended the local school (62–72). Schoenbaum states: "we need not doubt that Shakespeare received a grammar school education" (63). The phrase "we need not doubt" indicates the absence of any supporting evidence. He adds: "Shakespeare was lucky to have the King's School at Stratford-upon-Avon. It was an excellent institution of its kind, better than most rural grammar schools" (65). He uses the circular argument that Shakespeare was so well-read that he must have received a wonderful education in Stratford; consequently, he was so lucky to have received such a wonderful education! In his introduction, he notes that historical researches show how "children were educated, families worshipped, and officials busied themselves with the task of local government" (xi). The unspoken assumption is that the experiences of any one child somewhere in England during the Elizabethan period coincided with the experiences of any other. However, we are uncertain whether Shakespeare even attended the King's School at Stratford, what exactly was taught there, or even if he was in Stratford during this period at all: no record mentions William from his baptism in 1564 until his marriage licence in 1582.

Having ignored the undocumented years from 1564 to 1582, Schoenbaum considers as 'lost' only the years from 1585 to 1592 (95–117). He reports the anecdote about the drinking competition in Bidford, but is aware that "Shakespeare's drinking exploits [at Bidford] may have no more authoritative basis than (in Chambers's phrase) "the inventiveness of innkeepers' [WS ii. 286–87]." The drinking 'exploits' were first mentioned in 1762, nearly two centuries after the supposed events. Schoenbaum frequently quotes Rowe's 'biography' and in the absence of evidence to the contrary accepts Rowe's assertions with little or no doubt.

> But, if we may give credence to another and better established tradition, the Warwickshire lads amused themselves with more exciting – and dangerous – diversions than carousing tournaments (Schoenbaum *Documentary Life* 1975, 78).

He describes Rowe's myth that Shakespeare was caught stealing deer. Schoenbaum continues with Shakespeare's apparent punishment, as a result of which he wrote a ballad in revenge against Sir Thomas Lucy (95–109). He cites the differing version reported in the comments of the little-known Richard Davies (c.1690):

> Shakespeare was much given to all unluckiness in stealing venison and rabbits, particularly from Sir – Lucy who oft had him whipped and sometimes imprisoned and at last made him fly his native country to his great advancement.
>
> (WS ii 255–57)

This episode was demolished by Malone in 1790 who, among other observations, demonstrated that there was no enclosed deer park at Charlecote at the time and that Lucy's apparent punishment did not conform to the sanctions laid down by law. Malone states that a learned antiquary, Richard Fulman, who died in 1688, left many notebooks in which he mentioned Shakespeare's dates. Davies inherited these notebooks and made additions of his own, before leaving them on his death to Corpus Christi College, Oxford in 1708 (Boswell, ed.,1821 ii. 121–25). It is possible that someone at Corpus Christi read the deer poaching story and passed it on to Tonson in response to the advertisement for information in 1709. Schoenbaum also mentions versions of a ballad cited by Malone (1790, I, pt. 1, 106-7n) and by Steevens (1778 ii, 223n). Although Schoenbaum stops short of accepting its literal truth, the fact that Schoenbaum gives it so much prominence suggests significance. Furthermore, he invests it with a mythic quality by calling Shakespeare the 'Deerslayer' (78) as if he were covering the youthful exploits of Greek heroes such as Hercules or Theseus.[6] Schoenbaum calls it a "picturesque relation deriving, one expects, from local Stratford lore." He does not appear to realise that the anecdote was only written down with the first visitors came to Stratford in search of Shakespeare in the late seventeenth century. Paul Franssen (2016, 77–91) calls the anecdote "dubious" and shows how it has been altered in line with changes in society. In Davies and Rowe, the anecdote provides the 'call to adventure', the Fortunate Fall, which forces Shakespeare to leave his home and find expression for his genius in London, while taking revenge on Sir Thomas Lucy in a series of lampoons. Later in the twentieth century, the story was used to show how Shakespeare was making a class protest against landowners who were enclosing the land.

Returning to Stratford, he offers the opinion that "we are on safer ground of focusing on records" of visiting troupes to Stratford (115). He takes up a suggestion by A. W. Pollard (1909) that Shakespeare joined the Queen's Men when they played in Stratford in 1587, shortly after one of their company was killed in a fight. Schoenbaum asks: "If these players [the Queen's Men] came after 13 June [1587], they lacked one man. Before leaving Stratford, had they enlisted Shakespeare, then aged twenty-three, as their latest recruit?"[7] Like many other biographers, Schoenbaum asks questions rhetorically to direct readers towards doubtful claims. His chapter on London and the theatres is entirely contextual (118–142), prefaced by the assumption that Shakespeare made his way alone on foot to seek his fortune in London, ignoring the possibilities that he came with a group of players or even that he may have travelled with some of his townsmen or perhaps attended his father in the legal action against John Lambert heard at the King's Bench in 1588–1589 (Thomas 1964). Few biographers even mention this record but Jonathan Bate speculates that "Shakespeare's writing career may have begun in 1589, as he waited for the Lambert case to come before the Lord Chief Justice's court" (2008, 327). Schoenbaum accepts further myths of Rowe without question: that he enjoyed the patronage of Southampton (170–79); that he inspired envy in Jonson, basing his account on various anecdotes "however dubious" (256–59); and that he retired to Stratford (178–319). There is no evidence for any of these claims.

Despite his professed intention to avoid speculation, Schoenbaum believes that in "the absence of a firm chronology, one must speculate and some guesses are better than others" (161). While it is likely to be true that "some guesses are better than others," it is impossible to judge which guesses are better without external corroboration. The underlying assumption is that Schoenbaum relies on his own intuition as to which guesses are better than others. This fallacy is especially evident in guessing the order and dates in which Shakespeare composed the plays: there is no evidence on when Shakespeare composed any play or on his compositional practices regarding revision, alternative versions, co-authorship, preparation for publication, etc.

Although Schoenbaum discarded many conjectures, he indulged in some others. He asserted that the company who performed *A Comedy of Errors* at Gray's Inn on 28 December 1594 must have been the Chamberlain's Men (161) despite their documented performance on the same night at Greenwich, which he mentions (183). Schoenbaum gives his own opinion as to the original audience of a problem play: "To suggest that *Measure for Measure* was a royal play planned and written expressly for court performance is no doubt to strain credulity" (250). Schoenbaum has offered no definition for what might "strain credulity." Some have argued strongly that this play was indeed intended for court performance.[8] Schoenbaum shows his awareness of biomythography in his consideration of Richard Ryan's anecdote, first recorded in 1825:

> It is well known that Queen Elizabeth was a great admirer of the immortal Shakspeare, and used frequently . . . to appear upon the stage before the audience . . . dropped her glove, and re-crossed the stage, which Shakspeare noticing, took up.
>
> (*WS* ii. 300–1)

Schoenbaum is dismissive of this story: "'While not enhancing the biographical record, it contributes to the Shakespeare mythos" (1970, 308). Somewhat curiously, Schoenbaum is happy to accept other anecdotes, e.g. the "famous tradition" that Elizabeth commissioned a play about Falstaff in love which "first reaches print in 1702" (196). There is no earlier mention and therefore no tradition. Like many biographers, Schoenbaum is intrigued by the anecdotes of the 'Shakespeare-mythos' because "in some may reside a kernel of truth" (1970, 85). Thus Schoenbaum situates himself in the privileged positon of deciding which anecdotes have "the kernel of truth" and which do not. This is a subjective process as biographers are thus dependent on their own inclinations, since there is no contemporary evidence to corroborate the comments.

Overall, the original edition of *William Shakespeare: A Documentary Life* (1975) was an important resource for its high-quality, facsimile reproduction of so many documents. It has also served an important (but in my view undeserved) role for establishing the view in academic circles that it is possible to write a life of Shakespeare based on contemporary records. Its claim that more is known of Shakespeare's life than is usually realised has been frequently repeated, but remains questionable. It also sets the outline of the life allowing a few variables or "unknowns." However, as a narrative account of Shakespeare's life, it mainly relies on context and conjecture – in much the same way as the popular biographies which Schoenbaum had himself dismissed in *Shakespeare's Lives*. Moreover the records which he presents in *A Documentary Life* "afford no insight into the interior life of the artist, wherein resides the chief fascination of literary biography" as Schoenbaum elsewhere observed (1971, 1).

6.3 "Gentle" Shakespeare

Samuel Schoenbaum was not the first to refer to Shakespeare as "gentle" but he re-established it as the dominant view of his personality. Schoenbaum is using the term in the modern sense of amiable, courteous, and generous. However, in the early modern period 'gentle' was a word primarily used in terms of social status. In the works, the word 'gentle' is used in this sense: in *Henry V*, the king states on the eve of Agincourt that the soldier who fights bravely shall "gentle his condition" where he clearly means that such a soldier will enhance his social condition, not make himself tender and kind. Similarly, Romeo appeals to a sense of status when saying "Gentle Mercutio, put thy rapier up." The linking of the term 'gentle' with Shakespeare was not recorded until seven years after his death; it occurs three times in the preliminary matter to the First Folio. Heminge and Condell in the Epistle to the Reader describe Shakespeare "who, as he was a happie imitator of Nature, was a most gentle expresser of it." Jonson referred to "gentle Shakespeare" in the address to the reader and "my gentle Shakespeare" in the address to the memory. Herbert Howarth (1961) argues that Jonson is referring to the attempts by John (and William) Shakespeare to attain the status of gentlemen, not necessarily that he was kind or amiable.[9] Notwithstanding these observations, Schoenbaum is keen to present Shakespeare as a considerate and benevolent person, noting that "literary geniuses are not on the whole celebrated for their amiable disposition," Schoenbaum cites Greene in *Groatsworth* as the only person who saw Shakespeare in a bad light (1987, 255). Schoenbaum then quotes a number of contemporary writers who seem to have taken a favourable view of Shakespeare's personality. These citations, however, are not secure as they are brief, fragmentary, and ambiguous. If they do allude to Shakespeare, then it is as a poet and playwright. Donaldson (1996, 122-3) points out that the term "gentle" was often applied to poets for their facilty in writing. He quotes *Lucrece* "Deep woes roll forward like a gentle flood" (1118).

First, even though Henry Chettle does not mention Shakespeare by name in this or any other publication. Schoenbaum claims that Chettle reported that "divers of worship commended Shakespeare's uprightness of dealing" (255). This is a serious misquotation as the original text used the pronoun "his" four times but did not name any playwright in his address to the Gentleman Reader in *Kind-harts Dreame* (S. R. December 1592):

> . . . the diver of worship have reported his uprightness of dealing, which argues his honesty, and his facetious grace in writing that approves his art.
> (Henrie Chettle. *Kind Heart's Dream*. WS ii. 189)

Whereas Chambers thought it only "probable" that Chettle was referring to Shakespeare as the second playmaker (*WS*, i. 58–59), Schoenbaum has no doubts. However, this interpretation was attacked by Lukas Erne as lacking "any credible textual evidence" (1998, 430). Nevertheless, Schoenbaum's interpretation is followed by various modern biographers of Shakespeare (e.g. Honan 1998, 158–62; Greenblatt 2004, 212–15; Ackroyd 2005, 176–78; Duncan-Jones 2011, 37–44).

Another writer cited by Schoenbaum (1987, 255) who stated that Shakespeare had an amiable disposition is identified as "Anthony Scoloker." In the epistle to the reader's preceding *Daiphantus, or the Passions of Loue*, 1604 (WS ii. 214–15), the author refers to "Friendly Shake-speare's tragedies" and signs himself "An. Sc." Since this cannot refer to a printer called Anthony Scoloker from the time of Edward VI, it is usually taken to be an otherwise unknown relation.

> *Tasso*, he finds, by that of *Hamlet*, thinkes,
> Tearmes him a mad-man; then of his Inkhorne drinks . . .
> Puts off his cloathes; his shirt he onely weares,
> like mad-*Hamlet*; thus as Passion teares

The poem likens his protagonist to the character of Hamlet, as suffering the passions of love and for wearing just his shirt, which suggest that the author of *Daiphantus* did not know Shakespeare personally, but only through a performance of *Hamlet*. It is extremely tenuous to base an estimation of someone's character on the printed testimony of an unidentifiable writer without any known personal connection to the subject.

The third writer cited in support of a "gentle" Shakespeare is John Davies of Hereford, who referred to "good Will" in *The Scourge of Folly* (1611).[10] Schoenbaum over-interprets the allusion as the phrase "good Will" not only appears in parenthesis but also after a qualifying phrase "Some say":

> To our English Terence, Mr. Will. Shake-speare.
> Some say (good *Will*) which I, in sport, do sing,
> Had'st thou not plaid some Kingly parts in sport,
> Thou hadst bin a companion for a King;
> And, beene a King among the meaner sort.
> Some others raile; but, raile as they thinke fit,
> Thou hast no railing, but a raigning Wit:
> And honesty thou sow'st, which they do reape;
> So, to increase their Stocke which they do keepe.
>   John Davies, *Scourge of Folly* Epigram 159 (1611)

Davies's comment does not amount to any special praise, especially as the subtitle of the work "satyricall epigramms, and others in honor of many noble and worthy persons," suggests that there may be more than a touch of irony about the poems. Although Davies wrote extensively, there is no other mention of Shakespeare in his writings and he has no recorded connection with Shakespeare. Henry Brown speculated that Davies might have been the 'rival poet' of the sonnets (*The sonnets of Shakespeare solved*, 1870), a suggestion taken up by Bate who accepts that this interpretation might be "fanciful" (2008, 230–35).

Schoenbaum also refers to a minor poet, William Barksted, whose allusion in *Mirrha, or the Mother of Adonis* (1607) to a "deere lov'd" neighbor might be a reference to Shakespeare (*WS*, ii. 216). Barksted makes no suggestion as to his personality, only to his "worthie merit" as a poet. Taken together, these suggestions remain vague and do not confirm whether Shakespeare was gentle or not. Nonetheless, from these sparse references, Schoenbaum concludes:

> Shakespeare is enshrined in the consciousness as Gentle Will Shakespeare. One cannot imagine a more fitting designation for the innate gentleman who was not gently born.
>
> (1987, 255)

Schoenbaum also has to play down the less gentle references to Shakespeare. Regarding the 1596 writ of attachment against Shakespeare, Langley, and two women, Schoenbaum calls it a "minor legal drama" (1987, 198) and states that "somehow Shakespeare was drawn into this feud" rather than concede that Shakespeare may have had violent tendencies and was threatening the life of Wayte.

Nevertheless, Schoenbaum's interpretation of Shakespeare as a "gentle" person is followed by almost all modern biographers, with the exceptions of two female writers, Katherine Duncan-Jones (2001) and Germaine Greer (2007). Bevington finds it "comforting to realize that many people have wanted to think of him as not only a great writer but a splendid person" (2010, 28).

Samuel Schoenbaum's two great achievements, to survey previous attempts at a biography of Shakespeare and to provide a documented basis for Shakespeare's life, deservedly command respect among subsequent scholars. After academics had neglected the literary biography of Shakespeare in the first three-quarters of the twentieth century, Schoenbaum's *Documentary Life* established that such a life was both feasible and academically respectable, as well as providing the structure which modern biographies have followed. However, both his approach and his judgements need to be carefully re-evaluated in the need for a stricter adherence to the use and understanding of contemporary records than is evident in *A Documentary Life*.

Notes

1 Schoenbaum briefly dismisses the following popular biographies: Hazelton Spencer (1947); Charles Norman (1947); Leonard Dobbs (1948); Frank Ernest Hill (1949); Hesketh Pearson (1949); M. M. Reese (1953); F. E.

Halliday (1961); Hugh R. Williamson (1962); Peter Quennell (1963); Roland Mushat Frye (1968).

2 Maurice Charney (*Journal of English and Germanic Philology* 1971, 661–63) was looking for a new term to match 'historiography'. Other enthusiastic reviewers included Robert L. Montgomery (*Shakespeare Quarterly* 1972, 209–10) and Douglas Hamer (*Review of English Studies*, 1971, 482–85). Mark Eccles reiterated that no biography was possible (*Renaissance Quarterly* 1973, 83–85).

3 Samuel Schoenbaum's *William Shakespeare: A Documentary Life* was originally issued in 1975 as a hardback, large size format, approx. 36 cm × 26 cm, and included facsimiles of 218 documents. It was issued two years later as *Shakespeare: A Compact Documentary Life* (1977), a reduced format with the same text but smaller images. The small format was reissued in 1987 with changes to the introduction and brief additions to the text concerning the Lancastrian hypothesis, William Bott, a former owner of New Place, further evidence of John Shakespeare's business dealings, and Shakespeare's signatures. Schoenbaum issued a further large-sized volume dealing with subsidiary documents was published as *William Shakespeare, Records and Images* in 1981.

4 Susan Snyder. Review in *Shakespeare Quarterly* 27 (1976, 125–27). Similarly enthusiastic reviews were made by David Bevington in *Modern Philology* 77 (1979, 217–21) and by Douglas Hamer in *Review of English Studies* 27 (1976, 203–5).

5 Kenneth Muir. "A More Interesting Life." Review in *Shakespeare Quarterly* 29 (1978, 126). E. D. Pendry in *Shakespeare Survey* 31 (1979, 177) states that in "A Compact *Documentary Life* we are given the substance of the lavish parent volume in a more portable form." Among many other favourable reviews are Geoffrey Bullough in *Renaissance Quarterly* 31 (1978, 411–12); and J. Bernard Haviland in *College Literature* 4 (1977, 262–63).

6 While it is true that killing deer is a difficult undertaking, it does not have the heroic stature of Beowulf slaying Grendel or St. George slaying the Dragon. For the term used, Schoenbaum may have been influenced by the tale of Natty Bumppo in James Fennimore Cooper's novel *The Deerslayer* (1841) or in the film versions with the same name (1943, 1957).

7 Mark Eccles in *Shakespeare in Warwickshire* (Madison, WI: University of Wisconsin Press, (1961, 82–83) reported the record that the actor William Knell had been killed in a brawl with John Towne at Thame on 13 June 1587, and suggested that Shakespeare was recruited to take his place. Scott McMillin and Sally-Beth MacLean (1998, 160–61) see the speculation as "hard to resist" but believe that the matter cannot be settled. Katherine Duncan-Jones (2001) states it as a possibility and then proceeds as if it is firmly established. Others believe that a London-based acting company was unlikely to recruit personnel from the provinces.

8 Both Nina Bawcutt (ed. *Measure for Measure*, Oxford Shakespeare edn. 1991, 1–6), Alvin Kernan (*Shakespeare, the King's Playwright*, 1995 50–70) and Richard Dutton (*Shakespeare: Court Dramatist*, 2016) present strong cases for courtly composition.

9 Herbert Howarth 'Shakespeare's Gentleness' in *Shakespeare Survey* 14 (1961: 90–97), reprinted in *The Tiger's Heart* (Chatto & Windus: New York, 1970: 1–23).

10 John Davies. *The scourge of folly. Consisting of satyricall epigramms, and others in honor of many noble and worthy persons of our land* (1611). (WS ii. 214).

7   After Schoenbaum

> It is not possible to write a biography of William Shakespeare within the
> normally accepted meaning of the word.
> —(Robert Bearman 2016) Archivist, Shakespeare Centre,
> Stratford-upon-Avon.

Biographers of Shakespeare invariably make two claims: (1) that there
are more records concerning Shakespeare than are popularly supposed
and (2) that these are sufficient records for an evidence-based biography
of Shakespeare. These claims were made originally by John Payne Collier in 1844, when he resorted to fabricating records to satisfy them. The
claim was repeated by Sidney Lee (1899, 361) and by Schoenbaum (*Documentary Life* 1975, xi). In more modern times, Jonathan Bate states.
"We know a great deal more about Shakespeare's life than we do about
the lives of his fellow-dramatists and fellow-actors" (1997, 4), suggesting
also that there are more records for Shakespeare than for Jonson, which is
a glaring mistake. Park Honan echoes this claim "Research into the Eliz-
abethans is of such quality today that new material about Shakespeare,
his town, his parents, his schooling, his friendships, or his career contin-
ually come to light" (1998, ix). Duncan-Jones repeats the idea, stating
that there is a "remarkably substantial body of documents relating to
Shakespeare" (2001, ix). These writers seem unaware that no major contemporary document bearing Shakespeare's name has been discovered
since the Wallaces published the papers in the Bellott-Mountjoy case in
1910 and Hotson published the Langley writ (1931). The biographical
data for the life of Shakespeare remains very thin.

A further weakness of modern biographies is their dependence on
Schoenbaum. This is most clearly evident in the acknowledgements and
lists of further reading in Shakespearean biographies. Instead of noting
any debt to scholars who assembled the records, perhaps E. K. Chambers
(1930), or Roland Lewis (1940), or Catherine Loomis (2002) whose work is
completely overlooked, biographers of Shakespeare cite their debt to other
biographers. Anthony Holden (1999) pays tribute to Harold Bloom and
to Anthony Burgess, neither of whom are known for their work on the

biographical material for Shakespeare. Michael Wood (2003, 345) lists a wide range of over thirty historical studies of Elizabethan England as essential reading, before mentioning his debt to *Shakespeare's Lives* (1970) and *A Documentary Life* (1975), neither of which offer a comprehensive list of references to Shakespeare. Stephen Greenblatt (2004, 390) introduces his Biographical Notes with fulsome praise for Schoenbaum (1970) and for Taylor (*Reinventing Shakespeare* 1989), both being narrative accounts of the history of Shakespeare's reputation, not lists of records. Peter Ackroyd (2005, 511) begins his bibliographical list with a note of thanks to recent biographers (Duncan-Jones, Holden, Sams, Wells, Wilson, and Wood) but does not mention any historical records. Likewise, René Weis (2007, 420) starts his biographical note with a page of praise for Schoenbaum's *Documentary Life*, without noting that this is a narrative biography with its own assumptions and limitations. Laurie Maguire and Emma Smith characterised *A Documentary Life* as still "the standard life of Shakespeare" in which he gives "the documentary evidence and assesses difficult questions with even-handed restraint" by (2012, 207). Thus modern Shakespeare biographies are derivative, which necessarily has a limiting effect on their own accounts. However, it should be essential for any biographer to begin with primary evidence and then proceed only with caution.

7.1 Modern Shakespearean Biographies

It would be impossible to review the numerous biographies of Shakespeare which have been published since Schoenbaum's *Documentary Life*. Rather than make a historical review of biographies of Shakespeare as Schoenbaum had managed, David Bevington (2010) adopted a different approach by offering a thematic survey. Bevington relies on *Documentary Life* for records of Shakespeare's life, claiming that Schoenbaum was able to assemble the verifiable data and speculate as to their meaning only with great caution (2010, 13). His stated purpose is to study the "art" of Shakespearean biography, which would seem to suggest that accuracy and objectivity are not high on Bevington's criteria for evaluating a Life of Shakespeare. In the opening chapter he reviews the biographical data and accepts a lack of primary evidence regarding Shakespeare who "chose not to talk about himself." But he finds it "comforting to realize that many people have wanted to think of him as not only a great writer but a splendid person." For Bevington, contradictory interpretations (catholic v. protestant, republican v. monarchist, faithful husband v. adulterer) are praiseworthy and not simply the result of shoddy scholars resorting to the use of uncorroborated posthumous anecdotes, contextual description, intuitive conjectures, and selective biographical inferences from the works.

The sheer number of biographies is astounding (Table 7.1):

Table 7.1 Some biographies about Shakespeare since 1975

Bradbrook, M.	*Shakespeare: The Poet in His World*	1978
Honigmann, E.	*Shakespeare: The 'Lost Years'*	1985
Levi, P.	*The Life and Times of William Shakespeare*	1988
Kay, D.	*Shakespeare: His Life, Work and Era*	1991
Thomson, P.	*Shakespeare's Professional Career*	1992
Wilson, I.	*Shakespeare: The Evidence*	1993
Skura, M.	*Shakespeare the Actor and the Purposes of Playing*	1993
Wells, S.	*Shakespeare: A Dramatic Life*	1994
Honan, P.	*Shakespeare A Life*	1998
Shellard, D.	*William Shakespeare*	1998
Holden, A.	*William Shakespeare: His Life and Work*	1999
Southworth, J.	*Shakespeare, the Player: A Life in the Theatre*	2000
Duncan-Jones, K.	*Ungentle Shakespeare: Scenes From His Life*	2001
Wood, M.	*In Search of Shakespeare*	2003
Greenblatt, S.	*Will in the World: How Shakespeare Became Shakespeare*	2004
Holland, P.	*"William Shakespeare" (ODNB)*	2004
Ackroyd, P.	*Shakespeare: The Biography*	2005
Shapiro, J.	*1599: A Year in the Life of William Shakespeare*	2005
Weis, R.	*Shakespeare Revealed*	2007
Bryson, B.	*Shakespeare: The World as a Stage*	2007
Greer, G.	*Shakespeare's Wife*	2007
Nicholl, C.	*The Lodger: Shakespeare on Silver Street*	2007
Bate, J.	*Soul of the Age*	2008
Bevington, D.	*Shakespeare's Ideas*	2008
Pearce, J.	*The Quest for Shakespeare*	2008
Potter, L.	*Life of William Shakespeare: A Critical Biography*	2012
Fogg, N.	*Hidden Shakespeare: A Biography*	2012
Callaghan, D.	*Who Was William Shakespeare?*	2013
Shapiro, J.	*1606: William Shakespeare and the Year of Lear*	2015

It is impossible to offer a complete review of each work, so I will attempt only to describe their main characteristics. Muriel Bradbrook (1978) gave a more traditional biography in describing the plays and poems within an outline narrative of the life, as did Stanley Wells (1994) and Dympna Callaghan (2013). An early critic of Schoenbaum was Peter Levi (1988) who made a plea for the use of conjecture, and offered many speculations of his own. Dennis Kay's study was adopted in the Twayne's World Author Series. Peter Thomson (1992) emphasised Shakespeare's role as actor as did Meredith Skura (1993). In the misleadingly titled *Shakespeare: The Evidence*, Ian Wilson posits Ferdinando, Lord Strange as Shakespeare's first patron, identifies Elisabeth Lanier as the 'dark lady' and surmises that Shakespeare rode out the plague years 1593–4 at Titchfield with the third earl of Southampton. In 1998, Oxford University Press justified a new biography by Park Honan, an academic biographer of Jane Austen and Robert Browning, by stating in the blurb that "In the last ten years, virtually every previously known fact about Shakespeare has been modified by new research." Like earlier biographies, there is a considerable amount of critical opinion, e.g. *Antony and Cleopatra* considers "non-literal truth, in myth, fable, and implicit connections between historical epochs" (343) His claims of "a wealth of fresh information" which turns out to be largely contextual, suggesting that Shakespeare died from typhoid due an unusually warm spring which Honan believes turned the River Avon into a "fetid stream" (407). In the same year, OUP published Dominic Shellard's biography in the British Library Writers' Lives series, which was lavishly illustrated and very contextual. The celebrated biographer Anthony Holden (1999) was more speculative than previous studies, especially when imagining how Shakespeare worked as a tutor and actor at the home of a Catholic Lancastrian nobleman. Elsewhere he asks: "Is it entirely idle to wonder if Shakespeare himself was suffering sleepless nights while writing *Macbeth*?" (237), which might invite readers to suppose such a conjecture was entirely idle.

Biographies since the Turn of the Millennium

In a change of emphasis, the Arden Shakespeare published a biography of Shakespeare by Katherine Duncan-Jones, who unusually portrayed Shakespeare as ambitious and obsessed with "social class, sex and money" (x–xi). She also departed from the traditional narrative by describing Shakespeare as an "early starter" who joined the Queen's Men in the mid-1580s. Without any personal papers, it is not possible to form any reliable view as to whether Shakespeare was gentle or ungentle. There may have been a touch of irony when Jonathan Bate called *Ungentle Shakespeare* "unquestionably the best Shakespearean biography of the new century."[1] In 2003, Michael Wood presented *In Search of Shakespeare* as a miniseries for the BBC with an accompanying biography in print. For Wood, the key to Shakespeare's personality was his adherence to the old faith, fostered in both Stratford and Lancashire, which explains why he has left so little evidence of his literary career. Although he states that it is "dangerous to read auto-biography into the plays," he proceeds to do just that in linking the ghost of Hamlet's father with his own father's death in 1601 (240–41).

The most eagerly awaited biography of the twenty-first century was by Stephen Greenblatt *Will in the World: how Shakespeare became Shakespeare* (2004). As a key figure in the emergence of New Historicism, he more than anyone would be able to provide clear and causal links between the playwright's social setting and the works. At the outset of his biography, Greenblatt somewhat paradoxically noted

> the inward springs of his art... would be difficult enough to glimpse
> if biographers could draw upon letters and diaries, contemporary

> memoirs and interviews, books with revealing marginalia, notes and first drafts. Nothing of the kind survives, nothing that provides a clear link between the timeless work with its universal appeal and a particular life that left its scratches in the humdrum bureaucratic records of the age.
>
> (2004, 13)

He follows this with the following admission: "There are huge gaps in knowledge that make any biographical study of Shakespeare an exercise in speculation" (18). He opens *Will in the World* with the request: "Let us imagine" (23). In the absence of archival material regarding Shakespeare's childhood, he indulges in speculation based on the slimmest of inferences, e.g. William first heard poetry from his mother singing a nursery rhyme (23), or that John Shakespeare the ale-taster suffered from alcohol problems (66–67) which Greenblatt deduces from Hal's disdain for Falstaff (*1 Henry IV*). He openly follows Frank Harris (1909) in claiming that Shakespeare had an unhappy marriage. He asserts that the description of the death of Falstaff in *Henry V* is based on the account of the death of Robert Greene (219). Like Wood, he sees Shakespeare as an adherent of the old religion and imagines a casual meeting between the young William and the Edmund Campion. He adds: "Not surprisingly, Shakespeare never referred openly to Campion" (108–17). Such a line of argument could be made to support any contact with anybody as Shakespeare makes no reference to any person before his will.

Many academics were disappointed that Greenblatt relied more on his own imagination than on documentary evidence. The reviews of *Will in the World* were analysed by M. G. Aune (2006), who found that Greenblatt was "promoted as a celebrity scholar inside the profession and promoted as a popular author outside the profession." Terry Eagleton noted that "Greenblatt seems to have ditched the rest of his new-historicist baggage" (2004) and despite the conjectures and speculation, he praised "the stylishness and lucidity" of the narrative. Similarly Lois Potter accepts that when "a book's chief allegiance is to imagination, it is pointless to criticize it by the standards of biographical scholarship." She too admires how "Greenblatt writes beautifully and appreciatively." (2005b). However, other academics expressed disapproval. Colin Barrow was surprised that "the founding father of New Historicism" should resort to "the individuating anecdote" and the "simple psychologising of the plays" when constructing his biography of the bard. Katherine Duncan-Jones stated that "*Will in the World* includes "a strangely uncritical mish-mash of idées fixes and nonsense." After giving further examples of a similar nature, Bate concludes that many of Greenblatt's interpretations are "entirely arbitrary." In other words, they are merely unevidenced assertions or fictions. Colin MacCabe concurs: "There is a great deal of valuable history in this book, but of the historical

Shakespeare, there is hardly a trace." The most wide-ranging criticisms were made in a review article by David Ellis.[2]

Peter Holland's entry in the *ODNB* for "William Shakespeare" (2004) was seldom reviewed and is rarely cited; however, it offers a very reasonable view of Shakespeare's life. It considers alternate theories and states the writer's preference for one interpretation over another. Another good feature is its awareness of the limited evidence. A major shortcoming, however, is its use of the works as evidence of Shakespeare's life: he states that "Viola's passionate mourning for the apparent death of her twin brother in *Twelfth Night* could have been generated by the loss of Hamnet" and adds that it "is not too fanciful to see Shakespeare drawn as a result towards the subject matter of Hamlet." How can any reader tell the difference between what is "too fanciful to see" and what is not?. Holland served as the Director of the Shakespeare Institute at Stratford-upon-Avon and local affiliations may have clouded his judgement when he describes the school at Stratford as "splendid," despite the total absence of any records concerning the institution in the Elizabethan period. Coincidentally in 2004, Peter Holland was the editor of *Shakespeare Survey* when the journal decided to dispense with the review of biographical claims about Shakespeare. In the 1990s, these comments had become fewer, prompting the reviewer in 1993, Martin Wiggins, to ask: "Should *Shakespeare Survey* ever again review the year's work on Shakespeare's Life, Times and Stage?" (*SS* 1993, 192) Ten years later the editor decided that commenting on claims about Shakespeare's life was unworthy of the journal.

After Holden and Wood, Peter Ackroyd was the third professional biographer within a decade to undertake a life: *Shakespeare: the Biography* (2005). Among Ackroyd's original, but unevidenced claims were that Shakespeare's godfather was one William Smith, a haberdasher and a neighbour, apparently based on nothing more than the coincidence of Christian name (3). Ackroyd claims that Shakespeare was "known for playing kingly roles" for which he cites no evidence (27). Like Holden, he accepts uncritically many speculations, e.g. that he attended the funerals of his son (270–71) and his father (373) which he imagines in some detail. He decides that Shakespeare died of syphilis and describes the Protestant funeral which he received; there is no evidence to support either of these claims. Regarding the deer-poaching legend, Ackroyd states that "there may well be truth at the bottom of this well of conjecture" (69), which is meaningless. Overall, Ackroyd's biography follows the dominant narrative structure set out by Schoenbaum but with considerable addition of inferences and conjectures.

Two years later, the next biography emerged, this time by a Shakespeare editor, René Weis in his *Shakespeare Revealed* (2007). Weis again follows the traditional narrative but adds many inferences from the works. He believes that references to schoolboys in *As You Like It* and

Romeo and Juliet (20) are autobiographical. Weis imagines that Shakespeare's son Hamnet was resurrected briefly on stage in the person of Sebastian in *Twelfth Night* (268). He adds new speculation, e.g. that he built up a library at New Place (251). There is no contemporary evidence supporting either claim. Weis also repeats James Joyce's suggestion in *Ulysses* that Anne had an affair with a younger Shakespeare brother, "so that Hamlet remonstrating with Gertrude may reflect Shakespeare imagining his son arguing with Anne" (2007, 275–76). He takes the sonnets as autobiographical. In the same year, Bill Bryson was invited by the series editor of *Eminent Lives* to write a short and accessible biography for the general reader. Bryson openly admits the lack of information on many points (2007, 17).

Jonathan Bate wrote two books about Shakespeare which have been taken as biographical. He described the earlier study, *The Genius of Shakespeare* (1997), as a "biography of the poet's talent and reputation." In his later work, *Soul of the Age* (2008), attempts to be more historical, adapting the chronological approach of the traditional narrative into the more thematic pattern of Jaques' speech about the Seven Ages of Man. Bate states his main method lies in "[g]athering what we can from his plays and poems: That is how we will write a biography that is true to him" (5). Later he asserts that "we must always be wary of attempts to map Shakespeare's life on to his work" (52). When Bate summarily dismisses the Lancastrian hypothesis and describes Shakespeare's Warwickshire upbringing, he lays himself open to sharing a vested interest in the Shakespeare industry, according to Anthony Holden (2008), as Bate at that time held a professorial chair at nearby Warwick University. His own "instinctive sense" points to Shakespeare's self-portrait in Bassanio's wooing of the wealthy Portia in *A Merchant of Venice* (165). Bate's efforts to link the life and times with the works are for the most part idiosyncratic. Like Bate, David Bevington's *Shakespeare's Ideas* (2008) considers in an approximate chronological order how "the writings of Shakespeare reveal the workings of a great mind" (1). Lois Potter first conducted her own review "Having Our Will: Imagination in Recent Shakespeare Biographies" (2005a) before setting to work on her own study *The Life of William Shakespeare: A Critical Biography* (2012). She addresses key issues overlooked by Greenblatt (2005) such as "which of the constantly metamorphosing theatrical companies, separately or in combination, might have produced which plays, or how much Shakespeare might have collaborated with other playwrights." Her own study is indebted to the work of Brian Vickers on co-authorship (2002). She identifies many possibilities for Shakespeare's collaboration, but remains cautious as there is no evidence as to how co-authorship was conducted by Shakespeare. She is openly intuitive "the only Shakespeare I can imagine is one whose imaginative life was fed essentially by words" (vii). Potter's *Life* received a very positive review by David

Riggs in *Shakespeare Quarterly* (2013, 378–80), which was followed immediately by an equally enthusiastic review by Robert Bearman of David Ellis's *The Truth about William Shakespeare* (2012), which argued against the possibility of any biography of Shakespeare. Kathleen Kuiper's *Life and Times of William Shakespeare* (2012) was intended for children and shows commendably more caution when advancing an outline of his life than most biographies for adults.

Joseph Pearce in *The Quest for Shakespeare* (2008) is one of a number of biographers who view Shakespeare as a closet Catholic. Much of the content of this study is contextual, describing the situation of the Catholics under Elizabeth and their increasing persecution. Pearce attempts to show that Shakespeare was linked to a large number of adherents to the old faith, not least his father who signed a spiritual testament. Following Heinrich Mutschmann and Karl Wentersdorf (*Shakespeare and Catholicism*, 1952), he believes that Sir Thomas Lucy conducted a vendetta against Shakespeare. He claims that Shakespeare knew the Jesuit martyr Robert Southwell. He over-interprets the record in claiming that Susanna's failure to receive Easter communion in 1606 was a sign of recusancy. He believes that the Blackfriars Gatehouse was purchased because of its Catholic connections. Pearce ignores any arguments for a Protestant or Anglican Shakespeare, or for that matter a secular Shakespeare, whose values were rooted in tolerance, which is currently the majority view.[3]

Partial Biographies

Whereas most biographies follow much the same continuous, cradle-to-grave narrative outline of Shakespeare's life as established by Schoenbaum in 1975, some have adopted another approach by offering a partial biography, a slice of a subject's life. Ernst Honigmann in *Shakespeare: the 'lost years'* (1985) developed the Lancastrian hypothesis, first proposed by O. L. Baker (1937), that William Shakespeare spent much of his youth in Lancashire and returned to Stratford to marry in 1582. This case is based on identifying William Shakespeare, the future poet and playwright, with a person named "William Shakeshafte, now dwelling with me" in the 1581 will of Alexander Houghton. Much contextual material has been found to support this hypothesis, especially among those who view Shakespeare as a closet Catholic (Wood 2003; Greenblatt 2004; Wilson 2004). The theory does offer an explanation as to how Shakespeare might have been introduced to drama. The Hoghton family had links with Ferdinando Stanley, Lord Strange, whose company of players acted a number of Shakespeare's plays. However, the case lacks direct evidence (Bearman 2002). Glyn Parry has identified a 'William Shakeshafte' from Preston who had connections with the Hoghton and Hesketh family.[4]

Plate 7.1 Hoghton Tower, Lancashire.

Another study to offer a slice of Shakespeare's life was James Shapiro *1599: A Year in the Life of William Shakespeare* (2005). Shapiro attempts to describe a key year in Shakespeare's life but only manages to describe some of the important political and theatrical events of this year, e.g. the death of Spenser or the return from Ireland of Essex. Shapiro is unusual among Shakespeare biographers in recognising insufficient biographical material for a cradle-to-grave account of Shakespeare's life, as he explained in a review article of "Five Books" to do with Shakespearean biography: "I keep coming back to the impossibility of writing a cradle-to-grave story of Shakespeare's life" (2011). His entire study *1599: A Year in the Life of William Shakespeare* (2005) depends on many unverifiable claims: "In the course of 1599, Shakespeare completed *Henry the Fifth*, wrote *Julius Caesar* and *As You Like It* in quick succession, then drafted *Hamlet*" (xv). While these dates are often accepted (although many would place the drafting of *Hamlet* to 1600 or 1601), there are no entries for any plays of Shakespeare in the Stationers' Register for 1599; the three entries in 1600 for *Henry V, As You Like It* and *Much Ado* might indicate composition in any of the preceding years. Shapiro ignores *Much Ado* but it has an equal claim to a 1599 date for composition. The earliest reference to Shakespeare's *Hamlet* is usually taken to be in the SR in 1602. There are other references to a play about Hamlet (in 1589, 1594, and 1596) which might refer to a version by Shakespeare.

Shapiro is offering plausibility, not certainty, in his slice of Shakespeare's life, as a careful reading of the preface indicates:

> Rather than awkwardly littering the pages that follow with one hedge after another – "perhaps", "maybe", "it's most likely", "probably" or the most desperate of them all "surely", I'd like to offer one global qualification here: this is necessarily my reconstruction of what happened to Shakespeare in the course of the year.
>
> (2005, xxiii)

Shapiro's omission of such terms of uncertainty encourages readers to accept that what he is saying is factually based. As a matter of record, there are only seven documented references to William Shakespeare in 1599, none of which states which plays or poems (if any) Shakespeare was writing at this time. There

Despite Shapiro's claim that "we know a considerable amount of Shakespeare's life" in the year 1599, there are only seven documented references to him, three handwritten and four printed (Loomis 2002, 90–102):

1 named as tax defaulter in parish of St Helen's, Bishopsgate;
2 named as a sharer in the Globe in the post-mortem inventory of Sir Thomas Brend (*c.* 16 May 1599);
3 named as an original sharer in the Globe in the lawsuit Witter vs Heminges & Condell (1619).

A draft of the grant of arms in 1599 only mentions John Shakespeare and his "posteritie"; it does not refer to William (*WS* ii. 18–20). It might also be possible to date some allusions in the *Return from Parnassus* to 1599, but this play is generally dated to 1600–1 (Leishmann 1949). There are also four references in print to Shakespeare:

4 named on the dedication to *Venus & Adonis* (O5);
5 named on the title page of *1 Henry IV* (Q2);
6 named on the title page of *The Passionate Pilgrim* (1599);
7 mentioned in an epigram (iv. 22) by John Weever in *Epigrammes in the Oldest Cut, and Newest Fashion.*

These printed allusions to Shakespeare only contribute to our knowledge of Shakespeare's standing, not to his life: *Venus & Adonis* and *1 Henry IV* are reprints. *The Passionate Pilgrim* is a collection of poems by various authors. Weever's epigram gives a poetic tribute to the narrative poems, and to plays about Romeo and a King Richard as he only writes one epigram to Shakespeare out of a total of 160. None of these printed references shows what Shakespeare was actually doing in 1599. Nonetheless, this study won the Theatre Book Prize and the Samuel Johnson Prize in 2006 for the best nonfiction writing in the English language.

Shapiro repeated his trick of reimagining the historical events of 1606 and assuming Shakespeare's place in them. His *1606 William Shakespeare and the Year of Lear* (2015) suffers from a similar deficiency of evidence. There are only six allusions to Shakespeare during this year (Loomis 2002, 173–74): (1) The Survey of Rowington lists his tenancy of a 'domum mansionalem' perhaps the property in Chapel Lane in Stratford. (2) The inventory of Ralph Hubaud's property after his death stated that "There was owinge by Mr. Shakspre xxli" (£20). (3) William Drummond of Hawthornden listed four plays of Shakespeare which he had read that year. There are also allusions to performances of Shakespeare's plays (4) by Barnabe Barnes in *Foure Bookes of Offices* and (5) by Wm. Warner in *A Continuance of Albions England* and possibly (6) by the Venetian Ambassador (sometime from 1606 to Nov 1608). There is a record concerning Susanna Shakespeare, who was listed among twenty parishioners for not receiving communion at Easter (April 1606). Another record that omits Shakespeare's name states that "Burbidge and Heminges and others, the owners of the Playhouse called the Globe" were ordered to repair their sewers. There are two further records of payments to John Heminges on behalf of the King's Men for performances in October and Christmantide. None of these records, however, indicate what William himself was actually doing or where he even was.

A similar description of historical context was conducted by Charles Nicholl in *The Lodger: Shakespeare on Silver Street* (2007) which deals with the Bellott-Mountjoy lawsuit in 1612. Nicholl described the historical and archaeological records for the area around Cripplegate to give an his informative portrait of the Mountjoy home in the period 1601–3. These papers give the only occasion in his life when we can locate Shakespeare to a particular time and place: on 11 May 1612, he was making his deposition at Westminster Hall, London. There are no other accounts which locate him to any other precise location on any particular day. Another study which claims to offer oblique insights into Shakespeare's character and life was Germaine Greer's *Shakespeare's Wife* (2007). Most biographers of Shakespeare refer to the lack of material or the difficulty of writing about Shakespeare from contemporary records. That of Germaine Greer is one of the more curious: "All biographies of Shakespeare are houses built of straw, but there is good straw and rotten straw, and some houses are better built than others" (2007, 9). In fact, there are only six documented references to her: her marriage bond, her burial record, her epitaph, and three citations in her lifetime in the wills of men. She is also mentioned in some law suits after her death. Despite the paucity of records, Greer feels confident enough to dispute and revise previous claims about Shakespeare's relationship with his wife. Greer claims "We can find no evidence of Shakespeare having supported his family, especially during the lost years" (2007, 138). Greer needs to be reminded that we can find no evidence about Shakespeare at all during the period from 1585 to 1592, hence the term 'lost years'. Overall, Greer only manages to exchange one "set of unsupported hypotheses" with another set as Charles Nicholl observed in his review. He believes that the "best way to learn more about Ann Shakespeare would be actually to discover something new about her."[5] Katherine Scheil compares the widely different interpretations of Shakespeare's marriage in six recent biographies ("Filling in the 'Wife-Shaped Void': The Contemporary Afterlife of Anne Hathaway." *Shakespeare Survey* 63, 225–36).However, Lena Orlin has recently argued that apart from the family household at New Place, Anne managed other properties (a tract in Stratford Old Town, a cottage in Chapel Lane, the houses in Henley Street); took in a lodger, Thomas Greene; was a maltster (and grain hoarder), brewer, hostess (to a visiting preacher), and money manager (borrowing from the shepherd Thomas Whittington), concluding that Anne contributed greatly to the economic success of the Shakespeares.[6]

The number of biographies that have been published by academics who are experts in English Literature is astonishing for claiming that any biography can be attempted at all. There are various reasons as to why there have been so many biographies of Shakespeare. Perhaps the most important is that publishers have realised that the reading public's respect for Shakespeare means that a biography is likely to sell. F. E. Halliday (1961, 9) introduced his biography of Shakespeare with the apology that he had been asked to write it by his publisher. Colin Burrow notes that readers are a lot more likely to buy books about Shakespeare's life than they are to buy books by Shakespeare (2005). Greenblatt mentions the public's enduring interest in the "rags-to-riches" story (2004, preface). Additionally, it has been noted that there is a continuing attraction for writers such as Wood and Ackroyd to write about a great writer (the emphasis of Schoenbaum's study 1970). Anthony Burgess asserted the "the right of every Shakespeare-lover who has ever lived to paint their own portrait of the man" (1972, 11). Michael Dobson has called it a craving for "someone to feel grateful to" (reported by Higgins 2009). Furthermore, the continuing iconic status of Shakespeare (as explained by Taylor 1991 and Dobson 1992) entails that popular writers such as Bill Bryson will happily attempt the Life of Shakespeare as he did in 2007.

7.2 Critique of Modern Shakespearean Biography

Not all modern critics have welcomed this surge of biographies, but follow earlier Shakespearean scholars such as Malone, Halliwell-Phillips, and Chambers in asserting that the surviving records are by no means sufficient for a narrative account of Shakespeare's life. David Ellis (2005,

2012), Michael Benton (2009), and Graham Holderness (2011) have expressed further their doubts as to its feasibility. Ellis is mainly concerned to show how Shakespeare emerged as a national icon, which rather suggests that the title *That Man Shakespeare* is somewhat misleading. In so doing, Ellis highlights six dubious historical practices used to develop a biography (examined in more detail later in this chapter). To these, I add five more dubious practices. However, Ellis does not go far enough. First, he tends to overstate (8–9) the significance of the ambiguous allusion in Greene's *Groatsworth of Wit*, failing to acknowledge that the allusion might refer to another writer: Second, Ellis assumes that Shakespeare and Jonson were closely acquainted (2005, 29–32), against which I argue in Chapter 9. Next, he believes that the present monument in the Holy Trinity Church at Stratford showing Shakespeare with an upturned moustache, a pen, and some paper remains substantially unaltered from the time of Digges's reference to it in the First Folio (1623). Ellis does not mention that the present-day monument depicts a very different person from the one illustrated by William Dugdale in *Antiquities of Warwickshire* (1656, 520). Ellis also tends to find value in posthumous anecdotes: he calls John Aubrey's slight report about Shakespeare "testimony" (40).[7] David Ellis's *The Truth about William Shakespeare* (2012) adopts a more analytical approach to fourteen topics in Shakespeare's life, including a chapter on Boyhood and Youth. Ellis shows how recent biographers have speculated beyond the limited records. In *Nine Lives of William Shakespeare*, Holderness considers different interpretations of Shakespeare's life. Each one is fictionalised but cannot be disproved due to the lack of records, thus indicating that a biography of Shakespeare, based on contemporary documents is "an almost impossible brief" (2011, 16). I go further and argue that it is indeed an impossible brief. Holderness and Ellis limit themselves for the most part to modern studies.

Part of the problem lies in deciding what is, or at least what should be, a biography. Whereas Eagleton and Potter praised style and narrative flair, M. G. Aune states:

> Academics expect right Shakespeare, a historically accurate biography, fully informed by new historicist practices. Providing something conjectural betrays the commitment to the academic pursuit of truth, as well as the implicit commitment to propagating factual or right Shakespeare.
>
> (2006)

Aune was very critical on Greenblatt's reliance on imaginative interpretation. In another incisive review article, Bruce Smith (2007) considers nine modern biographies of Shakespeare (including Wells 2002; Wood

2003; Greenblatt 2004; Ackroyd 2006) and offers useful categories for distinguishing references to:

- The historical William Shakespeare
- The complete works of William Shakespeare
- William Shakespeare as Authorship Function
- William Shakespeare as Cultural Icon

Smith then shows how biographers claim that they are writing about historical person but frequently lapse in the other three categories.

Novelistic Trajectory

Smith also shows how the studies thought they could identify four key moments in Shakespeare's life: when Shakespeare decided to set out on his career, his confrontation with an antagonist, his greatest achievement, and his retirement. None of these key moments emerge from the record. Instead, they merely conform to *Campbell's Face of a Thousand Heroes*. The standard account of Shakespeare's life is largely derivative, following "novelistic trajectory of increasing prosperity and respectability" as outlined by Rowe in 1709 and Malone in 1790 (de Grazia 1991, 138). This interpretation was reinforced by Schoenbaum (1975).

Modern biographies of Shakespeare follow the standard pattern of biography which was identified in Chapter 1:

I **Introduction.** Significance of the subject. Biographers have no difficulty in describing the significance of Shakespeare. They invariably dismiss the notion of lack of information, often vaguely claiming "new evidence." It is usually the publisher's blurb which explains why the biographer is particularly qualified to present a new study, perhaps as a respectable scholar such as Rene Weis "a world authority on Shakespeare" or as a popular writer: "From bestselling author Bill Bryson comes this compelling short biography of William Shakespeare [2007]" (Promotional material from John Murray and HarperCollins respectively). Greenblatt spans both categories.

II **Family Background** is treated in much detail because there is so much actual documentation both in the Stratford records and in John Shakespeare's application for a coat of arms. Some of the description entails mention of his mother's family to the Anglo-Saxon period (e.g. Wood 25–27). Attempts to make such description relevant to William's life are rarely convincing. Bate wondered how Greenblatt could "possibly know that Mary Arden sang the song of Pillicock when Will was a babe in arms?"

The Life is then described in a series of episodes.

III **Early Life.** The birth scene at Henley Street is frequently described in detail, but has no foundation in any records, as noted by Julia Thomas (2012). Any description of the circumstances of Shakespeare's birth, therefore, is entirely conjectural.

IV **Childhood and Education.** Every description of William's youth is conjectural as there are no records that he was even in Stratford from the time of his baptism until the issue of the marriage license.

V **Call to Action.** Biographers often identify the key moment in Shakespeare's life, when William decides to leave Stratford and head to London. For some it is the deer-poaching episode; for others it is when he joined the Queen's Men or another touring company. For such episodes, there is no evidence.

VI **London and its Theatres.** There is much contextual description of the City and its playhouses, sometimes of the courts of Elizabeth and of James.

VII **Contemporaries: friends and enemies.** Shakespeare is assumed to have known a patron, a rival poet, a dark lady who is usually his mistress, and a fair youth of whom he is very fond – all of whom receive different identifications.

VIII **Return to Stratford.** After great success, Shakespeare apparently enjoys an easy and well-deserved retirement in Stratford, again undocumented.

IX His **death** and funeral are often described in detail (again no evidence) and his will is analysed for his fondness for his family and friends.

X His **surviving family** are considered summarily. The biographer mentions the subsequent history of his widow, his children, and his grandchildren.

XI The **afterlife**, concerning his publications and/or his reputation, usually receives very brief treatment. One exception is Holland (*ODNB*, 2004), who devotes over half of his entry to his posthumous reputation.

The first stage of the hero's journey, according to Rowe, came when young William was caught poaching inside Sir Thomas Lucy's enclosed park. After he was punished, it was claimed, Shakespeare wrote a satirical ballad against the landowner(according to Rowe 1709, i. v). This episode was accepted by Lewis Theobald (1733 i. vi) and enhanced by Edward Capell who cited the testimony of an old woman whose grandfather had heard it from one Thomas Jones who had died in 1703 aged upwards of ninety (1779 iii. pt. ii 75). This story was doubted by Malone, who showed that there was no enclosed park at Charlecote at that time and that Lucy's punishments described did not correspond to those laid down in law (1821, ii. 119–32). Nevertheless, biographers continue to accept it. Sidney Lee calls it "a creditable tradition" (1917, 34).

E. K. Chambers notes that the "story of deer-stealing has been the subject of much controversy" but he is inclined to accept it (WS, i. 19–20). Schoenbaum is also keen to accept the anecdote which he calls a "satisfying story – an exciting sequence of theft, discovery, punishment, and escape. What a dramatic scene!" (1970, 108–14) Margreta de Grazia defends Rowe's use of the anecdote as concerned not with "recording facts" but with "a significant occasion" when Shakespeare had to leave Stratford and seek his fortune in London; for de Grazia the deer poaching story "dramatized the critical juncture of his life" (1991, 107). Similarly, Greenblatt states that regarding the deer poaching story, the question is "not the degree of evidence but rather the imaginative life that the incident has" (2004, 151). For most biographers of Shakespeare, this anecdote remains the only Call to Adventure in the Shakespeare mythos even though it was not recorded until 1709.

Campbell's Eighth Stage, the Woman as temptress, is sometimes cast as Anne Hathaway, beguiling an innocent teenager into an early marriage. It is usually reserved for the 'dark lady' of the Sonnets, whom Shakespearean biographers like to identify with a historical person such as Emilia Lanier, Mrs. Florio (née Daniel), or Mary Fitton. Katherine Duncan-Jones rejects all such attempts at identification (1997, 50–55) because there is no external evidence as to the identity of the 'dark lady' or even if one or more historical persons were being portrayed. For the final stage of his life, most people follow Rowe's account in which he stated that Shakespeare returned to Stratford, ceased working, and enjoyed "Ease, Retirement, and the Conversation of his Friends" (Rowe 1709, i. xxxv). Rowe indicates that he is arguing from norms by adding "as all Men of good Sense will wish theirs may be." There is no evidence that Shakespeare ever retired, either in the sense that he stopped working or in the sense that he returned to make Stratford his principal home: he invested in the Blackfriars Gatehouse in 1613. Rowe introduced the notion of retirement to provide closure to Shakespeare's life and it has featured ever since. Overall, the process for biographers is to try and adapt the limited biographical data for Shakespeare to the standard pattern of a linear narrative.

Description of his death scene plays an important part in the biographies of Shakespeare, despite the absence of record as to the cause of death or any burial ceremonies. There are only two surviving records: his will in the National Archives, January 1616, with corrections dated 25 March 1616, and a parish record of his burial dated 25 April, 1616. Peter Ackroyd describes his ritual laying-out and burial according to the Protestant custom (2005, 485), whereas Michael Wood describes how he received the sacrament of extreme unction from a Catholic priest (2003, 377). One later anecdote recorded by the Reverend John Ward (at some time between 1662 and 1679): "Shakespear Drayton and Ben Jhonson had a merry meeting and it seems drank too hard for Shakespear died of a feavour there contracted" (Severn 1839, 183). Some biographers accept this story: Park Honan diagnoses the fever as typhoid (1998, 409). Others adopt a different line: Duncan-Jones (2001, 266) changes the cause of death from typhoid to syphilis, which Ackroyd follows: "Nothing in Shakespeare's life or character would exclude the possibility" (2005, 294). Germaine Greer (2007, 304) also believes he had contracted syphilis and later died of mercury poisoning used in the attempted cure. Although there is no evidence for the cause of death or the style of burial, biographers present their own speculations as fact. Due to the limited biographical material for William Shakespeare, a full-length biography can only be constructed by supplementary techniques, giving detailed exposition of the context or through the use of imaginative reconstruction and conjecture.

Six Bad Practices in the Biography of Shakespeare

David Ellis (2005, 273–305) is one of the few scholars to consider the various strategies used by Shakespeare biographers to fill the information deficit; he posits six strategies:

> (a) Argument from Absence: Ellis cites the argument used by Michael Wood (2003, 147), who said that during the early modern period, it was dangerous to adhere to the old religion in England, so if Shakespeare was Catholic, he would have had to practise in secret. Since there is no document linking Shakespeare to Catholicism, Shakespeare must have kept his Papist affiliations secret. Ellis then refers to Katherine Duncan-Jones (2001, 118–19) who states: "The fact that the leading player [Shakespeare] in Jonson's first *Humour* play took no part in his second is rather striking." Duncan-Jones uses this "striking fact" to support her contention of an on-going feud between Shakespeare and Jonson.

Biographers often begin sentences with phrases such as "There is no reason to suppose/doubt" that Shakespeare did or did not perform some action or feel some emotion. Greenblatt imagines that there was a relationship between Edmund Campion and Shakespeare, and that Shakespeare kept it secret to protect the Jesuit. Another way to explain why Campion and Shakespeare are not linked in any of the existing records is that they never met. Greenblatt suggests Shakespeare's delayed reaction to his son's death: "Nor is it implausible that it took years for the trauma of his son's death fully to erupt in Shakespeare's work" (emphasis added, 2004, 290). The metastatement "nor is it implausible" with its double negative indicates the absence of any evidence as to immediate or delayed grief or both. Similarly, Lois Potter maintains that Shakespeare portrays his grief at his son's death in his revised *Hamlet*: "It would not be strange if Shakespeare, the actor, found it easiest to dramatize his response to Hamnet's death by taking on another man's voice" (emphasis added 2012, 228). Potter's hedge "it would not be strange" indicates a lack of evidence.

> (b) Minding your Language (linguistic hedges and rhetorical questions): Ellis bemoans the use of "the weasel words of biography" such as "perhaps," "if," "probably," "could have," "may," as well as rhetorical questions which are used at first to raise suggestions, but which are subsequently dropped so that the conjectures are presented as established facts.

Expressions which imply various degrees of uncertainty about a proposition are now known as linguistic hedges. They have been widely used in Shakespearean biography. In 1910, a senior official in the American government, William Stoddard explained why he came to write his own small book in which he reported all the known records for Shakespeare "expurgated" of all conjectures:

> Naturally, I turned for information to the biographies of the poet-actor. But I was doomed to a disappointment. For there in the welter of quoted, copied, and sometimes photographed documents, among "allusions" that alluded to Shakespeare and "allusions" that did not allude to him at all, in the confusion of skilfully deployed adverbs implying various degrees of uncertainty in the mind of the biographer (as, "doubtless," "probably," "credibly," and all their kind)... I felt myself strangely lost.
>
> (Stoddard 1910, 3)

One set of examples comes from a biographical sketch by Stanley Wells (2006b), who begins with the usual claim "In spite of the legend that all we know about him can be written on the back of an envelope, in fact much information about his life and family survives in legal and other records." Wells then outlines Shakespeare's education in a series of unsupported claims:

–   Shakespeare would have taken his first steps in education at a "petty" (junior) school...
–   Yet the real foundations of his success were most probably laid at the local grammar school...
–   His education in Latin would perforce have originated in...
–   Among Shakespeare's favourite books that he would have studied...
    (Wells 2006b, 13, emphasis added).

Wells is clear that there are no contemporary documents about Shakespeare's education; his claims are possible, perhaps even likely, but by no means certain; they remain conjectures.

Biographers rarely attempt to explain either the absence of a record or the converse interpretation. Lois Potter offers an interesting suggestion: in 1604, James I made his triumphal entry into London and after noting that "the speeches were made by professional actors" she adds: "Shakespeare may have been among them" (Potter 2012, 306). What Potter fails to address is why Shakespeare's name was not mentioned in this context where she might reasonably have expected him to make a speech, or why there is no record of his making any of the speeches. Potter identifies many opportunities when Shakespeare might have co-authored works with other writers:

–   If Shakespeare visited his Peele in January [1596] to report on the success of their play [*Titus Andronicus*], he would have found his former collaborator very ill (203).
–   [Middleton] may have been involved in revising some Shakespeare plays, but this would have been a case of consecutive rather than concurrent collaboration (340).
–   Shakespeare's choice of Wilkins as collaborator [in the composition of *Pericles*] may have been inspired by a play that the latter wrote for another company, with two other dramatists, in 1607 (344).
–   The [Bellott-Mountjoy case] may have brought the former collaborators together again [i.e. Shakespeare with Wilkins who was in court in 1612 in different cases but]... they were not called on the same day (387).
–   Assuming that they did write *Cardenio* in 1612, Fletcher and Shakespeare probably began planning *Henry VIII* shortly afterward (393).

Potter's linguistic hedges clearly indicate the sense of uncertainty in each case. The evidence is so limited that many scenarios can be constructed. However, Potter fails to consider why direct evidence is lacking or to explore alternative interpretations.

As Stoddard noted above, expressions of certainty or near certainty imply lack of documentation. Sidney Lee used the use of the adverb "doubtless" on over seventy occasions. Among debatable assertions are the following: "The Rose Theatre was doubtless the earliest scene of Shakespeare's pronounced successes alike as actor and dramatist" (1898, 37). In fact, the earliest references to Shakespeare as a member of the Chamberlain's Men was to a performance at the Palace of Greenwich before the Court (and probably another at Gray's Inn). Lee believes that Christopher Beeston's son, William, was Aubrey's informant, adding in another conjecture, that Beeston Jr. was "doubtless in the main a trustworthy witness" (361) without stating in what ways Beeston might not have been trustworthy. When referring to plays published as so-called "bad" quartos, Lee asserts: "Criticism has proved beyond doubt that in these plays Shakespeare did no more than add, revise, and correct other men's work" (59). E. K. Chambers asserted: "There can be <u>no doubt</u> that the play [about Richard II, performed prior to the Essex Rebellion] of 7 February [1601] was Shakespeare's" (1930, i. 354). However, the author of the play is not stated explicitly and at least one academic historian has argued that it was not Shakespeare's play (Worden 2006). Michael Wood states somewhat pompously: "John Shakespeare was buried in Stratford. A father's death is important in a man's life. It is <u>inconceivable</u> that William did not go back to Stratford – if not for the funeral then <u>surely</u> to comfort his mother" (2003, 264). Wood uses the adverb 'surely' on more than twenty other occasions. Peter Ackroyd tells us that it was "inevitable" that Gilbert Shakespeare became a glover, without explaining why it was not inevitable for William to do so (45). Katherine Duncan-Jones states that it is "<u>almost certain</u> that William left the Grammar School precipitately" (Duncan-Jones 2001, 14). In stating that it is "almost certain," Duncan-Jones paradoxically indicates that there is a lack of evidence. Imagining a conflict between Shakespeare's personality and his marriage, Park Honan uses a string of negative words and prefixes in making the following claim: "Ambitious, <u>dis</u>satisfied, and rest<u>less</u> as he <u>undoubtedly</u> was with <u>no</u> outlet for the energy of his talents at Henley Street, he was <u>not</u> to behave as a man ensnared by an <u>un</u>suitable woman" (Honan 1998, 87). Peter Ackroyd imagines the burial of John Shakespeare in 1601. Although there is no record of any people in attendance, Ackroyd asserts: "His son was <u>undoubtedly</u> present" (2005, 373) and continues by describing William walking behind the coffin alongside the bailiff. Jonathan Bate wonders about Shakespeare's attitude towards his family: "<u>Perhaps</u> the hopes that he once placed in Hamnet, then in Edmund, and his son, now rested in Hall and his daughter" (2008, 54; emphasis added). He then supports this with reference to fathers longing for their absent daughters in *The Winter's Tale* and *Cymbeline*. However, in both of these plays, the father is estranged from his only daughter, which is not known to be the case with Shakespeare's daughter, Susanna.

> <u>(c) Using the Plays</u> to make biographical inferences about Shakespeare's inner life. Ellis observes that many people identify Shakespeare himself with Hamlet, Prospero, Touchstone and other characters. Ellis observes (286): "Almost any state of mind, opinion or feeling which biographers can conjecture in Shakespeare himself will be expressed by someone, somewhere in the plays."

Making biographical inferences from the works is the basis for much speculation on Shakespeare's thoughts and feelings. Biographers scour the plays and poems, selecting suitable quotations, characters, and episodes to project onto their life of Shakespeare. One example is offered by Park Honan, who, accepting the mention "Shake-shaft" as Shakespeare, suggests that Gloucester's image of the person stranded on a promontory would have been inspired by the Lancastrian coastline (1998, 62–63):

> Why then, I do but dream of sovereignty;
> Like one that stands upon a promontory,
> And spies a far-off shore where he would tread,
> Wishing his foot were equal with his eye,
> And chides the sea that sunders him from thence,
> Saying he'll lade it dry to have his way.
>
> (*3 Henry VI*, 3.2.134–39)

While it is true that such a description does not correspond with the inland county of Warwickshire, it might have been inspired by another stretch of coastline. It is also a common simile in Latin literature and used by Marlowe in *Hero and Leander* (ii. 148–51). Treating Shakespeare's works as a source of biography has been heavily criticised by Richard Altick who echoed T. S. Eliot when noting the following contrasting interpretations of Shakespeare "as a Tory and a Radical, a Protestant and a Catholic (or else a free-thinker), a widely-travelled cosmopolitan and a stay-at-home" (1965, 98). Similarly, Raymond Williams criticised the scraps of conjectural biography. He speaks of a central methodological error that involves the "isolation of speeches by particular characters" and then taking them as "authorial confession" (in his "Afterword" to *Political Shakespeare* 1984, 281). In 2008, Anthony Holden includes himself among modern biographers who over-rely on inference:

> All began by deploring the practice of deducing details of his character, values and curriculum vitae from his writings, then proceeded, in differing degrees, to do just that.
>
> (Review of Bate *Soul of the Age* in *The Guardian*,
> 9 November 2008)

Bevington (2010, 4–5) notes that Shakespeare could dramatise different aspects of a controversy, making it difficult to isolate his own beliefs on many issues. So when biographers select a character or a speech to support a case that Shakespeare was pro-establishment or radical, either a Roman Catholic or an Anglican Protestant, they could often find a character to mouth the opposite. As Antonio noted to Bassanio "The devil can cite Scripture for his purpose" (*Merchant of Venice* 1.3.98).

(d) Using the Sonnets to make biographical inferences about Shakespeare's inner life. Ellis contrasts A. L. Rowse (1973), who claimed that the sonnets were "autobiography throughout" with Jonathan Bate who warned that the sonnets were not to be read as autobiography (1997, 36–44). However, Bate then contradicts himself and identifies the 'fair youth' as a composite of the earls of Southampton and Pembroke and the 'dark lady' as Samuel Daniel's sister, the wife of John Florio (56–58).

William Oldys (d. 1761) seems to have been the first to make such connections, some of which were mentioned by Steevens in the *Johnson-Steevens* 2 edition of the works (1778, i.) In his supplement to the poems, Malone (1780, i. 633–36) reported these inferences, adding his own observations and Steevens's reservations. Malone made his points cautiously, mainly with reference to the sonnets and stated that "it must be acknowledged that the present hypothesis is built on uncertain foundation" (Malone 1780 ii. 653–54). Few biographers subsequently have shared Malone's misgivings over making such biographical inferences and identify personas in the sonnets as the 'fair youth', the 'rival poet', or the 'dark lady' as individual entities, linked to historical figures. Although he notes that the "so-called Dark Lady has proved a tempting pitfall to biographers," Michael Wood states that "it is really not doing Shakespeare justice if we do not take his words at face value" (2003, 184). Wood moves from questions of historical accuracy to questions of justice. He confidently believes that the 'fair youth' was William Herbert, Earl of Pembroke (179) and asserts that Shakespeare's 'dark lady' was Emilia Bassano after her marriage to Alfonso Lanier in 1592 (195). René Weis (2007), however, believes that Emilia Bassano was Shakespeare's mistress (undocumented) at the same time as she was Henry Carey's mistress (well documented), but only <u>before</u> her marriage in 1592. Weis also identifies the 'rival poet' as Christopher Marlowe (126), and the 'fair youth' as Henry Wriothesley, earl of Southampton (149). Against these biographers, Germaine Greer (2007) argues that Shakespeare's 'dark lady' was his wife Anne. The problem is that outside the works, there is no documented evidence to fix any of these identifications: no love letters, no court appearances, no contemporary gossip. Other biographers tend not to read the sonnets biographically (as Ackroyd 2005, 288; Shapiro 2010, 56–64; Edmondson and Wells 2004, 22–27, 2012). Various identifications of the 'fair youth' are considered in Chapter 8.

(e) History to the Rescue. Ellis points (293–94) out that much of what is written in Shakespearean biography is contextual, that lives of Shakespeare are "rather history books disguised as biographies" and cites Anthony Holden's study as a good example.

Almost all biographers spend much time describing contextual features, such as Shakespeare's family background, Stratford-upon-Avon in the Elizabethan period and the London theatres. All of this material can be related to a biography of Shakespeare but it cannot be used as a substitute for it. Since there are only two records about Shakespeare's youth (his baptism in 1564 and his marriage licence issued in 1581 when he was seventeen), any account of this period is therefore either contextual or speculative. Schoenbaum takes over 100 pages to describe Shakespeare's background prior to arriving in London (1987, 3–117), amplifying five allusions in contemporary documents); he then considers the London theatre in 1592 (28 pages; no allusions); the *Groatsworth* allusion (16 pages; one ambiguous allusion). Similarly, Michael Wood's biography (2003) devotes the first six out of sixteen chapters to describing Shakespeare's life before he arrives in London, amounting to 95 pages (pp. 14–105) out of his 344 page biography. This material may well be factually correct, but it is almost entirely contextual. Michael Benton may have been contemplating Wood's biography when he asserts:

> Biography can tell us a great deal about the social, cultural and political world Shakespeare lived in and can deduce from such history what Shakespeare might have experienced. But no amount of inference and imagination can produce the "Life".
>
> (2009, 67)

These studies concentrating on background attempt to find meaningful links with the author's subsequent life and works, but such links are, in the case of Shakespeare, entirely speculative.

(f) The Argument from Proximity: Ellis shows how biographers present people only distantly associated with Shakespeare as close friends. Ellis refers especially to Honigmann (1985) and Wood (2003).

Another argument from proximity concerns Shakespeare and Leonard Digges, who supplied some commendatory verses to the First Folio in 1623. Digges's mother Anne was remarried to Shakespeare's friend, Thomas Russell, whom Shakespeare appointed as overseer to his will in 1616. Leslie Hotson (1938) assumed that Leonard must have known Shakespeare in Stratford. However, Digges was studying at Oxford when his mother settled near Stratford in 1603. After graduating, he travelled to Spain with his friend James Mabbe. While it is possible that Shakespeare and Digges knew each other in Stratford or in London, there is no direct evidence, just an argument from proximity. A similar argument from proximity concerns Shakespeare's undocumented contact with the Sirenaicals at the Mermaid Club. Again, this is based solely on the fact that Shakespeare may have been in the area at the time, but both Shapiro (1950) and O'Callaghan (*ODNB*, 2004) argue that it is most unlikely that Shakespeare attended the Mermaid. The weak case for Shakespeare's acquaintance with Jonson is considered more fully in Chapter 9.

Five More Bad Practices in Biographies of Shakespeare

To the six strategies listed by Ellis, five others are also in evidence:

   (g) Invention of tradition.

The invention of tradition involves valuing the testimony of posthumous anecdotes Chambers was very cautious about posthumous anecdotes, which he relegates to the status of the Shakespeare mythos. Schoenbaum also held a low opinion of mythos, which he defines as "that accretion of legend and lore which comes to surround the names of famous men" (*Documentary Life* 1975, 72). Biographers however utilise all their intuition and acumen when deciding which posthumous anecdotes to accept. They reveal their own assumptions and agenda when deciding whether there is the possibility or likelihood of truth in any of the stories about Shakespeare recorded by later writers, especially Nicholas Rowe: that he spent his childhood in Stratford, where he attended the local school; that he was caught stealing deer and punished, writing a ballad in revenge against Sir Thomas Lucy; that he retired to Stratford; that he enjoyed the patronage of the Earl of Southampton and that he was closely acquainted with Ben Jonson, whose envy he aroused. Other less-followed examples include horse-holding at the public theatre and the spiritual testament which Wood calls "unquestionably" genuine (2003, 83) Not all investigators have been so moved: Malone was ambivalent over the reliability of later reports: "the most fictitious accounts which tradition has handed down to us, have generally had some little semblance or admixture of truth in them" (1821, ii. 72).

   (h) Self-projection of the biographer or biographical displacement.

The idea of biographical displacement is a common criticism of biography in general. It is also known as the psychologist's fallacy, when a psychologist reads into the mind under examination what is true of his or her own mind. Frederick Karl refers to this as "countertransference" and explains it as an "emotional tie that develops between biographer and subject and often leads to the former placing a subjective template on the latter" ('Art Into Life: the Craft of Literary Biography' 2005, 6). Graham Holderness (2011, 21) makes a similar point: "All biographical writing is to some degree autobiographical, always inflected by personal ideological and subjective considerations." He attempts to show how Shakespeare's biographers are more autobiographical than others. Samuel Schoenbaum (in *Shakespeare's Lives* 1970) repeatedly claims that biographers of Shakespeare are simply describing themselves. "I quickly recognised the truth of the observation that biography tends towards oblique self-portraiture." He added: "How much this must be so with respect to Shakespeare, where the sublimity of the subject ensures empathy and the impersonality of the life record teases speculation!" He describes how John Crow, a lecturer at King's College London, once told him:

> Desmond McCarthy had said somewhere that trying to work out Shakespeare's personality was like looking at a very dark glazed picture in the National Portrait Gallery: at first you see nothing, then you begin to recognise features, and then you realise that they are your own.
>
> (1970 viii–ix)[8]

When considering Rowe's *Account* in which Shakespeare emerges as a very well-mannered, mild tempered gentleman, Schoenbaum asks:

> Is it too fanciful that perhaps this author, like so many biographers of Shakespeare after him, is gazing into his own mirror and finding there his subject's reflection?
>
> (1970, 133)

This suggestion was noted in Chapter 3, where it was argued that Rowe's description of the patronage enjoyed by Shakespeare from the Queen and from the Earl of Southampton is a thinly disguised appeal for patronage from Queen Anne and the Duke of Somerset. The idea of biography as displaced autobiography is a motif of Schoenbaum's study. About Thomas Carlyle's 1840 lecture "The Poet as Hero," Schoenbaum remarks:

> He [Shakespeare] has always been a spring in which men discover, Narcissus-like, their own reflection, and so we need feel no surprise that Carlyle, who came of Ecclefechan peasant stock, should seize on the myth that the Bard was a "poor Warwickshire peasant," and in turn help to propagate it.
>
> (1970, 261)

Thomas Carlyle was born at Ecclefechan, a village in Dumfriesshire, southwest Scotland, in 1795. Schoenbaum attacks Carlyle for "seizing a myth" that Shakespeare was a "poor Warwickshire peasant," apparently wishing to distance Shakespeare from the modern pejorative associations of the word "peasant." Of Anthony Burgess's speculative *Nothing Like the Sun* (1964), Schoenbaum states (766): "One may also discern in the sexual degradation of the protagonist [named in the novel as "WS"], a working out of the author's obsession rather than the fictionalisation of fact... It is our last recurrence of our ubiquitous mirror."

Schoenbaum uses the biographer's mirror as a convenient way to dismiss any interpretation outside his own view. It is an *ad hominem* attack on biographers who "Narcissus-like" stray from the account of Shakespeare's life. However, Schoenbaum is not always able to offer compelling evidence that Shakespeare was different from such interpretations. It is of course possible that biographers might be depicting the subject accurately as well as talking about themselves.

(i)   Appeal to Norms.

The appeal to norms is usually sociological – how ordinary people behaved. In the case of Shakespeare, it is very useful to assume that he was no different from other people. Charles Knight (1843) had written of Shakespeare as following the norms of life in Stratford and London. J. O. Halliwell-Phillips stated that Shakespeare's marriage must have been normal for the age: "It can never be right for a biographer, when he is unsupported by the least particle of evidence, to assume that the subject of his memoir departed unnecessarily from the ordinary usages of life and society" (1887, i. 65). Park Honan (1998, 44) presents Shakespeare as a typical Elizabethan boy, kneeling to his father dutifully every morning. "Of course, somebody made the boy's satchel and one or two greasy Joans collected ashes and grease all winter to make soap for that shining face" because William as a grammar school boy "was part of an élite." None of this is documented for Shakespeare. The appeal to norms can also be psychological, but not always necessarily acknowledged as such. Many biographers assume that Shakespeare must have suffered grief at the deaths of his son and his father, which he portrayed in works such as *Hamlet*. These writers use or assume theories of bereavement to infer Shakespeare's state of mind, without external corroboration. It is possible that either John or Hamnet or both suffered from painful and debilitating illnesses, where eventual death might have been taken as a welcome release from suffering.

(j)   Conjecture as fact

We have seen that Shapiro in *1599* avoids all use of linguistic hedges, with only a blanket admission in the preface that he is offering a personal interpretation. Many other biographers assert propositions as factual which cannot be verified by reference to any known records. Duncan-Jones suggests that as a member of Leicester's Men from 1584 to 1586, which is undocumented, Shakespeare "would have quickly showed his versatility" and that he "would be a natural choice" to join the Queen's Men in 1587 (36). Duncan-Jones then has a whole section based on the supposition that from 1588 "Shakespeare was indeed a Queen's Man" (36). Similarly, Greenblatt imagines an encounter between the Jesuit Edmund Campion and a young William Shakespeare ignores "the degree of evidence [about an anecdote such as the deer-poaching story] but rather the imaginative life that the incident has" (Greenblatt 2004, 151). By calling it an "incident" rather than an "anecdote" or a "tradition," Greenblatt encourages readers to accept the undocumented story as authentic.

Another recent biographer who asserts unverifiable claims as facts is René Weis, who adopts assuming a novelist's insight into his protagonist's thoughts (*Shakespeare Revealed* 2007). One example is when Weis asserts that Shakespeare never intended for *Coriolanus* to be performed and that the play is a re-enactment of Shakespeare's relationship with a dominating mother (2007, 328–31). Weis can make such pronouncements because there is no evidence to the contrary: thus they cannot be proved wrong. Nonetheless, they remain speculations as there are no records (1) of Shakespeare's attitude towards any of his family members or (2) of his attitude towards the publication of any of his works; or (3) of the play *Coriolanus* in his lifetime. It was registered and published six years after his death in the First Folio of 1623. The assumed date of composition, *c.* 1608, cannot be proved or contradicted. It could equally be speculated as representing the downfall of a brilliant nobleman such as the Earl of Essex, who overreached himself and paid the ultimate price (Jorgensen 1956).[9] Either way, we do not know, but for Weis to present his opinions without reservation marks his life not as biography based on historical fact but as historical fiction or biografiction.

> (k) Suggestion by juxtaposition: Biographers express a puzzle about some aspect of the subject's life and then place a piece of contextual information next to it, thus encouraging readers to make a connection between the two halves of the sentence.

Ackroyd notes that the "cause of the death of Shakespeare's son is not known, although at the end of the year Stratford suffered a severe rise in mortality from typhus and dysentery" (2005, 270). Ackroyd does not actually state that Hamnet died of typhus or dysentery, but strongly suggests that he did. This suggestion, however, seems to contradict the record that Hamnet was buried in August, a good few months before the outbreak. Laurie Maguire and Emma Smith imply a different cause in a similar way: "The cause of Hamnet's death is not known (but August, the month in which he died, was always a bad month for plague deaths)" (2012, 81). Maguire & Smith use juxtaposition to link Hamnet's death to the plague. However, both claims are unlikely: there are only four other burials recorded in the Parish Book during the first three weeks of August 1596, ruling out any epidemic of typhus, dysentery, or plague. We are no more able to ascertain why Hamnet died than to posit a definite link between Shakespeare's son Hamnet and the character Hamlet in the play.

This broad critique indicates the many ways in which Shakespearean biographers overcome the lack of biographical material. The next chapter will demonstrate how these techniques have been used on one important topic in Shakespearean biography: his apparent patronage by the Earl of Southampton, which has occasioned a wide range of different interpretations by modern biographers.

Notes

1 Jonathan Bate. "Not Such a Sweet Swan of Avon." Review of *Ungentle Shakespeare*. In the *Sunday Telegraph*, 21 April, 2001.
2 Reviews of *Will in the World* include: Terry Eagleton. "The Stratford Man." *The New Statesman*, 15 November, 2004. Lois Potter. Review in *Shakespeare Quarterly* 56.3 (2005, 374–76). Colin Barrow. "Who Wouldn't Buy it?" *London Review of Books*, 20 January 2005. Katherine Duncan-Jones. "Will-o'-the Wisp Forever." *The Spectator*, 9 October, 2004. Jonathan Bate. "The Sweet Swan and the Porcupine." *The Daily Telegraph*, 17 October 2004. Colin MacCabe. "The Bard as a Chat-Show Celeb." *The Independent*, 5 November 2004. David Ellis. "Biographical Uncertainty and Shakespeare." *Essays in Criticism* 55.3 (2005, 193–208).
3 David Scott Kastan in *A Will to Believe: Shakespeare and Religion* doubts that Shakespeare was a closet Catholic (35). He thinks that Shakespeare was "a tolerant, largely habitual Christian" (37), one of many adaptable conformists.
4 Glyn Parry, "New Evidence on William Shakeshafte and Edmund Campion." *Shakespeare Yearbook* 17 (2009, 1–27).
5 Katherine Duncan-Jones states that Greer exercises her imagination with "scatter-gun attacks on shadow squadrons of other scholars" *Literary Review*, July 2007. Charles Nicholl believes that Greer's study is "marred by a tendency to play ideological ping-pong with her reputation." *Guardian*, 1 September 2007.
6 Lena Orlin. "Anne by Indirection." *Shakespeare Quarterly* 65 (2014, 421–54).
7 Ellis refers to Rowe's *Account* (1709) as the "first real attempt at a biography of Shakespeare" (37), against which I have argued strongly in Chapter 3. Ellis also shows considerable enthusiasm for Samuel Schoenbaum's *Documentary Life* (1975), failing to notice the weaknesses which I explore in Chapter 6.
8 John Crow (1904–69) wrote "Deadly Sins of Criticism, or Seven Ways to Get Shakespeare Wrong." *Shakespeare Quarterly* 9 (1958, 301–6), which dealt with literary criticism. Desmond McCarthy (1877–1952) was a member of the Bloomsbury Group and founder of *Life and Letters*, a London literary magazine, which he edited until 1934. The notion of the biographer's mirror can be found in Virginia Woolf's late essays 'Anon' and 'The Reader which were begun in 1940 (ed. Brenda Silver 1979, 431–32).
9 *Coriolanus* might even be dated to 1601 or 1602; William Barlow, Bishop of London, preached a sermon at St Paul's, shortly after the execution of Essex in February 1601. Barlow specifically argued that Coriolanus would "make a fit parallel for the late Earle, if you read his life" (M. MacLure, *The Paul's Cross Sermons 1534–1642*, Toronto 1958, 89).

8 Inventing a Patron
The Earl of Southampton

Any hopes of practical help cannot be shown to have been fulfilled.
Southampton proved never to have had large sums of money to hand.
—(Robert Bearman 2016)

In almost every narrative, the protagonist receives help at the outset of his
quest from a person identified as a mentor by Campbell (1949). This help
might be advice and the encouragement such as given by Pallas Athene
in *The Odyssey* or by Merlin in the stories of Arthur. In the life story
of a writer, a mentor might be either a literary advisor or a patron. The
Roman poet of the Augustan Age such as Virgil and Horace were well
known to have enjoyed the generosity of rich men. The most important
patron was Maecenas, whose name is known used to indicate enlightened patronage. In the history of English literature, Chaucer, Gower,
Lydgate, and Spenser had all enjoyed royal or aristocratic patronage.
By the time Rowe came to collect some thoughts about Shakespeare,
literary patronage had become well established: in 1668, John Dryden
was named officially as the Poet Laureate, a position which fell to Rowe
himself in 1715. However, in the case of Shakespeare, there was no obvious literary mentor nor was there any record of literary patronage. It
was clear that Ben Jonson enjoyed royal support from February 1616,
styling himself the King's Poet, and he also received an annual stipend
of £20 for books from the Earl of Pembroke (*Informations*, 239–240;
Donaldson 2011, 356).

Regarding Shakespeare, it has been impossible to find a literary advisor as so little is known about his life before his first publication in
1593. Nor was there any direct reference to any patron. Despite these
drawbacks, Nicholas Rowe confidently identified both Queen Elizabeth
and the Earl of Southampton as the patrons who enabled Shakespeare's
genius to flourish. Since then, writers on Shakespeare, including
Malone, Chambers, and Schoenbaum, along with three major biographies of Southampton, have accepted that the earl patronised the poet.[1]
Yet only the dedications to the two narrative poems *Venus and Adonis*
(1593) and *Lucrece* (1594) actually provide any kind of link between the

two men. To supplement the limited biographical material, biographers have made inferences from the works, especially the sonnets. In this chapter, the primary sources concerning Southampton, mainly the Wriothesley Papers at the Hampshire Archives in Winchester (Collection number, 5M53), are reviewed but no mention of Shakespeare has been found. Second, different interpretations regarding the patronage are assessed. Two writers noted that Southampton was not in a position to patronise any writer in the late Elizabethan period (Heinemann 1993; Honan 2004). Bob Bearman concurs: "Any hopes of practical help cannot be shown to have been fulfilled. Southampton proved never to have had large sums of money to hand" (2016, 41).

The general details of the life of Henry Wriothesley, third earl of Southampton (1573–1624) are easily accessed in the account by Honan (*ODNB*, 2004). Upon the death of the second earl, Henry succeeded to the title in 1581, shortly before his eighth birthday. The seat of the earldom was at Titchfield Abbey, Hampshire, and his many estates were legally established in an *Inquisitio Post Mortem* of 13 June 1582. The second earl died with heavy debts and it is not known how these were discharged (Akrigg 21).

The third earl remained a royal ward until his twenty-first birthday that is from 1581 until 6 October 1594. During this time, some of the estates were managed by his mother, Mary the dowager countess, and others by the Lord Admiral, Charles Howard earl of Nottingham. Southampton spent most of his wardship under the supervision of Lord

Plate 8.1 Titchfield Abbey, the seat of the earls of Southampton.

Burghley, at Cecil House on the Strand, London. He was allowed only a "pitifully small exhibition" as Burghley received the "necessary expenses and honorable maintenance of the young Earl" (Akrigg 1968, 34). At the age of 12, he was sent to St. John's College Cambridge and at the age of 16 he enrolled at Gray's Inn. He was still a ward when he was sent on the Earl of Essex's expedition to Normandy in 1591. In the following year, Southampton pleaded with Michael Hickes, one of Burghley's secretaries, confirming that he had no control over his income or his property:

> Whereas I am gyven to understand that my manor house at Beaulye [Beaulieu, Hants] with dyvers parcels of my inheritance there, are lyke to fall in greate decaye and daunger to be lost thoroughe wante of meanes to supplye the charges of the reparacions during my wardship – I would hartely request you to move my Lord Treasurer, according to the note I doe sends, to yielde me his honorable favor in taking sourse as shall seeme best to his wisdom whereby the sayd chardges and reparacions may be supplyed ... from my lodging in the Strand this 26 June 1592.
>
> *Lansdowne* MS. LXXI. 72 (quoted by Stopes 1922, 49)

When Southampton came of age in October 1594, his annual income was estimated to be in the region of £3,000 p.a. One third of his estates (about eleven manors) was reserved for his mother as dowager countess (Akrigg 1968, 20–38). These estates only reverted to the third earl on her death in 1607.

Southampton was not able to enjoy his net income of *c.* £2,000 p.a. for five main reasons. First, he had to "sue his livery," which involved payment of a large kind of registration fee for him to gain control of his estates. The exact amount is not known, but when the Earl of Oxford attained his majority in 1571, he had to pay £4,000 for suing his livery.[2] Secondly, he had to pay for his wardship, a kind of hotel bill, which in the case of Oxford had been about £3,000 for maintenance over an eight-year period, whereas Southampton was a ward for about thirteen years. Next, Southampton was fined £5,000 for refusing to marry his guardian's choice of bride, Burghley's granddaughter, Elizabeth Vere: the Jesuit priest, Thomas Garnet recorded in January 1595 (*Stonyhurst MSS., Ang.* i. 82): "The young erle of Southampton refusing the Lady Veere payeth 5000[li] of present payment." By "making him pay this great sum in one payment, Burghley probably forced Southampton to go to the moneylenders" (Akrigg 1968, 39). Fourthly, by the terms of the second earl's will, he had to pay for a lavish family monument in the village church at Titchfield (Stopes 1922, 14–15). The contract for the monument was only signed in May 1594, for its construction in expensive Italian marble under the supervision of Gerard Johnson (Gheerart Janssen), the Dutch sculptor.[3] Consequently, Southampton entered his majority heavily in debt in 1594. Finally, Southampton acquired further debts on the imprudent re-marriage of his mother. In May 1594, the dowager countess married Sir Thomas Heneage in May 1594. Mary might not have realised the extent of the loans which her elderly husband had taken out against future income as treasurer of the queen's chamber and of the duchy of Lancaster. When he died in October 1595, Mary was liable for Sir Thomas's debts of £7,800. Overall, when Southampton gained his independence, he owed his approximate income for the next ten years. To service his own debts, Southampton sold the manors of Faringdon, Portsea, and Bighton among others (Akrigg 1968, 49–51). Southampton, either before his twenty-first birthday, or in the decade afterwards, was never in a position to patronise anyone.

The extent of Southampton's financial indebtedness was probably unknown to himself or to the six writers who made literary dedications in the period 1591–1595, i.e. about the time he attained his majority. The earliest dedication was made in 1591, by John Clapham, a secretary to Lord Burghley, who dedicated a Latin poem entitled *Narcissus* to the young earl. The title and content suggests that Southampton was excessively aware of his handsome looks. In 1593, Barnabe Barnes published *Parthenophil and Parthenope* which included a sonnet to the "right noble and vertuous lord, Henry earle of Southampton." In 1594, Thomas Nashe has a dedicatory epistle to *The Unfortunate Traveller* praising Southampton as a "dere lover and cherisher you are, as well of the lovers of Poets, as of Poets themselves." Nashe's description has sometimes been interpreted as an indication that the earl enjoyed homosexual relations with various writers. In 1595, Gervase Markham also included a dedicatory sonnet to Southampton in *The Most Honorable Tragedy of Richard Grinvile, Knight*, an occasional candidate for the 'rival poet' of the sonnets. In the following year, William Burton dedicated to Southampton a translation of the Greek Romance *Clitophon and Leucippe*, which includes a lament by a homosexual who has to marry (Akrigg 1968, 54). None of these writers repeated the dedication and none of them have any other known connection with Southampton. Perhaps they were misled into thinking that he might patronise them.

One writer was associated with Southampton: John Florio (*c.* 1553–1625). Florio had been born in England, the son of Italian refugees and brought up in Oxford, where he gave lessons in Italian. He had enjoyed the patronage of Leicester, then Nicholas Saunders of Ewell. An official report on a fracas at Titchfield in October 1594 stated that Florio attended the earl there. A few years later, in the dedication to his *Italian Dictionary*, published until 1598, Florio described Southampton as the "most noble vertuous and most Honourable Earle of Southampton, in whose paie and patronage I have lived some yeeres."[4] What is not clear is Florio's actual position within the Southampton household; Frances Yates has suggested that Burghley planted Florio as Southampton's

Italian tutor so as to keep an eye on him. Coming from a Catholic family, the young earl's sympathies may have been suspected.[5] Florio did not mention Southampton in any other works and had no recorded contact with Shakespeare. Thus Florio's connection with Southampton is limited and no link with Shakespeare is established.

Florio also dedicates his *Dictionary* to Roger Manners, Earl of Rutland and Lucy Russell, Countess of Bedford. The dedication is long and obsequious, giving rise to the notion that Florio might be identified with the pedant Holofernes. By far the largest share of the eulogy is aimed at the Countess of Bedford, who later brought Florio into her household to finish his translation of Montaigne (Yates 1934). If Florio was one of the government's informers, he may have joined this household to monitor the activities of the Countess's husband, Edward Russell, third Earl of Bedford (1572–1627), who was a follower of Essex and was later convicted of taking part in the 1601 uprising. In contrast to the Earl of Southampton, the countess of Bedford was indeed a patron of writers. Ben Jonson thanked her for her support in Epigrams 76, 84, and 96. She also patronised Chapman, Daniel, Donne, and Drayton, but not Shakespeare (Lawson 2007).[6] Some commentators have linked all these writers into a 'Southampton circle' similar to the group known to have been promoted by Philip and Mary Sidney. Although possible connections have been reviewed by John Klause (*Shakespeare, the Earl, and the Jesuit*, 2008), there is no direct evidence of any 'Southampton circle'.

While it is usually taken that a dedication was intended to elicit some kind of reward, the system of royal and aristocratic patronage was breaking down towards the end of the Elizabethan era:

> Due to changes in the social, economic and literary conditions during Elizabeth's reign, patronage could no longer support literature as it had previously done. The growth of a middle class in prosperity demanding reading of their own, the widening popularity of poetry and especially of the drama begot writers as well as an ever increasing clientele of readers.
>
> (Gebert 1933, 20)

Alistair Fox has shown how writers in the 1590s complained that they were no longer receiving the patronage which they "they thought they deserved and once would have had a right to expect (1995, 240). Paul Voss (1998) has shown that to offset the decline in aristocratic patronage in the 1590s, stationers began to promote their publications directly to the buying public.[7] Overall, Southampton is the object of a number of dedications in the early 1590s, but no writer apart from Shakespeare makes a second dedication, suggesting that these writers made a pitch for Southampton's patronage without ever receiving anything in return.

A second reason for seeing Southampton as a patron of Shakespeare is the claim that Southampton frequented the public theatres. This claim is based on a letter about Southampton's visits in 1599 when avoiding Queen and Court. Rowland White wrote to Sir Robert Sidney on 11 October:

> My Lord Southampton and Lord Rutland come not to the court [then at Nonsuch Palace]: the one doth but very seldom. They pass away the time in London merely in going to plays every day.
>
> (*Sidney Papers* ii. 132)[8]

The mention of theatre visits is made somewhat disparagingly, although this might reflect the opinion of the writer more than Southampton's. During this time, Southampton was very involved with the political and military affairs of Essex. He joined the naval expeditions to Cadiz in 1596 and to the Azores in 1597. After secretly marrying Elizabeth Vernon, one of the Queen's maids, Southampton joined Essex in Ireland in the first part of 1599, where he was appointed General of the Horse despite the Queen's "express prohibition to the contrary."[9] After an unsuccessful campaign, Southampton accompanied Essex back to court. On 28 September 1599, Essex famously burst into the Queen's Bed-Chamber at Nonsuch Palace and a few days later was placed under house arrest (Akrigg 1968, 9–6). Southampton's absence from court soon after was therefore more a tactful retreat from the Queen's displeasure rather than any special interest in drama. He continued his courtly intrigues on behalf of Essex, revisiting Ireland in 1600 "in a futile attempt to recruit the lord deputy, Lord Mountjoy, for Essex's cause" (Honan *ODNB*, 2004). In 1601, he took part in the Essex Rebellion, for which he was arrested, tried, and sentenced to death. Thus from 1594, when he came into his estates, until Elizabeth's death in 1603, Southampton had little or no means to patronise poets and writers, and spent his time in political and military affairs.

James I released Southampton on 5 April 1603 and pardoned him on May 1603 (Hants Archives 5M53/1001). The King then granted him a lucrative monopoly in the farming of sweet wines, as well as estates in Romsey, Compton Magna, and Dunmow.[10] With his improved finances, Southampton was one of seven earls and over 650 other investors in the Virginia Company. He also invested in the East India Company and the North-West Passage Company. He contributed expensive titles to the new Bodleian Library in 1605 and 200 manuscripts along with 2000 printed books to a new library at St John's College, Cambridge (Stopes 1922, 372). He remained involved in politics at court and in parliament for the rest of his life. According to Margot Heinemann (1993, 135–41), Southampton patronised many writers only during the Jacobean period, but there is no evidence that Shakespeare was one of them. Southampton made no mention of the Shakespeare family in his will, nor had Shakespeare mentioned the Earl of Southampton in his will. Only two sources link Southampton with Shakespeare – the dedications to the narrative poems.

8.1 Shakespeare's Dedications to Southampton

It was during the last years of Southampton's minority that Shakespeare dedicated to him two narrative poems: *Venus & Adonis* was entered into the Stationers' Register on 18 April 1593, when the Earl was aged nineteen and six months; *Lucrece* was entered into the Stationers' Register on 9 May 1594, when the Earl was aged twenty years and seven months. Both poems are preceded by a short epistle. The dedications in *Venus & Adonis* and in *Lucrece* were printed as follows:

The opening of the first dedication ("I know not how I shall offend in dedicating...") suggests that Shakespeare was not personally acquainted with the nineteen-year-old earl. The phrasing of both dedications "fall well within the normal scope of dedicatory formulas," according to Chambers (*WS* i. 61–62). Gebert points out that in a writer's dedication to a nobleman, decorum is duly observed with regard to rank, where a writer of talent verbally prostrates himself before his superior patron, employing a false humility about his work which he describes as "vanities, shadows, imperfect patterns more mete for the pedlar than for the printer, toyes, trifles, trash, trinkets" (1933, 12; the list is quoted from Robert Greene's preface to *Mamillia*, 1593).

Shakespeare's dedications are shorter than the average (Gebert 1933). The author adopts the conventional pose of humility in contrast to the noble's greatness. The first dedication appears less assured with conditional clauses "if your Honour..." and "if the first heir..." Although Chambers cannot detect any "great advance in the poet's intimacy with his patron between the two addresses" (*WS* i. 61–62), most commentators see the second dedication as more intimate than the first, and therefore cite it as evidence that Southampton become Shakespeare's patron. Akrigg is aware that this does not constitute evidence, when he states, "<u>presumably</u>, Southampton generously rewarded both Shakespeare and Barnes" (1968, 38, emphasis added). Richard McCabe shows that the first dedication asked that the poet be accepted for the poem, but that the request was reversed in the second. Although Shakespeare surpasses the addresses by other Elizabethan writers, McCabe still calls the epistles "highly conventional," lamenting that they have "generated more vacuous speculation than any of their kind" (2012, 82).

Dedication to *Venus & Adonis* (1593)	Dedication to *Lucrece* (1594)

TO THE RIGHT HONORABLE

Henrie VVriothesley, Earle of Southampton, and baron of Titchfield.

Right Honourable, I know not how I shall offend in dedicating my vnpolisht lines to your Lordship, nor how the worlde vvill censure mee for choosing so strong a proppe to support so vveake a burthen, onelye if your Honour seeme but pleased, I account my selfe highly praised, and vowe to take aduantage of all idle houres, till I haue honoured you vvith some grauer labour. But if the first heire of my inuention proue deformed, I shall be sorie it had so noble a god-father: and neuer after eare so barren a land, for feare it yeeld me still so bad a haruest, I leaue it to your Honourable suruey, and your Honor to your hearts content, vvhich I wish may alvvaies ansvvere your ovvne vvish, and the vvorlds hopefull expectation.

Your Honors in all dutie
William Shakespeare

TO THE RIGHT HONOVRABLE HENRY

VVriothesley, Earle of Southampton, and Baron of Tichfield.

THE love I dedicate to your lordship is without end; whereof this pamphlet, without beginning, is but a superfluous moity. The warrant I have of your Honourable disposition, not the worth of my vntutord Lines, makes it assured of acceptance. VVhat I haue done is yours; what I haue to doe is yours; being part in all I haue, deuoted yours. VVere my worth greater, my duety would show greater; meane time, as it is, it is bound to your Lordship, To whom I wish long life, still lengthened with all happinesse.

Your Lordships in all duety,
William Shakespeare.

That Southampton was Shakespeare's patron was first asserted by Rowe who claimed that Southampton gave Shakespeare "many marks of favour and friendship" (1709, i. ix). Since then, this notion of Shakespeare's patron has remained constant. In his own preface, Pope refers to Southampton as Shakespeare's "noble patron" (1725, i). The prefaces of Rowe and Pope containing these assertions were reprinted in most subsequent editions of Shakespeare's plays in the eighteenth century (e.g. Warburton, 1747, i; Johnson 1765, i; Steevens 1766, i. 3). Edward Capell (1767, i. 10) makes a similar statement. Thus the claimed patronage by Southampton was repeated so often as to become established before scrutiny of evidence to examine the claim. Malone accepted the notion of Southampton's patronage without question, adding details about Southampton's public activities without offering any indications of how, if at all, he might have interacted with Shakespeare (1778, i. 402–3). Malone included an expanded version of his essay "Memoirs of Henry Wriothesley, third Earl of Southampton" in the final volume of the complete works (1790, x. 4–9), where he refers to the earl as "our great poet's patron" and accepts Rowe's anecdote about the £1,000 which alone will "immortalise" Southampton. Malone's third variorum contains a much longer account of the earl's life, including many eulogies written on his death (1821, xx. 427–68). In volume ii (477–80), Malone makes an effort to suggest how Shakespeare might have known Southampton. Malone offers two supporting allusions: the 1599 letter to Sir Robert Sidney about Southampton attending the plays and the Dowager Countess's marriage to Thomas Heneage "probably before 1580." As Heneage was treasurer to the Chambers of the Queen, he was responsible for payments to the players. Lord Southampton "would, of course, be a frequent visitor at his mother's" (emphasis added), a clearly signalled deduction. Malone cites dedications by Barnes, Nashe, and Gervaise Markham's 1617 sonnet as evidence of patronage. Malone concludes: "That Shakespeare partook of this nobleman's bounty, there can be no reason to doubt." The final phrase – "no reason to doubt" – indicates that someone had doubted the proposition. Malone's conclusion is not recorded in any document. Based on two brief dedications and two allusions, Malone has inferred how Southampton would have acted as Shakespeare's patron.

There are major difficulties in Malone's account. Southampton's mother, Mary dowager Countess of Southampton did not marry Thomas Heneage in the 1580s but in May 1594 (Akrigg 1968, 41), after the dedications in *Venus* and in *Lucrece* were published. Even if the marriage had taken place earlier, it is unlikely that Lady Mary could have taken her son on a visit to anyone as Henry was still a royal ward and his activities were dictated in minute detail by Lord Burghley. Finally, Malone was unaware that Southampton had no access to his income at the time to reward the dedications so does not comment on the parlous state of Southampton's finances when he came of age. Park Honan states clearly that he had no cash to spare:

> Southampton had little but enthusiasm to offer any poet. He hardly had funds to spare; he lived on a fixed allowance and faced paying a gigantic fine to Burghley, plus another vast sum to get his estates out of wardship. After he turned twenty-one in 1594, his need for money became desperate.
>
> (*ODNB*, 2004)

Nonetheless, most modern biographers, e.g. Schoenbaum (1987, 159–83), Bate (1997, 46–49), Honan (1998, 169–95), Holden (1999, 124–37), Duncan-Jones (2001, 58–81), Wood (2003, 154–63), Greenblatt (2004, 229–45), Potter (2012, 108–23) repeat the claim that Southampton was Shakespeare's only patron. They remain vague as to how such patronage might have been exercised. Colin Burrow is unusual in surveying the possible gifts that Southampton might have bestowed: "friendship, love, hospitality during the plague, or money, or any or all of those things" without doubting that some form of patronage must have occurred (2002, 10–15). Few biographers acknowledge that there is no record that Southampton ever gave any financial reward to Shakespeare or that Shakespeare's dedications were addressed to an aristocrat while still a minor with no control over his own finances.

A different reason might lie behind dedications to an aristocrat. As we have seen, aristocratic patronage declined during the 1590s. However, the author (probably at the request of the stationer) might present an aristocrat as an ideal reader for that work. In this way, Thomas Danett might have dedicated his translation of Lodovico Guicciardini's *Description of the Low Countries* to William Cecil, Lord Burghley (1593), to indicate his anticipated audience (government officials), a kind of celebrity endorsement. While Burghley probably welcomed the translation for his own purposes of state, he had no need to have the work printed. In 1599, John Hayward may have dedicated his prose *Life and Raigne of King Henry IIII* to Robert Devereux, Earl of Essex, as the most prominent aristocrat interested in the deposition of a prince (1599), but Essex does not seem to have paid for it.[11] According to this view, Shakespeare might have been interested in dedicating his narrative poems to a youthful earl more as a sales pitch to the reading public than for direct patronage, trying to persuade any buyer that if a volume is good enough for such and such an earl, it must be good enough for an ordinary person to buy. The notion of celebrity endorsement during the Elizabethan period has been explored by Miller (110–11). Richard McCabe has made the same point, that the dedications identify "an increasingly fashionable courtier" as an arbiter for the merit of Shakespeare's poetry (2016, 83–84).

8.2 Rowe's Mention of a £1,000 Gift

Southampton's supposed gift of £1,000 to Shakespeare also gained its first mention by Rowe in 1709, who claimed that the poet enjoyed both royal and aristocratic patronage. In *Some Account &c.*, Rowe writes: "Queen *Elizabeth* had several of his Plays Acted before her, and without doubt gave him many gracious Marks of her Favour" (1709, i. viii). Rowe is vague as to what these "marks of her favour" might have been. The phrase "without doubt" indicates the lack of evidence or authority for his assertion.[12] Having mentioned the royal patronage apparently enjoyed by Shakespeare, Rowe then assumes aristocratic patronage for the aspiring poet and playwright:

> He had the Honour to meet with many great and uncommon Marks of Favour and Friendship from the Earl of *Southampton*, famous in the Histories of that Time for his Friendship to the unfortunate Earl of *Essex*. It was to that Noble Lord that he Dedicated his *Venus* and *Adonis*, the only Piece of his Poetry which he ever publish'd himself,

tho' many of his Plays were surrepticiously and lamely Printed in his Life-time.

(Rowe 1709, i. ix–x)

Rowe is vague about dates and is apparently unaware that Shakespeare published and dedicated more than one poem. Pope corrected the mistake by omitting "the only Piece of his Poetry which he ever publish'd himself" when he reprinted Rowe's *Account* in his 1725 edition (Smith 1903, 305n6). Rowe then adds the story of the thousand pounds:

> There is one Instance so singular in the Magnificence of this Patron of *Shakespear's*, that if I had not been assur'd that the Story was handed down by Sir *William* D'Avenant, who was probably very well acquainted with his Affairs, I should not have ventur'd to have inserted, that my Lord *Southampton*, at one time, gave him a thousand Pounds, to enable him to go through with a Purchase which he heard he had a mind to. A Bounty very great, and very rare at any time, and almost equal to that profuse Generosity the present Age has shewn to *French* Dancers and italian *Eunuchs*.
>
> (Rowe 1709, i. x–xi)

Rowe can only say somewhat apologetically that he has been "assured" that the story originated with Davenant, who had died over forty years earlier in 1668, before Rowe was born. Rowe's use of "probably" indicates the hypothesis that Davenant was an authority on Shakespeare, which is unevidenced. The story also implies that Southampton only knew at second hand of the playwright's intended dealings but did not know Shakespeare personally. Rowe states that "he [Southampton] <u>heard</u> he [Shakespeare] had a mind to." Helen Hackett has noted that the playwright John Dennis's claim about the Queen's commission was "a polemical point about the contemporary neglect of playwrights by the Crown" (2009, 25–26). However, no biographer has suggested that Rowe carefully arranged this *Account* to follow his own dedication to the Duke of Somerset. Rowe may have been hinting at patronage for himself, both royal and aristocratic. At about this time, Rowe secured a post under James Douglas, second duke of Queensbury, who became Secretary of State for Scotland in the newly formed Union of England and Scotland. Rowe eventually achieved royal patronage when he was appointed Poet Laureate in 1715.

The lack of biographical material about Shakespeare means that most biographers refer to this anecdote in some way. Since Rowe's figure exceeded the combined total of all Shakespeare's property dealings,[13] Malone changed his mind as to the amount involved in the gift: he finds the sum of £1,000 to be "extravagantly exaggerated" and declares that it was "much more likely" to have been a gift of one hundred pounds in return for the dedications (1821, ii. 480). Most biographers subsequently accept that the amount was exaggerated. Lee (1899, 378) sees the story as evidence of Southampton's patronage but is otherwise vague. E. K. Chambers suggests that the figure was much less and that the purchase probably concerned a share in the newly-formed Lord Chamberlain's Men in 1594 (1930, i. 62). However, there is no mention of any such involvement in the extant records of the Lord Chamberlain's Men. J. Dover Wilson follows Chambers (1932, 66–67) as does Rowse (1965, 85) who reports the story as "an authentic tradition" without stating that the first mention of the tradition was in 1709, more than a century after it was supposed to have occurred. Nor does Rowse explain why he considers it "authentic." Akrigg also accepts Rowe's anecdote and Malone's reduction of the amount (1968, 220). Duncan-Jones agrees and reports a personal communication from Andrew Gurr that Shakespeare may have sold his playscripts to Southampton (2001, 85 and 295n). Gurr does not mention this conjecture in *The Shakespeare Company 1594–1642* (2004). However, Weis accepts the amount as literally true (2007, 114–15). On the other hand, Bearman calls the sum "preposterously large" and says that "such a story could have evolved simply through an imaginative misinterpretation of the dedications" (2016, 41–42).

Various other biographers who take Southampton to have been Shakespeare's patron, ignore Rowe's report of a £1,000 gift, including Stopes (1922), Holden (1999), Wood (2001), and Greenblatt (2004). Schoenbaum (1987, 179) is very doubtful and Burrow (2002, 13) calls it "wildly improbable." Potter (2012, 432) also finds the gift unlikely and believes that Rowe derived the story from Donatus's *Life of Virgil*. Overall, most biographers of Shakespeare accept that Shakespeare must have attracted patronage in his lifetime. However, the evidence that any tangible patronage came from Southampton during the late Elizabethan period is very thin.

8.3 Plays Written for Southampton?

It has also been suggested that Shakespeare wrote various plays when he apparently enjoyed a close relationship with Southampton, especially between 1593 and 1595; two plays in particular *A Midsummer Night's Dream* and *Love's Labour's Lost* are taken to reflect such a relationship. The date(s) of these plays, as with all others of Shakespeare, is conjectural since there is no allusion to either play before Meres in 1598. Following Stopes (1922, 75–76) and Acheson (*Shakespeare's Sonnet Story*, 1933, 184–88), C. C. Stopes (1922, 75) and later A. L. Rowse (1965, 86–87), claims that Shakespeare wrote *A Midsummer Night's Dream* for the wedding of Sir Thomas Heneage (then aged in his sixties) and the widowed Countess of Southampton (in her forties) in May 1594. While several editors accept that the play was probably written or revised for a wedding, they tend to prefer the wedding of William Stanley Earl of Derby with Elizabeth Vere in January 1595 (*WS* i. 358–59) or Thomas Berkeley with Elizabeth Carey in February 1596 (Alexander *Shakespeare's Life and Art* 1939, 105). Holland rejects the notion that the play was an epithalamium (Oxford edn. 1995, 112) and R. A. Foakes is skeptical (Cambridge edn. 2003, 2–3).

Another play which Shakespeare is said to have written for Southampton at that time is *Love's Labour's Lost* (Akrigg 1968, 207–15). Biographers have thought that the Earl of Southampton is likely to have seen it in performance in his town house (e.g. Lee 1918, 383–84) but such performances are not known to have happened until after his release from the Tower in 1603. Sir Walter Cope wrote to Viscount Cranborne (as Robert Cecil was known from 20 August 1604 until he was created Earl of Salisbury on 4 May 1605) saying:

> Burbage is come, and says there is no new play that the Queen [Anne] has not seen; but they have revived an old one called *Love's Labour's Lost*, which for wit and mirth he says will please her exceedingly. And this is appointed to be played to-morrow night at my Lord of Southampton's, unless you send a writ to remove the *corpus cum causa* to your house in the Strand. Yours most humbly, Walter Cope.
>
> *MSS Marquis of Salisbury, Hatfield House, vol.16, 415*

A further reference to Southampton hosting revels at this time occurs in a letter by Dudley Carleton to John Chamberlain on 15 January 1605:

> But it seems we shall haue Christmas all the yeare, and therefore I shall neuer be owt of matter. The last nights reuels were kept at my Lord of Cranborns, where the Q: with the D: of Holst and a great part of the court were feasted. and the like two nights before at my Lord of Southamptons.
>
> *TNA, London SP/14/12, f. 32r*

H. R. Woodhuysen accepts that the letters refer to the same events, although he is not sure whether the performance of *Love's Labour's Lost* took place at all, or if it did whether at Southampton House or at Robert Cecil's House (Arden3 1998, 83–85). It can only be assumed that Southampton witnessed the play and that Shakespeare was part of the playing company. It does not constitute evidence that Shakespeare wrote the play for Southampton.

Austin K. Gray (1924) offers a scenario in which Shakespeare wrote *Love's Labour's Lost* at the request of Southampton for performance before the queen and court at Titchfield on 2–3 September 1591. The Queen's Progress in that year had also taken her to Cowdray Park, where the entertainment for Elizabeth included masques.[14] Gray argues that

Love's Labour's Lost was specially written for this occasion at the time Southampton's marriage was being discussed. The intention behind the play would have been to demonstrate unwillingness on the part of the teenage earl to marry. Southampton had been with Essex in France and there he might have known or heard about Charles de Gontaut, duc de Biron, on whom the character of Berowne may have been based. Gray's scenario has not gained widespread support. Stopes describes Elizabeth's Progress and the entertainment at Cowdray but finds no evidence that "there were any masques prepared or performed" (1922, 45–48). Nor has the early date of 1591 for this play been accepted, with 1594–1595 suggested by Chambers (1930, i. 335) and accepted by most modern commentators.[15] Bullough does not mention Southampton in his review of the sources for *Love's Labour's Lost* (1957 i. 425–33) but believes that for this play Shakespeare drew principally on two accounts: de la Primaudaye's *L'Académie française* (1577) and Marguerite de Valois' *Memoires* (printed 1628). As these two texts seem to be the main sources for the plot of *Love's Labour's Lost* with the *commedia dell'arte* providing the stock characters, there is no need to posit any link between Shakespeare and Southampton's experiences in Titchfield.

8.4 The 'Fair Youth' of the Sonnets

Shakespeare's sonnets were first published by Thomas Thorpe in 1609. The order of the sonnets was changed for a second edition by John Benson in 1640. Most commentators believe that Shakespeare wrote his sonnets in the early 1590s when they were in vogue. Sir Philip Sidney's sonnet sequence was published in 1591 under the title *Astrophel and Stella*. Edmund Spenser called his sonnet sequence *Amoretti* (1595). Other Elizabethan sonneteers included Samuel Daniel (1592), Barnabe Barnes (1593), and Michael Drayton (1593–1594).[16] However, it is not known when Shakespeare composed his sonnets, whether they date to a short period of a year or two, or to a long time span of a decade or more, or in what sequence they were composed, or whether Shakespeare himself placed them in any sequence. Many commentators identify three personas within Shakespeare's sonnets: the 'fair youth', the 'dark lady', and the 'rival poet'. It is not known whether Shakespeare envisaged these as single or multiple entities, or even if they correspond to historical figures. Richard Dutton surveys the wide range of dates and identifications made by different writers for the sonnets (2007).

Almost all modern biographers of Shakespeare identify Southampton as the 'fair youth' against the prevailing opinion of editors of the sonnets, who tend to prefer Pembroke. Malone was the first editor to give critical attention to the sonnets in his 1780 supplement to the *Johnson-Steevens* 2 edition. In his own edition he stated that sonnets 1–126 were addressed to a young man (1790, x. 191). Although unable to adduce further details, Malone states: "To this person, whoever he was, one hundred and twenty six of the following poems are addressed. The remaining twenty-eight are addressed to a lady." Five years after Malone's death, Nathan Drake made a detailed case for identifying Southampton as the 'fair youth', pointing out verbal parallels between the phrasing of the sonnets with the narrative poems, and noting that Southampton was the only dedicatee named by Shakespeare in his lifetime (1817, ii. 62–73). He argued that the purpose of Sonnets 1–17 was to persuade Southampton to marry Elizabeth Vernon, despite the Queen's opposition to the match. Drake's identification of Southampton as the 'fair youth' was accepted by Lee (1898, 142) and most subsequent biographers including Stopes (1922, 40–41), Holden (1999, 116–17), and Greenblatt, who takes the sonnets as "a cunning sequence of beautiful locked boxes to which there are no keys" – except that Greenblatt provides two keys in identifying Southampton as the 'fair youth' and Marlowe as the 'rival poet' (2004, 227–36). Weis also accepts Southampton as the 'fair youth' and believes that Sonnet 104 ('To me fair friend you can never be old') was a gift to the earl on his twenty-first birthday in 1594 (2007, 122).

Editors of the sonnets on the other hand identify the 'fair youth' as William Herbert, Earl of Pembroke. This idea seems to have been first proposed in 1832 by James Boaden (1762–1839) and elaborated by Thomas Tyler (1890) and H. C. Beeching (1904) in their editions of the Sonnets.[17] The Cambridge editor, J. Dover Wilson (1966, lxxxviii–xci), believes that Shakespeare began writing the sonnets in the late 1590s, by which time Southampton could no longer be considered the youth. He believes that Sonnets 1–17, imploring the 'fair youth' to marry, were commissioned by Pembroke's mother, Mary Sidney, who wanted her wayward son to settle down. Pembroke had been betrothed to Lady Bridget Vere, but subsequently rejected her. He had also been imprisoned for an affair with Mary Fitton, a lady in waiting to the Queen (1966, xci–ciii; repeating ideas from 1963, 59–74). In the Arden3 edition, Katherine Duncan-Jones (1997, 55–69) agrees with Dover Wilson on the date and the identification. She does add a reservation:

> If some of the 'fair youth' sonnets, or versions of them, were written as early as 1592–1595, these may have been originally associated with Southampton... But as completed and published in 1609 the sequence strongly invites a reference to Pembroke.

Burrow also dates the majority of the sonnets to the late 1590s and 1600s and therefore inclines towards Pembroke (2002, 100–3). Two biographers agree with the Pembroke identification: Schoenbaum (1987, 269) finds that there is "no strained ingenuity" in presenting Pembroke as the 'fair youth', a surmise that is followed by Ackroyd (2005, 284–87).

Only a few scholars prefer not to read the sonnets biographically. Lee said: "While Shakespeare's poems bear traces of personal emotion and are coloured by personal experience, they seem to have been to a large extent undertaken as a literary exercise" (*DNB* 1897). He dismisses the notion that Mary Fitton, a mistress of the Earl of Pembroke, was the 'dark lady', noting that she was fair and also dismisses the notion that Shakespeare was "the *protégé* of Pembroke" or that the three were involved in a 'love triangle'. However, Lee was still inclined to think of Southampton as the 'fair youth' of the sonnets (1898, 134–43).

Kerrigan states outright that "the sonnets are not autobiographical."[18] Dutton also rejects any biographical reading of the sonnets (1989, 2007). Honan likewise believes that the sonnets "do not sketch 'real' characters, scenes, or experiences as candidly as modern sonnets may" (*ODNB*, 2004). Orgel in his introduction to the New Cambridge Shakespeare edition describes why it is difficult to offer any kind of date for the sonnets or any identification of the 'fair youth' (2006, 106–7). Edmondson and Wells (2012) give further detailed arguments as to why it is not possible to identify any historical figures with assumed personages in the sonnets. Overall, the identification of the 'fair youth' with either Southampton or Pembroke (or both) is very tenuous. The sonnets do not name any person or give any unambiguous allusion to any person. The uncertainties about the time of composition also makes it impossible to them link with historical figures or events.

8.5 The 'Classless' Green Room

Another question to puzzle biographers concerns where and how Southampton might have met Shakespeare. Most biographers suggest a first encounter at the playhouse, which they see as some kind of egalitarian environment where high and low members of the audience could happily mingle with members of the playing company.

> Only in the theatre did the professional writer find a natural context of colleagues: a classless society, in a sense, where noble patrons rubbed shoulders with apprentices.
>
> (Sheavyn & Saunders *The Literary Profession in the Elizabethan Age.* 1967, 100)

Biographers date this putative encounter in the year or two prior to the dedication in *Venus & Adonis*, which was entered into the Stationers' Register on 18 April 1593. After admitting that there is no evidence for any encounter, Stopes offers her own interpretation, detailing how Southampton left Dieppe sometime after 2 March 1591, spent his leisure time at the London Theatres (not attested until 1599), and met the promising playwright in the spring of 1591. She continues her description of this imaginary encounter by saying that Southampton would give advice "to the players, as is often the way with amateurs" and was drawn to

Shakespeare by "a subtle intuition," had private talks with him, and took him home to supper. None of this is recorded. Apparently, Southampton was able to stimulate the young playwright by showing him some of his books on poetry. These "feasts of reason" took place, according to Stopes's account, not in Cecil House but in Southampton House at Holborn. Stopes seems unaware that before he came of age in October 1594, Southampton was unable to control his time, his finances, or his place of residence (1922, 40–44). Akrigg follows Stopes to some extent, accepting a backstage meeting in a London playhouse (1968, 193), repeated by Greenblatt (2004, 227–28) and Ackroyd (2005, 190–95).

F. E. Halliday (1963, 120–24) thinks it likely that Shakespeare first admired Southampton when Elizabeth and her Court visited Oxford in September 1592: a poem in Latin by John Sanford includes fulsome descriptions of Essex and Southampton (Akrigg 1968, 35–36). As the poet returned to Stratford, according to Halliday, he composed Sonnet 104 ("To me, fair friend, you never can be old"). There is no evidence that Shakespeare was in Oxford at this time or whether he would have been admitted to courtly entertainments, or even if he ever admired Southampton. Other venues for this assumed first meeting have been suggested. Holden believes that they met through Catholic connections (1999, 112). Wood develops this possibility, but adds sagely: "We are never likely to know about them; these were not the sort of things people talked about" (2003, 147–48).

A. L. Rowse (1965, 58) admits that "we know nothing whatever of the player-playwright's introduction to the notice of the young Earl." Park Honan (2004) also realises that it is unclear how the earl might ever have met Shakespeare. He suggests two possibilities: Southampton attended the royal court with the younger Fulke Greville, whose father at Stratford had known a board of aldermen which included the dramatist's father: "Young Fulke Greville could have put the earl in touch with Shakespeare." This theory suggests that the elder Fulke Greville (1536–1606) visited Stratford, where he knew John Shakespeare, took notice of William whom he introduced to his own son (born 1554), who in turn presented him to nobles such as the young earl of Southampton. Honan offers another suggestion: that Southampton, as a keen playgoer, might have met the dramatist at Gray's Inn (1998, 172–79). Weis believes that Shakespeare and Southampton met even earlier – in the summer of 1590, when Southampton was 16 years old. He conjectures that Southampton may have been introduced by Nashe or Greene, two playwrights with connections to St. John's College Cambridge (2007, 112). The range of dates and venues for the assumed first meeting between Shakespeare and Southampton indicate the lack of any record that they ever met at all.

Some biographers have seen the strong attachment between Southampton and Shakespeare as a homosexual relationship. That Southampton enjoyed homosexual relations was implied in various dedications mentioned earlier (Nashe *The Unfortunate Traveller* 1594; Markham *Tragedy of Richard Grinvile, Knight* 1595; Burton *Clitophon and Leucippe* 1596). It was also described, in a letter of 1601 to Sir Robert Cecil. The writer, William Reynolds, had served with Essex and Southampton in Ireland, and was describing a man wanted in connection with the Essex Rebellion:

> [Piers Edmonds] was corporal general of the horse in Ierland under the earl of Sowthampton. he eate & drancke at his table and lay in his tente.... the earl sowthampton would cole and huge [embrace and hug] him in his arms and play wantonly with him.
>
> (Cecil Papers, 83, 62)

Duncan-Jones dismisses this testimony saying that Reynolds may have been a paranoid schizophrenic, as by his own admission he had written over 200 protest letters to the Queen, Privy Council, and members of the clergy to complain of "al the abewses and vilent opresseones & sodometicall sines over flowing this land" (1993, 481–84). Shakespeare is also thought to have shown homosexual tendencies, not from the testimony of observers but from a reading of his own poems. W. H. Auden argued that the sonnets showed that he too was gay and that they amounted to "naked auto-biographical confession."[19] In Sonnet 20, the speaker addresses the younger man as the "master-mistress of my passion." Duncan-Jones describes the tone to this poem as homoerotic (1997, 150–52). Burrow considers whether Shakespeare was expressing homosexuality in this and other sonnets without coming to a conclusion (2002, 124–30). Most biographers stopped short of stating that Shakespeare and Southampton were lovers. Perhaps because of this implication, Steevens had expressed distaste for the poems (1793, i. vii). Peter Levi (1988, 100) thinks that Southampton and Shakespeare were very close but were not "complete lovers" and that "the sonnets are not about buggery."

More recently, biographers have been more forthright about the possible homosexuality of Shakespeare and/or Southampton. Honan (1998, 177) believes that Southampton had bisexual and homosexual tendencies while Shakespeare's sonnets shows his understanding of homoerotic attraction. Greenblatt (2004, 308, 254) sees Shakespeare and Southampton as part of an intimate circle of close friends who would understand the covert references in the poems (234) and that Southampton was Shakespeare's "patron, friend and possible lover" (308). Weis makes the unrecorded claim: "That Shakespeare knew Southampton well is a matter of record." He states without any evidence that Shakespeare's relationship with Southampton was not of a physical nature but was still a kind of infidelity (2007, 112).

Only a few biographers have imagined a detached acquaintance between Southampton and Shakespeare. John Southworth, who emphasises the acting career, claims without any evidence that a proper distance was maintained between the poet and his patron (*Shakespeare the Player* 2000, 70–72). In his account of Southampton, Honan also states that Shakespeare "cannot have intruded often in Southampton's set, or some notice of this would have survived... In all probability, Shakespeare's meetings with his patron were few" (*ODNB*, 2004). Bate raises a far more pressing issue about Shakespear' assumed access to and intimacy with either Southampton or Pembroke:

> How likely is it that so great a figure as an earl would have allowed a player and a play-maker of lower middle-class origins, however talented and successful he may have been, sufficient access to achieve the kind of intense intimacy that the sonnets purport to describe?
>
> (Bate 2008, 221–22)

According to this view, Shakespeare might have been patronised early in his career through an agent.

The variety of interpretation as to the degree of friendship between Shakespeare and Southampton arises from the lack of evidence which would associate them. There are only two contemporary documents linking Shakespeare and Southampton: the dedication to *Venus & Adonis* in 1593 and *Lucrece* in 1594. Shakespeare might have dedicated his poems to the earl in the hope of patronage but there is no evidence he ever received any rewards, financial or otherwise. The earl lacked access to funds when these dedications were written as he was still a minor. He was very unlikely to have patronised Shakespeare or any other writer during the remainder of Elizabeth's reign as he was heavily in debt. When Southampton enjoyed the grace and favour of James I, there are records that he patronised writers, but Shakespeare is not listed among them. It is also possible that Shakespeare dedicated his poems to Southampton not as a patron but as an ideal reader as the author and more likely the publisher believed he could be used to help promote the product. The social distance between the playwright and the nobleman suggests that any close relationship was unlikely. Overall, the enormous variation shown by biographers as to how Shakespeare and Southampton may have known other clearly illuminates the unevidenced nature of their biographical imaginings, or 'biografiction'.

Notes

1 C. C. Stopes, *The Life of Henry Third Earl of Southampton, Shakespeare's Patron* (1922). A. L. Rowse, *Shakespeare's Southampton: Patron of Virginia* (1965). G. P. V. Akrigg, *Shakespeare and the Earl of Southampton* (1968).

2 *Salisbury MSS* VI, 533 mentions the need to make the payment but does not state the amount. The matter is described by Joel Hurstfield. *The Queen's Wards: Wardship and Marriage under Elizabeth I*. London: Longmans Green (1958, 171–79). See also Daphne Pearson *Edward de Vere (1550–1604)* Ashgate: Aldershot (2005, 35–36) for the disastrous consequences of non-payment of these fees.

3 Contratct survives at 5M53/262 in the Hampshire Record Office. Cf. Nikolaus Pevsner. *The Buildings of England: Hampshire and the Isle of Wight.* Harmondswoth: Penguin (1967, 624).

4 John Florio. *A vvorlde of wordes, or Most copious, and exact dictionarie in Italian and English,* London: Edw. Blount (1598, sign. a3v).

5 Frances Yates. *John Florio: The Life of an Italian in Shakespeare's England.* Cambridge: Cambridge University Press (1934, 126).

6 Lawson, Lesley. *Out of the Shadows: The Life of Lucy, Countess of Bedford.* London: Hambledon Continuum (2007).

7 Alistair Fox. "The Complaint of Poetry for the Death of Liberality: The Decline of Literary Patronage in the 1590s." In *The Reign of Elizabeth I: Court and Culture in the Last Decade,* ed. J. Guy. Cambridge: Cambridge University Press (1995, 229–57). Paul J. Voss. "Books for Sale: Advertising and Patronage in Late Elizabethan England." *The Sixteenth Century Journal* 29 (1998, 733–56).

8 Arthur Collins, ed. *H. Sydney and Others, Letters and Memorials of State* (1746, ii. 132); reported by Malone (1778, i. 402) and by Akrigg (1968, 96). Sir Robert Sidney was at the time governor of Flushing and had sent Roland White to keep him informed of events in England in the late 1590s.

9 Letter from the Privy Council at Greenwich to Essex, 10 June 1599, *Calendar of State Papers (Ireland), 1599–1600,* 62 (quoted by Akrigg 1968, 83).

10 Akrigg derives these from the *Salisbury MSS,* XVI, 187 and the *Cal. S. P. (Dom)* 1603–1610, 137 (1968, 135–42).

11 John J. Manning, ed. *The First and Second Parts of John Hayward's Life and Raigne of King Henry IIII,* London: RHS (1991, 18–19).

12 Helen Hackett (2009) finds no evidence that Elizabeth ever patronised Shakespeare directly as a poet, only indirectly as a member of the Lord Chamberlain's Men. Moreover, Elizabeth never attended the public playhouses and there is no record of any private audience with Shakespeare or any other actors.

13 According to Chambers, Shakespeare spent £60 on New Place, £320 on land at Old Stratford, £440 on the tithes, and £140 on the Blackfriars gatehouse, totalling £960.

14 A short account was published as the *Honorable entertainment giuen to the Queenes Maiestie in progresse, at Cowdrey in Sussex, by the right Honorable the Lord Montacute.* 1591 (Reprinted in C. Nicholls, *Progresses* 3.27).

15 Peter Alexander. *Shakespeare's Life and Art* (1939, 58) suggested *Love's Labour's Lost* was written by Shakespeare in his "first period" of play-writing in London, 1592–1594, before he joined the Chamberlain's Men. H. R. Woudhuysen notes that the play is usually dated to 1594–1595 but that "the evidence for it is fairly thin"; he considers attempts to date the play through its French associations or the Gray's Inn revels as "unsatisfactory," and other topical allusions as "not convincing" (1998: 59–60).

16 J. W. Lever. *The Elizabethan Love Sonnet.* London: Methuen (1956).

17 Boaden's essay first appeared in *The Gentleman's Magazine* (1832, CII: 217–21, 308–14, 407) and was published separately in 1837. It has been reprinted in Boaden and Wivell (2013). Thomas Tyler, ed. *Shakespeare's Sonnets.* London: David Nutt (1890). Henry Charles Beeching, ed. *The Sonnets of Shakespeare.* Boston, MA: Ginn (1904).

18 John Kerrigan, ed. *Shakespeare's Sonnets and A Lover's Complaint.* Harmondsworth: Penguin (1986, 11).

19 Richard R. Bozorth. "Auden: Love, Sexuality, Desire." In *The Cambridge Companion to W. H. Auden.* Cambridge: CUP (2005, 178).

9 Inventing a Rival

Ben Jonson

Jonson's commendation in the First Folio "has something of the flavour of a blurb, designed to sell a book;" and is "primarily a literary composition, entertainingly making use of literary conventions."
— (T. J. B. Spencer 1974)

Most narratives contain a foil to the protagonist, some kind of rival or opponent. Often, this person is originally a friend or relative. In Joseph Campbell's *Hero of a Thousand Faces* (1949), the protagonist has to overcome the friend-turned rival to achieve the goal set out. In the plays of Shakespeare, the protagonists often have friends and allies who become rivals and opponents, among them Hotspur, Banquo, and Laertes. In the recorded events of his life, however, there is no person or entity to stand in the way of Shakespeare's success. Various attempts have been made to identify such an antagonist as the 'rival poet' in the sonnets, including Samuel Daniel, Michael Drayton, and Barnabe Barnes, but there is no evidence that any of these were Shakespeare's rival in love or in any other sense. Thus when writing about the life of Shakespeare, Ben Jonson (1573–1637) was cast by critics after the Restoration in the role of Shakespeare's friend who turned into a jealous rival. Jonson was portrayed as surly, ill-natured, proud, and disagreeable, whereas Shakespeare was gentle, good-natured, easy, and amiable. Holland is typical in referring to Shakespeare's "close friendship and genial rivalry with Jonson" (*ODNB* 2004). A review of allusions, however, shows that few records link Jonson directly with Shakespeare, and that there is only limited evidence to suggest that Shakespeare and Jonson were personally acquainted. Malone had reached this conclusion in his essay on Ford and Jonson (1790, i. 387–414). As with Southampton, biographers imagine that Shakespeare had a far closer relationship with Jonson than is evident in the records.

The biographical material for Ben Jonson differs enormously both in kind and in extent from the material about Shakespeare. Anne Barton (whose biography of Jonson appeared in 1984) explains in her collective review of five biographies of Shakespeare:

Our knowledge of Jonson's year-by-year existence is not only enormous compared with the totality of what can be gleaned (mostly from scattered and laconic legal or church records) about Shakespeare's but of a strikingly different provenance and kind.

She continues:

We have many of the private letters Jonson wrote, a detailed record of his conversation, and an impressive body of explicitly self-revelatory poetry and prose. We know exactly who Jonson's many friends and patrons were, where he travelled and with whom he stayed, when and why he suffered prison sentences, and when his private library (along with several as yet unpublished works) was destroyed by fire.[1]

These personal writings by and about Jonson have allowed four additional literary biographies in the last thirty years.[2] Despite all this material, Donaldson sums up Jonson's life as "mainly a matter of gaps, interspersed by fragments of knowledge" (2011, 9).

Born in 1573, Ben Jonson was about nine years younger than Shakespeare. He was a member of Pembroke's Men in the 1590s and was arrested in 1597 for contributing to the play *Isle of Dogs*. His earliest publication was *Every Man out of his Humour* (*EMO*), which was performed in 1599, entered into Stationers' Register on 8 April 1600 (Arber iii, 159) and published in 1600. Although Jonson published fewer plays in the next decade, eight compared to about fifteen of Shakespeare's,[3] he also published various masques and panegyrics.[4] By 1616, with the publication of a folio of his works, more of Jonson's plays and poems had appeared in print than Shakespeare's. Jonson's popularity remained greater until the Restoration (Bentley 1945). Given their interrelated activities and overlapping careers, it is obvious that biographers should look for contacts between them. After the Restoration, the tendency was to depict Jonson's pique at his own inferiority. Dryden doubted Jonson's sincerity in his commendation (1693, vii). Rowe asserted that Jonson was proud, insolent, and very jealous of Shakespeare (1709, i. viii). Steevens claimed that Jonson was overly critical of Shakespeare while Malone declared that Jonson viewed Shakespeare with "scornful and yet jealous eyes" (1778 iv. 153). Not all critics at this time took such a view: Betterton repeatedly stated that no rivalry existed between Shakespeare and Jonson.[5] This envy was reimagined in the nineteenth and twentieth centuries when critics tended to depict a friendly relationship. Octavius Gilchrist in 1808 and William Gifford in more detail, in 1816 challenged the notion of Jonson's bad temper, finding no evidence of any feud or jealousy in the connection between the two (ccli).[6] Some modern commentators follow this: Holden asserts that "Shakespeare and Jonson show every sign of having remained firm friends until Shakespeare's death" (1999, 158). Holden does not say what these signs were. Donaldson imagines "the two men working and talking together, watching and pondering each other's inventions, observing and retaining certain phrases, ideas, names, turns of plot" (2006, 249).

Most modern biographers, however, see them in opposition, (e.g. Shapiro *Rival Playwrights*, 1991, and Bednarz *Shakespeare and the Poets' War*, 2001). Just a few biographers of Shakespeare, notably Levi (1988) and Greenblatt (2004), find little or no suggestion of any significant relationship between the two men.

9.1 Did Shakespeare Purge Jonson?

Whatever is claimed about this relationship originates in Jonson's biographical record: Shakespeare never mentions or alludes to Jonson (or any other writer). In his will, Shakespeare did not remember Jonson or the Jonson child once mentioned as his godson. While Shakespeare was named among the members of the newly-formed King's Men in 1603, Jonson was not mentioned in any document concerning them. The only allusion linking Shakespeare in his lifetime to Jonson occurs in the anonymous Cambridge play *Return to Parnassus* Part 1, (4.3), where the following speech is assigned to Will Kempe:

> Why heres our fellow Shakespeare puts them all downe, I [aye] and Ben Jonson too. O that Ben Jonson is a pestilent fellow, he brought up Horace giving the Poets a pill, but our fellow Shakespeare hath given him a purge that made him beray his credit.
> (Leishman 1949, 337)

The *Return to Parnassus* seems to have been performed in 1602 (there is a reference to Elizabeth as still alive) but it was not published until 1606. The passage may be part of a broader 'War of the Poets', a view elaborated by James Bednarz (2001, 19–52). Bednarz is unsure whether Shakespeare was directly involved or was merely an observer. Malone expressed the opinion that the purge did not refer to any particular play (1790 i. ii. 321), a view followed by Lee (1898), Chambers (*ES* iv, 40), and Donaldson (2011, 173–74).

Various interpretations have been offered as "the purge" which Shakespeare is said to have given Jonson. In the late nineteenth century, Fleay identified Shakespeare's it with his depiction of Ajax in *Troilus and Cressida* at 1.2.19 (1886, 45). E. K. Chambers accepted that this passage might parody Jonson as it "seems unnecessarily elaborate for its place, refers to 'humours', and has not much relation to the character of Ajax as depicted in the play" (*WS*, i. 72). Fleay also declared that "Sir Toby represents Jonson and Malvolio Marston" (1886, 220). G. Sarrazin in

1904 suggested that Jonson was portrayed as the insignificant Nym in *Henry V* and in *Merry Wives of Windsor* as he rarely speaks without using the word 'humour', a point accepted by Sir Arthur Quiller-Couch in 1921. David Riggs (1989) also sees Malvolio as a comic satire, especially with Malvolio's conversion in prison mirroring Ben Jonson's. Henk Gras (1989) agreed that *Twelfth Night* was a direct response to overt criticisms made by Jonson in his Humours plays, an interpretation developed by Janet Clare in 2005.[7] Henry Gray (1932) suggested that *Hamlet* was Shakespeare's purge on Jonson. However, any reference to the so-called War of the Poets is very brief:

> *Rosencrantz*: Faith, there has been much to do on both sides; and the nation holds it no sin to tar them to controversy: there was, for a while, no money bid for argument unless the poet and the player went to cuffs in the question.
> *Hamlet*: Is't possible?
> *Guildenstern*: O, there has been much throwing about of brains.
> *Hamlet* 2.2.352–59 (Folio 1623, not in Q2)

Arthur Gray (1928) put forward the view that the melancholic Jaques in *As You Like It* was Shakespeare's satire on Jonson.[8] Duncan-Jones accepts this and believes that Shakespeare "engaged in increasingly fierce and hostile competition with Jonson" in the late 1590s and early 1600s (2001, 123–24; 136). There is little to suggest that Shakespeare is specifically referencing Jonson in any of these passages. It seems that almost any unfavourable depiction of a character in a Shakespeare play can be interpreted as an attack on Jonson – or any other supposed enemy.

Against this 'offensive Shakespeare', some critics have seen Shakespeare writing in a 'defensive' or 'reactive' mode against Jonson. Ernst Honigmann (1982, 111) sees Shakespeare defending himself against Jonson's demand to maintain the unities with this speech: "The lunatic, the lover and the poet / Are of imagination all compact" (*Midsummer Night's Dream* 5.1.7–8), but this play is usually dated to 1595–1596, earlier than Jonson's first recorded play. Honigmann also sees a response in *A Winter's Tale* where the Chorus asks the audience: "Impute it not a crime / To me or my swift passage that I slide / O'er sixteen years." (4.4.90). In these passages, as in the speeches by the Chorus to *Henry V*, Shakespeare may have been answering more general criticism by writers such as Philip Sidney, whose *Apologie for Poetrie* was published in 1595.

Overall, there is no record in which Shakespeare mentioned Jonson and no confirmed allusion in any of the works to Jonson. Jonson might, or might not, have been satirised in the portrayal of Ajax, Sir Toby, Corporal Nym, or Malvolio, or in the plays *Troilus and Cressida, As You Like It, Merry Wives of Windsor*, and *Twelfth Night*. Shakespeare might, or might not, have been answering Jonson's criticism in

A Midsummer Night's Dream, A Winter's Tale, Othello, and *Hamlet*. Whichever allusion is selected, none constitutes evidence of any respect, rivalry, or even acquaintance on the part of Shakespeare.

9.2 "Shakespear Wanted Arte"

While Shakespeare's opinion of other writers is carefully concealed, Ben Jonson's opinions of other writers, including Shakespeare, is well documented in various ways: (i) in private conversations recorded by William Drummond in 1619; (ii) in his own works, especially his plays, especially where he speaks in *propria persona* in the prologue or epilogue; (iii) in his commendatory poems to Shakespeare in the 1623 Folio; (iv) in his own notes, collected and published posthumously as *Timber or Discoveries* (1641). These references, taken to indicate the relationships between the two playwrights, will be considered in turn.

In 1619, Ben Jonson visited Scotland and spent some time over Christmas with William Drummond (1585–1649) at Hawthornden Castle near Edinburgh. The host made notes of Jonson's opinions which were eventually published as *Informations to William Drummond of Hawthornden* (Sage and Ruddiman 1711; Patterson 1923). Drummond was very interested in contemporary poetry and owned a large library, including plays of Shakespeare (MacDonald 1971). He also owned an edition of Jonson's *Works* (1616) and many books by other English writers, including Lily, Chapman, Dekker, Marston, and Middleton. In his journal, Drummond noted books which he had read, including *Romeo and Juliet, Love's Labour's Lost, A Midsummers Night's Dream, Lucrece*, and *Venus & Adonis*. With such an interest in poetry and drama, Drummond would pay close attention to Jonson's views on poets and playwrights, especially Shakespeare. Yet Drummond only records two comments by Jonson on Shakespeare, fewer than his opinions about other writers. Jonson's opinions about Shakespeare were juxtaposed by Sage and Ruddiman who added the phrase "and sometimes sense" (1711, 225), but as these comments were recorded in separate parts of the manuscript, they were likely to have been spoken at different times. According to Drummond:

– He said, Shakespear wanted Arte (Patterson 1923, 5).
– for in one of his Plays he brought in a Number of Men, saying they had suffered Ship-wrack in Bohemia, where is no Sea near by 100 Miles (Patterson 1923, 20).

It is unlikely that Jonson ever suspected that his comments would be reported in print. Thus, its is likely that Jonson was expressing an honest opinion that he did not rate Shakespeare highly. This comparison can readily be made in Sage & Ruddiman's edition as they collected Jonson's opinions under the title "Jonson's Censure of the English Poets" (see Appendix C).

The reproach "that Shakespear wanted Arte" is usually linked with Jonson's more famous suggestion that Shakespeare had "small Latine and lesse Greeke." Patterson believes that Jonson's criticism was "fair" (1923, 5) probably because Shakespeare did not imitate classical models in following the unities as Jonson did. The second of Jonson's adverse judgements concerns Shakespeare's geography and most commentators accept that Shakespeare made a mistake. It is possible to exonerate Shakespeare of geographical error by one or two simple arguments: Shakespeare was following Robert Greene's 1588 prose romance, *Pandosto the triumph of time*, the main source for *The Winter's Tale*, in which Bohemia is given a sea coast. Geoffrey Bullough (1975, viii. 118–25) describes how Shakespeare reverses the locations. Greene's story involves drifting from the sea coast of Bohemia to Sicily and back. Jonson's attack should therefore be directed at Greene. However, both Greene and Shakespeare might be correct, and Jonson wrong, because the Kingdom of Bohemia did have a sea coast from the time of Ottokar II (1233–1278), according to Pafford (Arden 2 edition, 1962, 66). The Austro-Hungarian Empire retained its Adriatic port until the end of the First World War when the citizens of Trieste opted to join Italy.[9] Jonson's criticism of Shakespeare's geography reveals his own limited knowledge rather than Shakespeare's.

In the 1616 *Workes*, Jonson included 133 epigrams, four of which praised contemporary writers such as John Donne. Jonson did not name Shakespeare in any epigram, which again suggests that they did not have a close relationship. In fact, Shakespeare is only named twice in *Works*: his name is included among the list of players of *Every Man in his Humour*, (*EMI*) "acted, in the yeere 1598," and *Seianus* "acted, in the yeere 1603." Four other playlists do not include Shakespeare's name: *Every Man out his Humour*, (*EMO*), *Volpone*, *The Alchemist*, and *Catiline*. The lists are otherwise consistent in naming Richard Burbage and John Heminges, often with William Sly (until his death in 1608) and Henry Condell. While it is not clear who prepared these lists and upon what authority, the absence of a particular actor's name may suggest that the actor had little or no part in the play. Duncan-Jones uses the argument from absence to support her idea that Shakespeare was angry at his apparent portrayal in *EMI* and so boycotted *EMO* a year later. She states: "The fact that the leading player [Shakespeare] in Jonson's first 'Humour' play took no part in his second is rather striking" (2001, 118–19). Duncan-Jones uses this "striking fact" to support her contention of an ongoing feud between Shakespeare and Jonson. Donaldson finds any such feud unlikely (2011, 438–39), contrasting the many records which show a feud between Jonson and Inigo Jones (423). Shakespeare might have been ill or injured and unable to play a part. He might have been busy in 1599 writing various plays as Shapiro suggests (2005). He might have been devoting his energies to obtaining a coat of arms for his father. It is also conceivable that Shakespeare's name was included as he was a sharer in the company and not an actor. Overall, Shakespeare's appearing twice in the list of players does not provide evidence that the two were either friends or rivals.

Ben Jonson appears to refer to Shakespeare in *EMI* a version of which was performed in 1598 by the Lord Chamberlain's Men (according to the title page). The play was entered into the Stationers' Register on 14 August 1600 (Arber iii, 169) and published in 1601. The play was among those performed at court in 1605. In the Prologue to the play, which was not printed in the 1601 quarto but appears in Jonson's *Workes* in 1616, Jonson criticises various aspects of contemporary comedies:

> Though need make many Poets, and some such
> As art and nature have not bettered much;
> Yet ours, for want, hath not so loved the stage,
> As he dare serve th'ill customs of the age,
> Or purchase your delight at such a rate,   5
> As, for it, he himself must justly hate.
> To make a child, now swaddled, to proceed
> Man, and then shoot up, in one beard and weed,
> Past threescore years; or, with three rusty swords,
> And help of some few foot-and-half-foot words,   10
> Fight over York and Lancaster's long jars;
> And in the tiring-house bring wounds to scars.
> He rather prays you will be pleased to see
> One such, today, as other plays should be.
> Where neither Chorus wafts you o'er the seas;   15
> Nor creaking throne comes down, the boys to please;
> Nor nimble squib is seen, to make afeared
> The gentlewomen; nor rolled bullet heard
> To say, it thunders; nor tempestuous drum
> Rumbles, to tell you when the storm doth come;   20
> But deeds, and language, such as men do use;
>
> Ben Jonson *Every Man in his Humour* Prologue (1616)

Although Jonson does not mention the name of any particular author or play, many of the criticisms readily apply to Shakespearean drama. Jonson's first point concerns characters depicted across a large period of time: "To make a child, now swaddled, to proceed Man, and then shoot up, in one beard and weed, Past threescore years" (vv. 7–9). Perhaps he is referring to Perdita in *The Winter's Tale* or Marina in *Pericles*. Henry VI is depicted growing from a baby to a man aged about fifty when he is murdered, but this takes place across a trilogy. Jonson's second points concerns the theatrical practice, using a small number of actors to represent large gatherings: "with three rusty swords, And help of some few foot-and-half-foot words, Fight over York and Lancaster's long jars" (vv. 9–11). Jonson apparently alludes to the *Henry VI* trilogy (normally dated 1590–1595) in performance. His third main criticism, the use of a Chorus to announce changes of scene (v.15), seems to refer to *Henry V* although the Chorus's speeches were not printed in the 1600 or 1602 quartos but only in F1 in 1623. His derisory mention of the descent of a "creaking throne" (v. 16) might refer to Juno in *The Tempest* or Jupiter in *Cymbeline*. Jonson criticises the use of speeches by actors rather than stage effects for a drum or a storm (vv. 18–21). This might refer to the witch who announces, "A drum! A drum! Macbeth doth come!" Only one criticism might relate to any of the plays of Shakespeare which were then being performed at Court in 1604–1605.[10] These criticisms, if they were aimed at Shakespeare, were completely at odds with the adulation expressed in the commendatory verses in the First Folio.

In trying to establish a link between Shakespeare and Jonson, a few critics have suggested that one character in *EMI*, Bobadilla, owed something to Shakespeare's Falstaff – who had been presented on stage by the same company a few months earlier (Miola 2000, 33). However, the braggart soldier was a stock character in Comedy, stretching back from Plautus' *Miles Gloriosus*. There are differences between them: Bobadilla is not witty and "has no talent for the monstrous and witty lie that ingeniously wrenches a true cause" (Barton 1984, 50). Few scholars accept a direct link between Bobadilla and Falstaff.

Another character from *EMI* may have had a great influence on Shakespeare. In the Q1 version of Jonson's play, a jealous husband called Thorello, broods over the imagined infidelities of his wife and complains of headaches. Not only is the character's name a near anagram of Shakespeare's hero, Othello, he also undergoes similar mental torment. The Italian setting of *EMI* in Q1 was altered to London when published in the Folio of 1616. The names of the characters were similarly changed and many references to contemporary city life were added. Nevertheless, the jealous husband features largely in the revised version. J. W. Lever lists many verbal echoes between the two plays while MacDonald considers similarities of characters and structure.[11] Miola offers this connection:

> Shakespeare's experience acting in the original *Every Man In His Humour* bore fruit several years later in *Othello* (1604) – his tale of jealous husbands and innocent wives. Shakespeare remembers Thorello in the choice of name for Cinthio's Moor; perhaps also in his addition of a subordinate instance of male jealousy.
>
> (2000, 65)

Not every editor is so persuaded. Michael Neill plays down the similarity of name and counters that Othello is close to 'Ottoman'. The similarity between Thorello and Othello is ignored by both M. R. Ridley and E. A. J. Honigmann (the Arden 2 and the Arden 3 editors) and by Geoffrey Bullough (1973, vii. 193–208).[12]

If there is a link between Thorello and Othello, the direction of influence depends on the relative date of composition. Most commentators follow Chambers and date *Othello* to 1603–1604, due to the mention of a performance of *The Moor of Venis* "in the Banketinge house att Whit Hall on Hallowmas," i.e. 1 November 1604 (*WS* ii. 331). Such a date for *Othello* would place it after *EMI* appeared on stage and in print. However, an earlier date for *Othello* might be inferred from an entry in Henslowe's Diary. On 14 December 1594, Henslowe recorded a performance of 'the mawe', and again on 2, 17, and 28 January 1595 (Foakes 2002, 26–27). This play has not otherwise been identified, but might refer to *The Mawe/Moor of Venice*. If Henslowe is recording a performance of Shakespeare's play (or a version of it), then it could be Jonson who borrowed the details from *Othello*. The case of Thorello and Othello indicates the perils in assuming that the dates of composition of Shakespeare's plays are well-established.

In *EMO*, Jonson again seems to mock Shakespeare, but this time on a more personal or familial level. At 3.1.2010-47, the character of Sogliardo proudly announces his new coat of arms with the motto "Not without mustard." This phrase echoes Nashe's *Pierce Penilesse* (1592), in which a shipwrecked character promises to give up Haberdine if he is saved; when he steps onto land, he shouts: "Not without mustard, good lord, not without mustard as though it had been the greatest torment in the world to have eaten Haberdine without mustard." Nashe's protagonist is not, however, obtaining a coat of arms. Jonson's Sogliardo announces: "I can write myself a gentleman now. Here's my patent, it cost me thirty pounds, by this breath." Jonson thus appears to be mocking families, perhaps even the Shakespeares, for buying, rather than deserving, their coat of arms which seems to have had the motto *Non Sanz Droict* "Not Without Right." The grant of arms to John Shakespeare occurred sometime between 1596 and 1599 (*WS* ii. 23–24). A few years later, in 1602, the York Herald of Arms, Ralph Brooke, made a complaint against Sir William Dethick (Garter King-of-Arms) and his associate William Camden (Clarenceux King-of-Arms) "for elevating base persons, and assigning devices already in use," naming Shakespeare as the fourth in a list of 23 cases (Loomis 2002, 126). If Jonson was satirising a cash-for-honours scandal, he would have been implicating his headmaster at Westminster, William Camden. There is further irony as Jonson himself acquired arms by 1606 when he is described as 'armiger' (Donaldson 2011, 163). Greenblatt imagines that Shakespeare endured Jonson's taunt in rehearsals and "probably laughed uncomfortably"

(2004, 79–81). Maurice Hunt compiles a long list of reasons to identify Sogliardo with Shakespeare (2008, 107–9).

Other commentators do not accept that Jonson is satirising the upwardly mobile Shakespeare in his character of Sogliardo. Schoenbaum notes that Sogliardo is not a man of the theatre and that the motto *Non Sanz Droict* does not appear to have been used by Shakespeare or his family (1987, 229). Duncan-Jones simply asserts that "Sogliardo, a country bumpkin of manifest stupidity, could not possibly be construed as a portrait of Shakespeare" (2001, 96). The reference is ignored by Bate (1997), Holden (1999), Wood (2003), Ackroyd (2007), and Potter (2012). E. A. J. Honigmann makes an alternate case for identifying Sogliardo with John Weever (1987, 45). However the most detailed treatment is by Donaldson (2011, 159–60), who concludes that Jonson could not have been satirising Shakespeare.

A third play *Bartholomew Fayre* (performed in 1614, published 1631) also seems to criticise Shakespeare: the speaker of the Induction ridicules theatre-goers who have old-fashioned tastes:

> Hee that will swear *Ieronimo*, or *Andronicus* are the best plays, yet shall pass vnexpected at, heere, as a man whose Iudgement shewes it is constant, and hath stood still, these fiue and twentie, or thirtie yeeres.

Jonson seems to be alluding to Kyd's *The Spanish Tragedy* (c. 1589; Q 1592) and *Titus Andronicus* (Q1, 1594). Jonson reiterates this criticism in his 1629 Ode to Himself, in which he views *Pericles* as "some mouldy tale" and "stale as the Shrieve's crusts." He censured its episodic nature as having "scraps out of every dish Throwne forth, and rak't into the common tub." Jonson might also be satirising Shakespeare in *On Poet-Ape* as one who steals from the work of others (Epigram 56, 1616). This is the only Jonsonian epigram to follow the scheme of a Shakespearean sonnet (*abab cdcd efef gg*). These passages seem to indicate that Jonson held Shakespeare in low regard, quite different from the excessive praise which he made of Shakespeare in the 1623 folio.

While Shakespeare and Jonson are said to have co-written plays with other authors, there have been very few suggestions that Shakespeare and Jonson ever worked together. There are many records showing that Jonson worked with many other playwrights of the time: with Dekker and Porter in the composition of *Hot Anger Soon Cold* in 1598 and with Marston and Chapman in *Eastward Ho!* in 1605 (Donaldson 2011, 126; 206). While Shakespeare was not known as a co-author until the publication of *The Two Noble Kinsmen* (1634), he seems to have co-authored works with other playwrights: *Titus Andronicus* with George Peele, *Timon of Athens* with Thomas Middleton, *Pericles* with

George Wilkins, and *Henry VIII* and *The Two Noble Kinsmen* with John Fletcher (Vickers 2002). Further analysis by Gary Taylor has suggested that Thomas Middleton added scenes to *Macbeth* and Christopher Marlowe was responsible for parts of *1 Henry VI*.[13] It is therefore surprising that two prolific playwrights, connected with the same company and known to have collaborated with other authors, are not known to have worked together. Malone suggested that Shakespeare might have been the unnamed author who had originally helped Jonson with *Sejanus* (Boswell 1821 i. 356). Few if any subsequent critics have accepted this. Barton thought it more likely that the other writer was George Chapman (1984, 91–94), which is accepted by Donaldson (2011, 472n33).[14] There are many allusions by Jonson to Shakespeare's plays, showing that he was very conversant with them on stage, but they do not indicate that the playwrights knew each other personally.

9.3 Dedications in the First Folio

Seven years after Jonson's *Works*, *Shakespeare's Comedies, Histories and Tragedies* appeared in a publication that has become known as the First Folio (F1). In the preliminary matter there were two poems signed by Jonson, three commendatory poems or literary puffs, a dedication to the Incomparable pair of Brethren, the earls of Pembroke and Montgomery, and an epistle to the Reader. The sequence of the preliminary matter varied in the final arrangement of different copies (Greg 1955, 449–51). Franklin B. Williams states that in "Stuart times, it is clear from scattered evidence, the task of soliciting puffs was frequently, if not customarily, assumed by the publisher or stationer" (1966, 7). In the case of F1, the main publishers were Edward Blount and William and Isaac Jagger. Two other stationers, John Smethwick, and William Aspley, played a lessor role in the enterprise (Greg 1955, 2–4).

The shorter poem of Jonson accompanied the engraving by Martin Droeshout, and consisted of ten lines. Jonson's point was that the engraver is unable to do justice to the wit of "gentle Shakespeare" and that the reader of the poem should read the volume:

> *This Figure, that thou here seest put,*
> *It was for gentle Shakespeare cut,*
> *Wherein the Graver had a strife*
> *With Nature, to out-doo the life:*
> *O, could he but have drawne his wit*
> *As well in brasse, as he hath hit*
> *His face; the Print would then surpasse*
> *All, that was ever writ in brasse.*
> *But, since he cannot, Reader, looke*
> *Not on his Picture, but his Booke.*

That this is a generic comment appears from a comparison with the beginning of Jonson's Folio (1616), where two lines of verse in English express the same sentiment:

> *O could there be an Art found out that might*
> *Produce his Shape so lively as to Write.*

Lee (1915, 525) believes that this point derives from the French poet Malherbe, who attached similar verses to the portrait of Montaigne in the 1611 edition of the *Essaies.*

> *Voicy du grand Montaigne une entiere figure,*
> *Le Peinctre a peinct le corps et luymesme l'esprit:*
> *Le premier par son art égale la Nature*
> *Le second la surpasse en tout ce qu'il escrit.*

> [Here is a full portrait of the great Montaigne
> The painter has painted his body and illuminated his soul
> In the first part, his art equals nature
> In the second he surpasses it in all that he has written.]

T. J. B. Spencer (1974, 25) draws attention to the same sentiment expressed by the Roman poet Martial about a portrait of Marcus Antonius Primus:

> *Ars utinam mores animumque effingere posset!*
> *Pulchrior in terris nulla tabella foret.*
>
> (Martial X, 32)

> [If art could show his mind and character!
> No picture in the world would show lovelier.]

Jonson's references to French and/or Latin literature raise the question as to whether he was more interested in showing off his own learning than in praising Shakespeare. However, most modern commentators follow Schoenbaum who accepts the commendation at face value, stating that only an "over-subtle reader will detect a latent irony in Jonson's conclusion" (1987, 317).

The commendatory poem to the memory of "my beloved" Follows the address to the reader. While Jonson calls Shakespeare the "Soul of the age! The applause, delight, the wonder of our stage" and "Sweet swan of Avon," the praise remains general and directed at the works, not at the author. This address contains 80 lines, forty couplets, arranged in the following formal manner:

1	Introduction	eight couplets (1–16)
2	Address to Shakespeare	twelve couplets (17–40)
3	Address to Britain	twelve couplets (41–64)
4	Peroration	eight couplets (65–80)

In the introduction, Jonson claims that he will not offer excessive praise to Shakespeare out of "seeliest ignorance" (v.7), "blinde Affection," (v.9) or "crafty malice" (v.11), which suggests that Jonson has such a reputation. Lynn Meskill (2009) calls the opening couplet "one of the strangest openings in the history of panegyric," explaining that it was a ritual denial to prevent the gaze of envy from the evil eye. She states that Jonson was commissioned to write the commendation. Marlin Blaine (2009) finds that Jonson's "disavowal of envy" is important to counteract his growing reputation as a "a contemner and scorner of others."[15] Jonson then marks his address to Shakespeare in the second section with "I therefore will begin." He praised Shakespeare as superior to many recent writers, e.g. Lily, Kyd, and Marlowe (vv.29–30), and to the Greek tragedians, Aeschylus, Euripides, and Sophocles (vv.34–35). In the third section, which invites "my Britaine" to triumph, he compares Shakespeare favourably to the ancient comic writers, Aristophanes, Terence, and Plautus (vv.51–52). In the final section Jonson attests to the enduring influence of the work. Jonson calls him "Sweet Swan of Avon" (v.71) and is glad that he appeared on the River Thames to delight both Elizabeth and James. Jonson also calls on him as "thou Starre of Poets" (v.77). Overall, Jonson pays great tribute to his achievement but offers virtually no personal details about the person who wrote them.

In the commendatory poem, Jonson appears to suggest that Shakespeare had limited knowledge of the classics: "Though thou hadst small *Latine*, and lesse *Greeke*" (v. 31). Most writers have seen this as censure. Yet, immediately afterwards Jonson praises Shakespeare as superior to the Greek tragedians. Jonson's apparent criticism is usually linked with his comment reported by Drummond "that Shakesperr wanted Arte." This opinion has sparked a debate which continues into modern times. Like many other of his opinions, Jonson's comment about Shakespeare's "small *Latine*, and lesse *Greeke*" derives from a foreign writer. Antonio Minturno in *L'Arte Poetica* (1564) wrote:

> Perciocche alcuni, i quali per avventura sanno poco del Latino, e pochissimo del Greco, non pur nella Tragedia Seneca appena da' Latini scrittori consociuto ad Euripide, ed a Sofocle da tutti principi nella Tragica Poesia riputati antipongano.[16]
>
> ['For this reason there are some, who happen to know little Latin and even less Greek, who rate Seneca (who was barely known to Latin writers) above Euripides and Sophocles (famously the best tragic poets) – even for tragedy!']

This allusion was recognised by J. E. Spingarn in 1905,[17] and repeated by Herford and Simpson in *Ben Jonson Complete Works* (1952, ix. 145) but it seems to have escaped the notice of most Shakespearean biographers. The derivative origin of Jonson's opinion and its ambiguous interpretations only mark it as significant for our understanding of Jonson, not for Shakespeare. Perhaps the most famous tribute by Jonson was the line (43): *He was not of an age, but for all time!* Few (if any commentators) have noted the generic element in this praise. The classical Greek historian, Thucydides, intended his work for posterity: "In fine I have written my work not as an essay with which to win the applause of the moment but as a possession for all time."[18]

Most modern biographers believe that the poem offers Shakespeare the highest praise. Halliwell-Phillipps (1883, 271) calls Jonson's commendation "a matchless eulogy." Chambers believes that "Jonson's considered judgement of Shakespeare is to be found in his First Folio lines and in his later *Timber*. It shows both admiration for the poet and affection for the man" (*WS* i. 70). Sydney Musgrove stated that Jonson's eulogy was "the greatest praise that any poet could be given" (*Shakespeare and Jonson* 1957, 9). Schoenbaum affirms that we "may rest assured" that Jonson "would not have penned so noble a tribute if he did not esteem Shakespeare as an artist and treasure him as a comrade" (1970, 18–19). Others who accept the praise as literal are Barton (1984, 258), Marcus (1988, 2–25), Donaldson (1996), Honan (1998, 405), and Holden (1999, 326). Weis begins his biography with quotations from this poem and asserts that Jonson knew Shakespeare well (2007, 7–8). Bate uses Jonson's phrase "Soul of the Age" as the title of his intellectual biography of Shakespeare, accepting Jonson's praise as literal (2008, 429). Although these poems constitute by far the most important commendation of Shakespeare among contemporaries, some biographers do not even mention them at all, including Brown (1949), Halliday (1961), Bradbrook (1978), and Greenblatt (2004). One reason might be that the content is predictable. Every literary panegyric claims that the subject rivalled and surpassed both contemporary and classical authors.

So Jonson's commendations to Shakespeare in the First Folio need not have arisen from any close relationship between the two men, but they may be down to Jonson's mercenary status. In Epigram 73 (*Works* 1616), he demands payment for various compositions on behalf of "Fine Grand." In this satirical poem, structured like a detailed invoice, the poet appears to list a wide range of compositions for which he should receive payment. It ends: "For which, or pay me quickly, or I'll pay you." Jonson is admitting that he was a pen for hire. So the commendations to F1 might not be genuine. Certainly, various critics during the next two centuries thought them insincere. Dryden found the address "insolent, sparing and invidious" (1693, vii). Malone referred to Jonson's comments as "clumsy sarcasm and many malevolent reflections" (1790 i. ii. 321). A few modern commentators have followed. Wesley Trimpi finds the poem formulaic (1962, 149–51). T. J. B. Spencer finds it obscure, especially in the references to the little known Roman tragedians, Pacuvius and Accius. Spencer adds that few readers could see Jonson's debt to Horace *Epistles* II i. 55–56 or Quintilian *Institutio Oratoria* (X 97). He argues that Jonson's poem "has something of the flavour of a blurb, designed to sell a book;" and that it is "primarily a literary composition, entertainingly making use of literary conventions" (1974, 39–40). Richard Peterson takes a similar view that Jonson was mainly interested in imitating and adapting quotations from classical authors. He has appreciated the poem as a lyric in the form used by the Roman poet Horace, and finds that Jonson was more concerned with emulating a classical panegyric than in praising a friend (1980, 129–58).[19]

The only previous publication of so many plays in the expensive folio format was Jonson's own *Works* (1616) which was prefaced by a dozen commendatory verses by established writers such as Hayward, Chapman, and Beaumont. While their tributes might well be genuine, the main purpose of any printed commendation was to entice readers to buy the volume in hand. The 1623 folio was a greater undertaking, "by far the most expensive playbook that had ever been offered to the English public."[20] Yet apart from Jonson's commendations, only three minor poets, Digges, Mabbe, and Holland, contributed commendations to Shakespeare's 1623 Folio. Thus, Jonson may have been invited, and paid, to write the dedications by the publishers or by his patron, William Herbert, Earl of Pembroke, one of the "incomparable brethren" to whom Shakespeare's First Folio was dedicated. Jonson's dependence on Pembroke seems to date twenty years or so before the publication of the First Folio. While in prison in 1605, Jonson wrote to Pembroke: "You have ever been free and noble to me" (Folger Shakespeare Library, MS V. a. 321). Jonson dedicated *Catiline* (1611) and his *Epigrams* (1616) to Pembroke and was grateful to the earl for an annual allowance of £20 towards new books (reported in *Informations* 239–40). Pembroke contrived Jonson's award of an honorary degree from Oxford in 1619 (according to Donaldson 2011, 268). As Lord Chamberlain from 1615 until 1626. Pembroke was responsible for the theatre. So Jonson would readily acquiesce in praising Shakespeare's *Folio*. Thus Jonson's eulogy, apparently the greatest tribute to Shakespeare paid by any contemporary writer, might only be an exercise in panegyric intending to promote the sale of an expensive volume of plays.

Overall, it is hard to accept that Jonson was praising Shakespeare in a simple and direct manner. His commendation of Shakespeare in the 1623 folio is inconsistent with the superior attitude that he shows elsewhere towards the plays. Jonson is likely to have been pressed into writing the panegyric (and paid for it) either by the publishers, Blount and Jaggard, or by the dedicatees, Pembroke and Montgomery, or by a combination of them. Jonson's fulsome praise of another writer is completely at odds with the view formed by Drummond.

Ben Jonson is also thought to have ghost written the epistle, apparently signed by Henrie Condell and Iohn Heminge. The opening statement has many echoes in Jonson's works:

> To the great Variety of Readers
>
> From the most able, to him that can but spell: There you are number'd. We had rather you were weighd. Especially, when the fate of all Bookes depends vpon your capacities: and not of your heads alone, but of your purses. Well! it is now publique, & you wil stand for your priuiledges wee know: to read, and censure. Do so, but buy it first. That doth best commend a Booke, the Stationer saies.
>
> Then, how odde soeuer your braines be, or your wisedomes, make your licence the same, and spare not. Iudge your sixe-pen'orth, your shillings worth, your fiue shillings worth at a time, or higher, so you rise to the iust rates, and welcome. But, what euer you do, Buy.

Steevens suspected Jonson of writing this address (1803 i, 166) due to the resemblance of phrases concerning the statement about the importance to the stationer of sales, citing Epigram 3 (*Works* 1616) in support. Pollard agreed (1909, 122), W. W. Greg found many verbal similarities between this address and the works of Jonson and concluded that Jonson probably wrote this address (1955, 17–21).

Another point to emerge upon consideration is that Condell and Heminges would have had no financial interest in the sales of the book. They had worked with Shakespeare as members of the King's Men and apparently collected the texts in manuscript. But it is very unlikely that they were offered a percentage of the sales of the First Folio. Yet the main purpose of their apparent address in the Shakespeare folio was to encourage readers to purchase the volume: "But, whatever you do, Buy." Chambers realised that the address was intended as an "advertisement, rather than an affidavit" (*WS* i, 144). Like Jonson's commendation, the address apparently signed by Heminges and Condell was composed to encourage readers to buy – and does not constitute personal evidence about Shakespeare by his colleagues in the King's Men.

The names of John Heminge and Henry Condell also appear at the end of the dedicatory epistle to the Incomparable Pair of Brethren, the earls of Pembroke and Montgomery. Various commentators have noticed the inconsistency between the epistle, in which readers are urged to buy, and the dedication, in which they claim that their sole intention was to preserve the memory of their friend. One reason to suspect Jonson's involvement in the dedicatory epistle is that it follows the classical model of Pliny's dedicatory epistle to Vespasian, prefixed to his *Natural History*: the author(s) of the Epistle in F1 had a high standard of Latin as the wording does not follow Philemon Holland's translation (1601). Malone (1790, i. ii. 99) thought it unlikely that Heminges and Condell would be responsible. Leah Scragg (1997) has argued in detail that it was the stationer, Edward Blount, who wrote the dedication. He held the copyright of sixteen Shakespeare plays and was responsible with William Jaggard for publishing the First Folio. He had published works by Jonson and had himself composed a number of dedications, including one for the 1598 translation of *Hero and Leander* and another for the 1632 collected edition of Lyly's plays. While Blount was an important stationer in the Jacobean period, he was not known as a publisher of Shakespeare's plays. Since Blount had no direct connection with Shakespeare and his works, there appears to be no biographical value in his (contribution to the) Dedication to Pembroke and Montgomery.

Holland, Digges, and Mabbe

The first stationer to include commendatory verses to promote a play in print was Edward Blount for Jonson's *Sejanus* in 1605. Jonson himself became the most prolific writer of literary puffs in the Jacobean period, writing commendations for thirty printed works (not counting his own). That there was an element of doubt about the sincerity of such commendations was expressed in the preface to the translation of *The Consolation of Philosophy* (1609):

> To the Reader: What need my lines to recommend these leaves, So frequently by learned hands perus'd, Since customarise praise suspicion weaves. For I mistrust a gorgeous Frontispiece, of mercenary penns.
>
> (signed by G.G.)

A similarly sardonic stance was adopted in an address preceding *The Bondman*, by Philip Massinger (1624): "By the Author's Friend: The Printers House Calls on. I must not drive My time past six though I begin at five" (signed W. B.).

There were only three other writers who contributed commendatory verses to the First Folio: Hugh Holland, Leonard Digges, and I. M., usually thought to be James Mabbe. While these writers had little or no connection with Shakespeare, all three, however, were known to Ben Jonson and to Edward Blount. Like Jonson, Hugh Holland attended Westminster and became a catholic convert. After travelling abroad, he returned to England and was a member of the Mermaid Club from about 1605. Holland wrote a number of commendations (over ten) including one for Ben Jonson's *Sejanus* in the 1605 quarto.[21] Holland's heavily alliterative sonnet in the First Folio has the rhyming scheme *abba abba cdcd ee* and concentrates on the popularity of Shakespeare's plays which "made the

Globe of heav'n and earth to ring." This is conventional praise for the works, not the man.

The third contributor of a literary puff for F1 was Leonard Digges, who also composed a second tribute to Shakespeare which was published in John Benson's 1640 edition of the poems. The earlier tribute is a 22-line poem, in which he advises Shakespeare that "thy Workes" shall outlive "thy tomb" and "thy Stratford Moniment." According to John Freehafer (1970, 63), Digges's commendations showed "unprecedented enthusiasm" for Shakespeare's works and his tributes "reveal an exceptional enthusiasm for those plays" – the beginnings of the excessive regard for Shakespeare which became known as bardolatry.[22] Leslie Hotson (1938. *I, William Shakespeare*) claimed that Digges was personally acquainted with Shakespeare in Stratford, as his widowed mother had married Shakespeare's friend, Thomas Russell. The view that Digges knew Shakespeare seemed to gain support in 1963 when a previously unknown handwritten note by Digges about Shakespeare was discovered. On the flyleaf of this book, which is a copy of *Rimas* by the Spanish poet Lope de Vega (published in 1613). According to Digges, Lope de Vega enjoyed as great a reputation for his sonnets in Spain as Shakespeare did in England. The comment is not dated but seems to have been written between 1613, when the work was published, and 1617, when Digges at least was back in England.

Freehafer accepts Hotson's suggestion that Digges was "associated with the Shakespeare circle in both Stratford and London" (63). Shakespeare certainly knew Thomas Russell as he appointed him one of the overseers to his will, and left him £5. It is not so clear if he knew his stepson. Thomas Russell (1570–1634) was already a widower when he married the widow Anne (née St. Leger) Digges in August 1603. The couple lived in the village of Alderminster (about five miles south of Stratford). Leonard (1588–1635) was her second son and entered University College Oxford early in the same year as her wedding, where he was deemed a very good scholar of the classics. After graduating in 1606, Leonard travelled to Spain with James Mabbe. For Shakespeare and Digges to know each other, they would have to have been visiting family in Stratford at the same time or Digges would have been spending time in London during his time at Oxford. So it seems likely that Shakespeare and Digges could have been anything more than slightly acquainted, if they were at all.

There may, however, be a different explanation for Digges's literary puff. The publisher Edward Blount was probably responsible for soliciting commendations for the 1623 folio from Leonard Digges, two of whose translations he had already published: Claudian *The Rape of Proserpine* (1617) and the Spanish novel *Gerardo, the Unfortunate Spaniard* (1622). *Gerardo* was dedicated to the same "incomparable paire of brethren" as the First Folio. In 1622, both Digges and Jonson contributed commendatory verses to James Mabbe's translation of Aleman's *The Rogue: Or the life of Guzman de Alfarache* (1623), also published by Blount. Thus Digges was widely involved with Blount, Jonson, and Mabbe in writing literary puffs. His poem in the *First Folio* might be attributed to the intervention of the publisher, and not therefore entirely genuine in his sentiments.

The fourth contributor of commendatory verses for the First Folio was I. M., who has been identified as James Mabbe, fellow of Magdalene College Oxford from 1594 to 1633.[23] Previous identifications with John Marston and Jaspar Mayne have now been discounted. There are three main reasons for identifying I. M. as Mabbe: first, like Jonson and Digges, he was writing commendations at about this time, including one for Florio's *Queen Anna's new World of Words*, which Blount had published in 1611. Second, he had a more recent association with Blount, who published his 1622 translation of *The Rogue* in 1622. Third, there is a similarity of phrasing with *The Rogue*. There, James Mabbe had written "that when the play's done, (which cannot be long) he must presently enter into the Tyring-house of the grave," the last phrase apparently a translation of "el vestuario del sepulcro." In I. M.'s tribute in F1, the poet wonders that Shakespeare went "so soone From the World's-Stage to the Graues-Tyring-roome."

Regarding the commendations as a whole, Sidney Lee (introduction to his 1902 facsimile) states that no comparable folio of the period was done in so slipshod a fashion or provided with so little commendatory verse. Ben Jonson's *Works* (1616) had a dozen commendatory verses by established writers such as Edward Hayward, George Chapman, and Francis Beaumont among others. James Mabbe's *The Rogue* (1622) was commended in eight sets of verses by five authors: Ben Jonson, Leonard Digges, I. F. (probably John Fletcher), William Browne, and Edward Burton. To conclude, the addresses signed by Heminge and Condell, and the commendations of Jonson, Holland, Digges, and Mabbe are open to doubt as to their sincerity and contribute little or no personal information about Shakespeare.

9.4 Jonson's *Timber or Discoveries* (1641)

Among the papers found after Jonson's death in 1637 were many judgements about contemporary writers, which were published under the title *Timber or Discoveries* in 1640–1641. This book consists of a collection of striking passages mainly from classical and continental authors (Donaldson 2011, 11–13). What is surprising is that within the dense text amounting almost to 50 folio pages, (originally numbered 85–132 inclusive), only one paragraph deals with Shakespeare. It is not known whether Jonson had collected these opinions together or whether it was the editor. The original printer gave it a marginal title "De Shakespeare nostrat." usually taken to mean "About our Shakespeare":

I remember the players have often mentioned it as an honour to Shakespeare, that in his writing (whatsoever he penned) he never blotted out a line. My answer hath been, "Would he had blotted a thousand," which they thought a malevolent speech. I had not told posterity this but for their ignorance who chose that circumstance to commend their friend by wherein he most faulted; and to justify mine own candour, for I loved the man, and do honour his memory on this side idolatry as much as any.

He was, indeed, honest, and of an open and free nature, had an excellent phantasy, brave notions, and gentle expressions, wherein he flowed with that facility that sometimes it was necessary he should be stopped. "*Sufflaminandus erat,*" as Augustus said of Haterius. His wit was in his own power; would the rule of it had been so, too.

Many times he fell into those things, could not escape laughter, as when he said in the person of Cæsar, one speaking to him, "Cæsar, thou dost me wrong." He replied, "Cæsar did never wrong but with just cause;" and such like, which were ridiculous.

But he redeemed his vices with his virtues. There was ever more in him to be praised than to be pardoned.[24]

These comments have been accepted as approval about Shakespeare. Schoenbaum states: "From Jonson, there can be no higher praise" (1987, 259). The comments, however, do not form a coherent view but contain contradictory estimations of Shakespeare's writing ability. They may well have been written down at different times.

There are four points about Shakespeare's ability, all of them derivative:

1 That he never blotted a line, which recalls the Epistle to the Reader signed by Heminges and Condell in Shakespeare's First Folio. Jonson sees the facility of composition as a fault, lacking revision and crafting.
2 His estimation of Shakespeare's character as "honest, and of an open and free nature" seems to derive from Iago's cynical view of Othello ("The Moor is of a free and open nature / That thinks men honest that but seem so" *Othello* 1.3. 398–99).
3 He criticises Shakespeare's prolixity and compares himself to the Emperor Augustus in wanting to stifle it.
4 He concludes with a generalisation from Seneca: "he redeemed his vices with his virtues."

Many critics, however, doubt that Jonson is praising Shakespeare as so many of the opinions are derived from Seneca the Elder's *Controversiae*. John Atkins (1952) reviewed literary criticism from the time of antiquity and observed: "Few things in critical history are indeed more remarkable than the use made of this volume of Seneca by Ben Jonson." Atkins refers to many of Jonson's opinions in *Discoveries* and cites the following as direct borrowings:[25]

Seneca's Controversiae	*Translation of Seneca*	*Jonson on Shakespeare*
Tanta erat illi uelocitas orationis, ut uitium fieret. itaque diuus Augustus optime dixit: Haterius noster sufflaminandus est... In sua potestate habebat ingenium, in aliena modum (4.7)	So fast was his speech, that it became a fault. As a result, the divine Augustus cleverly said: Our Haterius must be checked.... His wit (*ingenium*) was in his own power, its regulation under someone else's.	he flowed with that facility that sometimes it was necessary he should be stopped. "*Suffla-minandus erat,*" as Augustus said of Haterius. His wit was in his own power; would the rule of it had been so too!
Saepe incidebat in ea quae derisum effugere non possent. (4.10)	He often used to fall into those things which could not avoid derision...	Many times he fell into those things could not escape laughter.
redimebat tamen vitia virtutibus et persaepe plus habebat quod laudares quam cui ignosceres. (4.11)	However, he redeemed his vices with his virtues and frequently he had more to praise than to be pardoned.	But he redeemed his vices with his virtues. There was ever more in him to be praised than to be pardoned.

Overall, those few opinions which Jonson expressed about Shakespeare in *Discoveries* are derivative. As Jonson's comments about Shakespeare only consist of a very small fraction of his comments about other authors, it is impossible to maintain that Jonson professed admiration for Shakespeare.

There is further reason to doubt that Jonson admired Shakespeare. If imitation is the sincerest form of flattery, it is interesting that Jonson did not rate Shakespeare as a dramatist highly enough to have imitated his style. Whereas Shakespeare's plays involve "jumping o'er times, / Turning the accomplishment of many years / Into an hour-glass," Jonson proudly observed the unities in his own plays. Furthermore, in the prologue to *The Alchemist* (1610) he implicitly criticises Shakespeare for the overseas settings of his plays.

In addition, Jonson does not seem to have owned any copies of Shakespeare's works. Jonson had an extensive library, some of which was lost to a disastrous fire in 1623.[26] Nevertheless, he probably replaced many of these and added others, aided by the Earl of Pembroke's annual grant of £20. Over 200 books in 40 libraries have been identified as owned by Jonson (McPherson 1974).[27] Of these, McPherson found only nine books by English authors: Chaucer, Spenser, Daniel, Drayton, Fulke Greville, and Marston, but no copy of any work by Shakespeare. If Jonson's was expressing genuine admiration in the preliminary matter to the 1623 folio of Shakespeare's works, we might reasonable expect him to have owned a copy of this folio (and the F2 of 1632). However, McPherson found none.

Anecdotes which linked Jonson with Shakespeare did not emerge until both authors were dead. One story stating that one was the god-father to a son of the other concerned a pun on latten/Latin, was recorded in a book of over 600 jests recorded by Sir Nicholas L'Estrange (1629–1655), which states that Shakespeare was godfather to a son of Jonson and gave "a douzen good Lattin Spoones" (Harleian MS 6395, fo. 2r; *WS* ii. 243).[28] L'Estrange makes no further mention of Shakespeare. There are serious doubts about the historicity of the tale. In his will, Shakespeare mentions only one godson, William Walker, the son of a Stratford bailiff, Henry Walker, baptised in 1608. There is no mention of Ben Jonson or of his children. This anecdote is discarded by most biographers as the same story appeared in notebook *c.* 1657 by Thomas Plume with the roles of Shakespeare and Jonson reversed (*WS* ii. 247). The next anecdote was published after the Restoration by Thomas Fuller, who described the wit-combats between Shakespeare and Jonson in a laboured simile (1662, *History of the Worthies of England* iii. 284). John Ward reported a story about Shakespeare, Drayton, and Jonson in "a merry meeting, and it seems drank too hard" (Severn 1839, 1–24). Michael Drayton (1563–1631), however, was not known for his ale-house bravado: *The Returne from Parnassus* (*c.* 1601) satirises him for lacking "one true note of a Poet of our times, and that is this, hee cannot swagger it well in a Taverne, nor domi-nere in a hothouse" (Leishman 1949, 240). Although Drayton came from Hartshill near Atherstone, Warwks, about 30 miles north of Stratford, there is no other suggestion that they knew each other personally. Drayton wrote letters to Ben Jonson, William Drummond, and to others. Some of his works were collected and published in a folio edition in 1619, for which various other poets such as Jonson wrote commendatory verses. Drayton, however, did not write anything for Shakespeare's First Folio of 1623.

It is sometimes said that Shakespeare drank with Jonson and other companions at the Mermaid Tavern (e.g. Ackroyd 2005, 324). This myth cannot be traced earlier than Gifford's biography of Jonson (1816) and features strongly in historical fiction.[29] Shakespeare certainly knew the owner of the Mermaid, William Johnson, whom he named among the trustees of the recently-purchased Blackfriars Gatehouse in 1613 (*WS* ii. 154–58). There is no evidence, however, that Shakespeare ever attended the Mermaid (Shapiro 1950) or was ever part of the political club which met there (O'Callaghan, "Mermaid Club" in *ODNB* 2004). The earliest testimony that Shakespeare knew Jonson comes from an anecdote recorded by Nicholas Rowe in 1709, who believes that Jonson wrote a play which Shakespeare recommended "After this they were profess'd Friends; tho' I don't know whether the other [Jonson] ever made him an equal return of Gentleness and Sincerity" (Rowe 1709, i. xii). Rowe does not mention the authority for this anecdote, the place or time of the supposed encounter, nor does he state which play Jonson had shown Shakespeare. This story runs counter to the known method by which the Companies selected their plays (*WS* i. 95). Donaldson believes that the anecdote was invented to contrast the "imagined characters of Shakespeare and Jonson: the one, gracious, gentle, generous, gifted; the other surly, grudging, envious and ungrateful" (2011, 128). The posthumous anecdotes regarding Jonson and Shakespeare are not reliable as evidence that the two writers knew each other well or were even acquainted.

Overall, there is no firm basis for stating that Jonson and Shakespeare were ever known to each other personally. Shakespeare made no direct reference to Jonson and the possible references in Shakespeare's plays to Jonson's works are oblique and could have been intended for other authors. Jonson expressed more opinions about Shakespeare than any other contemporary did, but these comments concern the works and offer little indication of direct personal acquaintance. He clearly knew Shakespeare's plays well enough to criticise them both on stage and in private, but he does not seem to have known the person. There is no evidence either of a "close friendship" or of any "genial rivalry." As with Southampton, so with Jonson, the biographers of Shakespeare have imagined a relationship, which goes far beyond the existing evidence.

Notes

1 Anne Barton. "The One and Only." *New York Review of Books*, 11 May 2006, (collective Review of Shapiro, *1599*, Richard Wilson *Secret Shakespeare*, Clare Asquith *Shakespeare Hidden Beliefs*, Peter Ackroyd *Shakespeare*, David Ellis *That Man Shakespeare*).

2 Anne Barton. *Ben Jonson: Dramatist* (1984). Rosalind Miles. *Ben Jonson: His Life and Work* (1986). David Riggs. *Ben Jonson: A Life* (1989). W. David Kay. *Ben Jonson: A Literary Life* (1995). Ian Donaldson. *Ben Jonson, a Life* (2011). Donaldson also contributed the entry for Jonson in the *ODNB* (2004).

3 Jonson's plays were published as follows: *Every Man Out of His Humour* (1600), *Every Man in His Humour* (1601), *Cynthia's Revels* (1601), *The Poetaster* (1602), *Seianus His Fall* (1605), *Eastward Ho!* (with Chapman and Marston, 1605), *Volpone* (1607), and *The Case is Altered* (1609). *Catiline His Conspiracy* was published in 1611.

4 Jonson's first six masques were published as follows: *Arch's of Triumph* (with Dekker, 1604); *King James Royal Entertainment* (1604), *Hymenaei* (1606), *The Masque of Blackness* and *The Masque of Beauty*, and *The Masque of Queens* (1609).

5 Joseph Spence. *Observations, Anecdotes, and Characters of Books and Men*. London: John Murray (1820). page 81 in an entry for 1728).

6 Octavius Gilchrist. *An Examination of the Charges Maintained by Messrs. Malone, Chalmers and Others, of Ben Jonson's Enmity &c. Towards Shakspeare* (1808). William Gifford. "Proofs of Ben Jonson's Malignity, From the Commentators on Shakspeare." *The Works of Ben Jonson*, I (1816, ccxlix–ccxci).

7 G. Sarrazin. "Nym und Jonson." *Shakespeare Jahrbuch* 40 (1904, 213). Arthur Quiller-Couch, ed. *Merry Wives of Windsor.* Cambridge: Cambridge University Press (1921, xxxi). Henk Gras. "*Twelfth Night, Every Man Out Of His Humour*, and the Middle Temple Revels of 1597–98." *Modern Language Review* 84 (1989, 545–64). Janet Clare. "The Complexion of *Twelfth Night.*" *Shakespeare Survey* 58 (2005, 199–207).

8 Arthur Gray. *How Shakespeare Purged Johnson: A Problem Solved.* Cambridge: Heffer (1928). Henry David Gray. "The Date of Hamlet." *Journal of English and Germanic Philology* 31 (1932, 51–61).

9 Maura Elise Hametz. *Making Trieste Italian 1918–1954.* London: Boydell (2005, 11–12).

10 For the Court performances of 1604–1605, Jonson provided two plays: *EMI* and *EMO.* Seven plays of Shakespeare seem to have been performed: *Othello, Merry Wives, Measure for Measure, Comedy of Errors, Henry V, Love's Labour's Lost,* and *The Merchant of Venice (ES* ii. 211).

11 Russ McDonald. "Othello, Thorello, and the Problem of the Foolish Hero." *Shakespeare Quarterly* 30.1 (1979, 51–67). J. W. Lever, ed. *Every Man in His Humour.* Lincoln: University of Nebraska Press (1971, xxiv–xxvi).

12 Michael Neill, ed. *Othello.* Oxford: Oxford University Press (2006, 193). M. R. Ridley, ed. *Othello.* London: Methuen (Arden2, 1958). E. A. J. Honigmann, ed. *Othello.* London: Thomas Nelson (Arden3, 1998).

13 Gary Taylor. "Empirical Middleton: *Macbeth*, Adaptation and Authorship." *Shakespeare Quarterly* 65 (2014, 239–72). Gary Taylor et al. *The New Oxford Shakespeare: Complete Set* (Forthcoming).

14 In the Address to the Reader, Jonson wrote: Lastly, I would inform you, that this book, in all numbers, is not the same with that which was acted on the public stage; wherein a second: pen had good share: in place of which, I have rather chosen to put weaker, and no doubt, less pleasing, of mine own, than to defraud so happy a genius of his right by my loathed usurpation." Donaldson believes that the second pen was Chapman (2011, 472n).

15 Lynn E. Meskill. *Ben Jonson and Envy.* Cambridge: Cambridge University Press (2009). Marlin E. Blaine. "Envy, Eunoia and Ethos in Jonson's Poems on Shakespeare and Drayton." *Studies in Philology* 106 (2009, 441–45).

16 Antonio Minturno. *L'arte poetica del Signor Antonio Minturno.* Venice: Valvassori (1563, Quotation comes from Book 2 of the 1725 edition, published in Naples by Stamperia di G. Muzio, page 158).

17 J. E. Spingarn. *A History of Literary Criticism in the Renaissance.* New York: Columbia University Press (1899, 89n).

18 Thucydides, *The Peloponnesian War.* London: J. M. Dent (trans. E. P. Dutton, 1910, i. 22). Jonson had been taught Greek at Westminster School, so he did not need to wait until this work was first published in an English translation by Thomas Hobbes in 1628. Interestingly, Hobbes and Jonson were close friends (Donaldson 2011, 84–85; 409–10).

19 Wesley Trimpi. *Ben Jonson's Poems: A Study of the Plain Style.* Stanford, CA: Stanford University Press (1962, 148–52). T. J. B. Spencer. "Ben Jonson on His Beloved, the Author Mr. William Shakespeare." In *The Elizabethan Theatre IV,* ed. G. R. Hibbard. Hamden, CT: Archon Books (1974, 22–40). Richard Peterson. *Imitation and Praise in the Poems of Ben Jonson.* New Haven, CT: Yale University Press (1980, 158–94).

20 Peter Blayney. "Introduction to the Second Edition." In *The Norton Facsimile: The First Folio of Shakespeare* New York: Norton (1996, xxviii).

21 Colin Burrow. "Hugh Holland," *c.* 1563–1633 (*ODNB* 2004).

22 John Freehafer. "Leonard Digges, Ben Johnson, and the Beginning of Shakespeare Idolatry." *Shakespeare Quarterly* 21 (1970, 63–75).

23 Bolton Corney in 1861 was the first to identify I. M. as James Mabbe in "The Commendatory Verses of the First Folio Shakespeare." *Notes and Queries* 9, 3. A. W. Secord. "I. M. of the First Folio, Shakespeare, and other Mabbe Problems." *Journal of English and Germanic Philology*, 47 (1948, 374–81).

24 Paragraph breaks added; Ralph Walker, ed. *Ben Jonson: Timber; or, Discoveries* (1953, 52).

25 John Atkins. *Literary Criticism in Antiquity: A Sketch of Its Development.* London: Methuen (1952 ii. 154).

26 Jonson described the fire in his poem "Execration against Vulcan" in *The Underwood*, 43 (1640, 85–106).

27 The Folger Library adds: an updated version of McPherson's catalog has been included in the electronic version of *The Cambridge Edition of the Works of Ben Jonson.* . . . This catalog includes the whole list of books from McPherson (minus doubtful and spurious ones) and adds in newly discovered ones. Altogether there are 296 entries. Updated location information and, in many cases, more detailed descriptions of copies have been provided by Henry Woudhuysen. (This work seems to be a work-in-progress.)

With close to 300 titles, Ben Jonson's collection was one of the most important private libraries in England at the time. It was a working library consisting mainly of works of literature: Ben Jonson's trade. A fluent reader in Latin and somewhat proficient in Greek, he owned many editions of the Classics in these languages, as well as some translations into English. He also owned numerous books in the original English, but few in other vernacular languages.

Jonson's copies of classical texts came from the Continent, largely from Northern Europe, which indicates the presence of Continental book agents in London (from the Plantin firm for example) feeding the English market with such books. Interestingly, some of the same books returned to the Continent either after Jonson sold them (McPherson notes that the writer sometimes sold his books when he needed money) or after his death. (https://collation.folger.edu/2016/10/ben-jonsons-library/),

28 Sir Nicholas L'Estrange (*c.* 1650) '606 Jests & curious Stories':
"Shake=speare was Godfather to one of Ben: Johnson's children, and after the christning, being in a deepe study, Johnson came to cheere him vp, and askt him why he was so Melancholy? No faith Ben: (sayes he) not I, but I haue beene considering a great while what should be the fittest gift for me to bestow vpon my God=child, and I haue resolu'd at last; I pr'ythe what, sayes he? I faith Ben: I'le e'en giue him a douzen good Lattin spoones, and thou shalt translate them."
The anecdote may have been transferred to Jonson as a result of his assertion of Shakespeare's "small Latin and less Greek" in F1. Chambers gives it no credence (*WS* ii. 243).

29 Alfred Noyes's *Tales of the Mermaid Tavern* (1913); George Cronyn's *Mermaid Tavern: Kit Marlowe's Story* (1937); Shirley Barker's *Liza Bowe: A Novel of Elizabethan Times and the Mermaid Tavern* (1956); Robert Nye's *The Late Mr. Shakespeare* (1998); Patrick Page's play *Swansong* (2002); Robert Brustein's play *The English Channel* (2008).

Conclusions and Inconclusions

It is not possible to construct a biography of Shakespeare – a narrative account of his life – as there are insufficient documents. Personal notes, letters, and journals would have given insight into the thoughts, feelings, and motives of the poet and playwright but he left none. The few contemporaries who allude to him in letters, business notes and literary allusions give no insight whatsoever into the character and personality of the man. Moreover, there are three glaring sets of 'lost years' in the surviving records: his childhood and youth (from baptism to marriage at eighteen), his early adulthood (from the birth of his twin children to when he was paid as a member of the Chamberlain's Men; aged twenty to thirty) and in his maturity (aged forty to forty-eight). He remains a complete enigma. The recent flurry of such attempts at a biography of Shakespeare have depended on Schoenbaum's *Documentary Life* (1975), in which contextual description and intuition play a predominant part. To write his life story often involves making inference from the plays: whereas a literary biography usually explains how a writer came to compose his or her works, a biography of Shakespeare uses the works to inform the life.

In the two centuries after his birth, there was little interest in the life of Shakespeare. Certain anecdotes such as the deer-poaching story and the wits-combats with Jonson were repeated but are unlikely when scrutinised carefully. The earliest claims about Shakespeare's life, in Fuller's *Worthies* (1662) and Rowe's *Account* (1709) are mostly without foundation and were poorly valued by later writers. There was no serious attempt at a narrative account of Shakespeare's life until the publication of Charles Knight's highly fictionalised biography in 1843. Biographies began to emerge in the late twentieth century for a variety of reasons: first because publishers realise that the reading public has an endless fascination with the man due to his iconic status. Second, many people enjoy the novelistic approach to reading the life story, interspersed with a few famous quotations. Third, the traditional view of Shakespeare is akin to Dick Whittington, a rags-to-riches story of a young man from a small provincial town – a man without independent wealth, without powerful family connections and without a university education – moves to London in the late 1580s and, in a remarkably short time, becomes the greatest playwright not only of his age alone but for all time. A New Historicist approach is welcome and enlightening for the study of Shakespeare's works but only so far as suitable primary sources exist and causal connections can be made. Reasons given for writing a biography of Shakespeare include claims of new research, never involving Shakespeare directly, and the presentation of new interpretations – based of course on the latest writer's superior knowledge. The very lack of biographical materials allows biographers to indulge their own narrative flair and imaginative insight, usually within Schoenbaum's life trajectory. Such biographers are unhampered by the need for extensive preliminary reading, as in the case of a life of Ben Jonson.

Since 1975, there has been some skepticism regarding the prospect of writing the life of Shakespeare. Notable among these are two monographs by David Ellis in 2005 and 2012, and one by Graham Holderness (1988, 2001, and 2011). In addition, Helen Hackett (2009) has demonstrated a very cautious approach in considering those myths which have linked Shakespeare with Elizabeth. Many other excellent reevaluations of Shakespeare myths have been advanced: Laurie Maguire and Emma Smith (2012) considered myths surrounding Shakespeare's life, as well as other myths concerning his works and his reputation.

The works of Shakespeare are an essential element of our culture and the implications of my findings are important for almost the full range of Shakespearean criticism. Every editor of a Shakespeare play or poem, and every director of a theatrical production, includes a section on the date of composition, invariably choosing a date suggested by Chambers and reaffirmed by Wells and Taylor, despite the lack of direct evidence. These chronologies are arbitrary and subjective: they depend on the undocumented assumption that Shakespeare started to compose plays in the early 1590s. The date of composition thus assigned is then considered for resonance in Shakespeare's personal life, echoes of contemporary events in London and a literary debt to sources. It is possible, however, to assign earlier dates, perhaps by as much as five years, to Shakespeare's plays. One of the few editors who admitted to doubt was Edward Burn: in his introduction to *1 Henry VI* (Arden3, 2000), he reminds his readers of important limitations: "We should always bear in mind the paucity and obliquity of the contemporary documentation of Elizabethan theatre. Any supposition that we build on such 'evidence' must be precarious."

There seems no prospect of an end to speculative accounts of Shakespeare's life. Both publishers and authors seem assured of a title that will sell. Works of historical fiction by Dame Hilary Mantel and Philippa Gregory are widely read and admired, even though there are considerable more sources for the historical figures they depict than there are for Shakespeare. However, historical fiction concerning Shakespeare (e.g. by Robert Nye and Gary Blackwood) does not enjoy such prestige as a work entitled "biography." Thus many academics present their own work as biography rather than as fiction.

My most important recommendation is that those who wish to adopt a biographical approach to Shakespeare should follow Schoenbaum and beware the biographical fallacy of pretending to deduce details about a writer's life from the works; instead, the investigator should only undertake skeptical examination of topics for which there are primary sources. It is important not to accept the opinion of previous editors or merely to refer to evidence which respected predecessors have used or even to offer a summary of the sources. Instead, it is essential to restate the primary sources (showing where a full transcription can be found) before undertaking an analysis of the topic in question. To some extent, this has been undertaken by the more skeptical of modern scholars. Any picture of Shakespeare will thus be very limited, but will have the merit of being historically based and verifiable, and not simply biografiction. My second recommendation is that writers who wish to present a single and consistent view of Shakespeare as man and as writer should use historical fiction. My third recommendation is that those who admire the works of Shakespeare should accept that little is known about Shakespeare: in other words they should take to heart the view of Sir Edmund Chambers (*WS* i. 26): "after all the careful scrutiny of clues and all the patient balancing of possibilities [regarding Shakespeare], the last word of self-respecting scholarship must be that of nescience."

Appendix A

The Records for William Shakespeare

The following documents the mention of the name William Shakespeare in records dated between 1564 and 1616. In total there are about 80 manuscript records and about 16 unofficial, hand-written references to Shakespeare in his lifetime. There are 18 references in print, plus about 46 attributions on printed works. This outline does not take into account allusions to the plays or poems.

References:

WS   Chambers. E. K. 1930. 2vols. *William Shakespeare: A Study of Facts and Problems.*

PRO   Thomas, D. 1964. *Shakespeare in the Public Records.* Document Numbers.

SSR   Bearman, Robert. 1994. *Shakespeare in the Stratford Records.*

Shakespeare in the Stratford Records

Robert Bearman (*SSR*) states that there are 30 or 31 documents in Stratford which refer by name to William Shakespeare up until his burial. Further documents which may also refer to Shakespeare are reported by Chambers (*WS*). There are thus about 35–40 documents relating to William Shakespeare in Stratford.

1564	Baptism 'Guliemus filius Johannes Shakspere' Holy Trinity Church, Stratford (*SSR* 1a).
1582	Licence for Marriage for 'Willelmum Shaxpere' to Anna Whately; Surety for Marriage for 'Willm Shagspere' to Anne Hathawey; Bishop of Worcester's Register (*WS* ii. 41).
1583	Baptism of Susanna 'daughter to William Shakspere' (*SSR* 1b).
1585	Baptism of 'Hamnet & Judeth sonne & daughter to William Shakspere' (*SSR* 1c).
1596	Burial, Hamnet filius 'William Shakspere'. Holy Trinity Church, Stratford (*SSR* 1d).

1597	Purchase of New Place for £60 from William Underhill (*SSR* 2).
1597	Stratford Corporation Payment for stone to 'Mr. Shakespere' [? father or son] (*SSR* 31).
1598	Letter from Abraham Sturley to Richard Quiney about 'Mr. Shaksper' (*SSR* 3).
1598	Stratforde Burrowghe, noate of corn and malt: 'Wm. Shackespere. x [10] quaerts' (*SSR* 4).
1598	Letter to 'Wm. Shackespere' from Richard Quiney requesting loan of £30 (*SSR* 5).
1598	Letter from Adrian Quiney to his son, Richard Quiney about 'Mr Sha' (*SSR* 6).
1598	Letter from Abraham Sturley to Richard Quiney about our countriman 'Mr Wm Shak' (*SSR* 7).
1601	Will of Thomas Whittington lists a debt of "xls [40 shillings] that is in the hand of Anne Shaxspere wyffe unto Mr Wyllyam Shaxspere" (*WS* ii. 42).
1602	conveyance of 107 acres of arable land and 20 acres of pasture to 'William Shakespeare' from William and John Combe (*SSR* 8).
1602	counterpart of document of conveyance of 107 acres of arable land (*SSR* 9).
1602	Transfer of cottage in Chapel Lane, Stratford from Walter Getley to Shakespeare (*SSR* 10)
1604	Survey of Rowington Manor confirms 'William Shakespere lykewise holdeth there one cottage' (*WS* ii. 112).
1604	Stratford Court of Record: 'Willielmus Shexpere' sued the apothecary Philip Rogers (*SSR* 11).
1605	Assignment of an interest in a lease of Tithe Lands to 'William Shakespear' from Ralph Hubaude (*SSR* 12).
1605	Ralph Hubaud's Bond of £80 with 'Willielmo Shakespear' (*SSR* 13).
1605	Draft of assignment of an interest in a lease of Tithe Lands from Ralph Hubaude (*SSR* 14).
1606	Inventory of Ralph Hubaud's property showing 'Mr. Shakspre' owed xxli (*Calendar of Worcester Wills*).
1608–1609	Court of Record for Stratford (seven documents). Addenbrooke suit (*SSR* 15–21)
1609	Conveyance of a Property adjoining a property of Shakespeare in Henley Street (*SSR* 22).
1611	Shakespeare's name added to List of 71 Contributors to a Highways Bill (*SSR* 23).
1611	Draft Bill of Complaint confirms Shakespeare's lease of the tithes of Stratford (*SSR* 24).

1611	Inventory of goods of Robert Johnson states he held a barn of Mr Shaxper (*WS* ii. 32).
1612	Survey of Stratford Corporation records Shakespeare as tithe tenant (*SSR* 25).
1613	Conveyance of property in Henley Street, next to a property of Shakespeare (*SSR* 26).
1614	Thomas Greene notes Mr Shakspeare among Freeholders in Oldstratford and Welcombe and mentions him on four other occasions (*SSR* 27 & 29).
1614	Welcombe Enclosure: covenant with William Replingham (*SSR* 28).
1603–1616	Endorsement on lease of a barn beside Mr William Shaxpeare's property (*SSR* 30).
1616	Burial of 'Will. Shakspere, Gent' (*SSR* 1e).

Shakespeare in Official London Records

Document Numbers follow D. Thomas, (1964) *Shakespeare in the Public Records*. Thomas lists 28 documents which mention Shakespeare. Of these, two do not mention him by name and four date from after his death. There are a few other public documents in London which mention William Shakespeare in his lifetime, about 25 in total.

1588–1589	Court of King's Bench: mentioned in Bill of Complaint about Estate at Wilmecote: (*PRO* 1).
1595	Treasurer of the Queen's Chamber paid £20 to Kempe, 'Will Shakespeare' and Burbage as members of the Lord Chamberlain's Men (*PRO* 2).
1596	Court of King's Bench: 'William Shakspere' bound over in in Writ of Attachment made by Francis Langley (*PRO* 3).
1597	Purchase of New Place by 'Willielmus Shakespeare' from Thomas Underhill (*PRO* 9).
1597	'William Shackspere' listed among tax defaulters in St. Helen's Parish, Bishopsgate (*PRO* 4).
1598	'Willelmus Shakespeare' listed as tax defaulter in St. Helen's Parish, Bishopsgate (*PRO* 5).
1599	'Willelmus Shakepeare' listed as tax defaulter in Bishopsgate (*PRO* 6).
1599	Shakespeare listed as tax defaulter in St. Helen's Parish, Bishopsgate (*PRO* 7).
1599	Thomas Brend's post-mortem inventory mentions 'Shakespeare' at the Globe (*PRO* 10).

1600	'Willelmus Shakspeare' in Lord Treasurer's Remembrancer as tax defaulter (*PRO* 8).
1600	Stationers' Register: 'Henry iiij... written by Mr Shakespere' (*WS* i. 377).
1602	Confirmation that 'Willielmum Shakespeare' purchased New Place in 1597 (*PRO* 14).
1602	York Herald mentions 'Shakespear ye Player by Garter' in a complaint about issuing of arms (*WS* ii. 22).
1603	Warrant for Letters Patent: 'Wilielmum Shakespeare' was listed as one of King's Men (*PRO* 15).
1603	Letters Patent: 'Wilielmum Shakespeare' listed as one of King's Men (*PRO* 16).
1604	Master of the Great Wardrobe grants red cloth to 'William Shakespeare' and others (*PRO* 17).
1604	Survey of Rowington lists 'William Shakespere' as property holder (*PRO* 18).
1604–1605	Revels' Accounts mentions 'Shaxberd' four times as the author in connection with performance of plays (*PRO* 21).
1605	Augustine Phillips bequeaths 30s. 'to my ffellowe william Shakespeare' (*WS* ii. 73).
1606	Exchequer, Land Revenue lists Shakespeare as property holder in Rowington (*PRO* 19).
1607	Stationers' Register: 'Master William Shakespeare his historye of Kynge Lear' (*WS* i. 463).
1608	Stationers' Register: 'A Yorkshire Tragedy by Wylliam Shakespere' (*WS* i. 535).
1609	Stationers' Register: 'a booke called Shakespeares sonnettes' (*WS* i. 556).
1610	Confirmation of land purchase by 'Shakespere' from William and John Combe in 1602 (*PRO* 24).
1611–1612	Revels' Accounts mentions two plays of Shakespeare but not him by name (*PRO* 22).
1612	Bellott-Mountjoy Case: Shakespeare is mentioned 18 times in 25 documents (*PRO* 25).
1613	Payment for an Impresa to Mr. Shakespeare (*WS* ii. 153).
1613	Purchase of Blackfriars Gatehouse for £140; mortgaged to Henry Walker (*PRO* 26).
1613	Bequest of five pounds by John Combe to Mr William Shackspere (*WS* ii. 127).
1615	King's Bench. Shakespeare mentioned as Sharer in Globe in case Ostler v Heminges (*PRO* 11).
1615	Mentioned in Bill of Complaint by Sir Thomas Bendish regarding Blackfriars (*PRO* 27).

1616	Last will and testament of William Shackspeare (*PRO* 28).
1617	Court Roll of Rowington confirms transfer of property to Susanna and John Hall (*PRO* 20).
1619–1620	Court of Requests mentions Shakespeare in case Witter v. Heminges and Condell (seven documents, *PRO* 12).
1632	Court of Requests: Cuthbert Burbage mentions Shakespeare as sharer in the Globe (*WS* ii. 67).
1635	Lord Chamberlain's Department. Cuthbert Burbage mentions Shakespeare (*PRO* 13).
1636–1637	Warrants from Lord Chamberlain mentions three plays of Shakespeare, but not him by name (*PRO* 23).

Unofficial, Manuscript References to Shakespeare

In addition to the six references listed in the Stratford section, there are about ten unofficial, hand-written references to Shakespeare in his lifetime.

1593	H. B. in *Willobie His Avisa* refers to Shakespeare (*WS* ii. 191).
1598–1603	Northumberland Manuscript contains unsigned scribbles, mentioning Shakespeare on various occasions (*WS* ii 196–97).
1598–1601	Gabriel Harvey in a manuscript note in a copy of Speght's translation of *Chaucer* (1598) mentions Shakespeare (*WS* ii. 196).
1599–1601	*The Returne from Parnassus* I and II mentions Shakspeare nine times (*WS* ii. 199–201).
1599–1605	'W. Shakespear' mentioned in an anonymous manuscript note in *The Pinner of Wakefield*, attributed to Robert Greene (*WS* ii. 201).
1601	Francis Davison's note in *Catalog of the Poems contayned in Englands Helicon* (*WS* i. 372).
1602	John Manningham in his diary reports an anecdote about Burbage and Shakespeare (*WS* ii. 212).
1613–1635	Leonard Digges in a manuscript note in a copy of Lope de Vega's *Rimas* mentions Shakespeare (*Shakespeare Survey* 16, 1963).
1614	William Drummond mentions Shakespeare (from notes published in 1711, *WS* ii. 220).
1615	F. B. [Francis Beaumont] in a poem to Ben Jonson mentions Shakespeare (*WS* ii. 222).
1618–1621	Edmund Bolton lists Shakespeare in his manuscript for *Hypercritica* (*WS* ii. 225).
1616–1633	William Basses's poem on the death of Wm Shakespeare (*WS* ii. 226).

References in Print to Shakespeare

There are about 18 references to Shakespeare in print until the end of 1616.

1592	Robert Greene's *Groatsworth of Wit* mentions a 'Shake-scene' (*WS* ii. 188).
1595	Thomas Covell in *Polimanteia* refers to 'sweet Shak-speare' (*WS* ii. 193).
1598	Richard Barnfield in *A Remembrance of Some English Po-ets* mentions Shakespeare (*WS* ii. 195).
1598	Francis Meres in *Palladis Tamia* mentions Shakespeare among others (*WS* ii. 193–95).
1599	John Weever dedicates one epigram (out of 160) to 'Honie-tong'd *Shakespeare*' (*WS* ii. 199).
1600	John Bodenham mentions Shakespeare once in his Epis-tle to *Bel-vedere or The Garden of the Muses* (*WS* ii. 211).
1600–1604	Anthony Scoloker in *Daiphantus, or the Passions of Love* refers to 'friendly Shake-speare's tragedies' (*WS* ii. 214).
1603	In *A Mourneful Dittie, entituled Elizabeths Losse*, Shakespeare is listed with Johnson and Greene (*WS* ii. 212).
1603–1625	I. C.[John Cooke] in *Epigrames* lists Shakespeare with Johnson and Greene (*WS* ii. 212).
1605	William Camden (1551–1623) in *Remaines of a greater Worke concerning Britaine* mentions Shakespeare (*WS* ii. 215).
1607	William Barksted in *Myrrha* mentions Shakespeare (*WS* ii. 216).
1612	John Webster in his *Epistle to The White Devil* mentions Shakespeare among others (*WS* ii. 218).
1614	Richard Carew on the *Excellencie of the English Tongue* mentions Shakespeare (*WS* ii. 219).
1614	Thomas Freeman in *Runne and a Great Cost* writes a son-net to Shakespeare (*WS* ii. 220).
1615	Edmund Howes in his continuation of Stow's *Annals* men-tions Shakespeare (*WS* ii. 221).
1615	Thomas Porter in his book of epigrams mentions Shake-speare (*WS* ii. 222).
1616	In *The workes of Beniamin Ionson*, Shakespeare is men-tioned on lists of actors for *Every Man in his Humour* and for *Sejanus* (*WS* ii. 71).

Publications Attributed to Shakespeare

There were about 46 publications attributed to Shakespeare by the end of 1616, either in quarto or in octavo. Twelve works are attributed to Shakespeare on their earliest known printing. Some works, e.g. *Richard II*, were published anonymously at first. Other works are thought to use Shakespeare as a pseudonym, e.g. *The Passionate Pilgrim*. A few remain doubtful as to their attribution, e.g. *Troublesome Raigne of King John*.

1593   Q1 *Venus*

1594   Q2 *Venus*; O1 *Lucrece*

1596   O3 *Venus*

1598   O2 *Lucrece*; Q1 *Love's Labour's Lost*; Q2 *1 Henry IV*; Q2, Q3 *Richard II*, Q2 *Richard III*.

1599   O4 *Venus*; O1 *Passionate Pilgrim*; Q3 *1 Henry IV*.

1600   O3 *Lucrece*; Q1 *2 Henry IV*; Q1 *MN Dream*; Q1 *Merchant of Venice*; Q *Much Ado*; *Sir John Oldcastle*.

1601   'The Phoenix and the Turtle' attributed to 'William Shake-speare' in Robert Chester's *Loves martyr: or, Rosalins complaint*.

1602   O5 *Venus*; Q1 *Merry Wives of Wndsor*; Q3 *Richard III*.

1603   Q1 *Hamlet*.

1604   Q2 *Hamlet*; Q4 *1 Henry IV*.

1605   Q4 *Richard III*.

1607   O6 *Venus*; O4 *Lucrece*.

1608   O7 *Venus*; Q1 *King Lear*; Q4 *Richard II*; Q5 *1 Henry IV*; *A Yorkshire Tragedy*.

1609   Q *Sonnets*; Q1, *Troilus*; Q1, Q2 *Pericles*.

1610   O8 *Venus*.

1611   Q3 *Hamlet*; Q3 *Pericles*; Q2 *Troublesome Raigne*,

1612   O2 *Passionate Pilgrim*; Q5 *Richard III*.

1613   Q6 *1 Henry IV*.

1615   Q5 *Richard II*.

1616   O5 *Lucrece*.

1617   O9 *Venus*.

1619   Q3 *Contention*, Q3 *True Tragedie*, Q4 *Pericles*, Q2 *Merry Wives*, Q2 *Merchant*, Q2 *Lear*, Q2 *MND*. (Pavier Quartos); *A Yorkshire Tragedy*.

1620   O10 *Venus*.

1622   Q1 *Othello*, Q6 *Richard III*, Q7 *1 Henry IV*, Q3 *Troublesome Raigne*, Q4 *Hamlet?* Q4 *Romeo?*

1623   First Folio (36 plays).

Unattributed Publications

The following plays, published without attributing an author, have at various times been considered Shakespeare's plays

1591   **Q1** *Troublesome Raigne of King John.*
1594   **Q1** *Titus Andronicus;* **Q1** *The First Part of the Contention* [*2 Henry VI*]; **Q1** *Taming of a Shrew.*
1595   **O1** *The True Tragedie of Richard Duke of York* [*3 Henry VI*].
1597   **Q1** *Richard II;* **Q1** *Richard III;* **Q1** *Romeo & Juliet.*
1599   **Q2** *Romeo & Juliet.*
1600   **Q1** *Henry V;* **Q2** *Titus Andronicus;* **Q2** *The First Part of the Contention;* **Q2** *The True Tragedie of Richard Duke of York* [*3 Henry VI*].
1602   **Q2** *Henry V.*
1609   **Q3** *Romeo & Juliet.*
1611   **Q3** *Titus Andronicus;*
1619   **Q3** *Henry V.*

Appendix B
Rowe's Biographical Comments about Shakespeare

Rowe's *Account* originally contained about 8,200 words, most of which concern his judgement as to Shakespeare's merit. Only the following extracts amounting to about 1,020 words are biographical (approx. 12% of the total). Alexander Pope reprinted Rowe's essay in 1725 but omitted sections amounting to about 1,165 words, none of which refer to Shakespeare's life. Thus the biographical content of the abridged version is about 1,000 words out of 7,000, about 14% of the total. Margreta de Grazia (in "Shakespeare's anecdotal character" *Shakespeare Survey* 2015, 1–14) agrees that Rowe's anecdotes "are less a form of biography than of literary criticism: they record not the life Shakespeare lived between 1564 and 1616 but the impression his works made after his death." (Paragraph numbers have been added in brackets.)

Some Acount of the Life &c. of Mr. William Shakespear by Nicholas Rowe

(2) He was the Son of Mr. *John Shakespear*, and was Born at *Stratford* upon *Avon*, in *Warwickshire*, in *April* 1564. His Family, as appears by the Register and Publick Writings relating to that Town, were of good Figure and Fashion there, and are mention'd as Gentlemen. His Father, who was a considerable Dealer in Wool, had so large a Family, ten Children in all that tho' he was his eldest Son, he could give him no better Education than his own Employment. He had bred him, 'tis true, for some time at a Free-School, where 'tis probable he aquir'd that little *Latin* he was Master of: But the narrowness of his Circumstances, and the want of his assistance at Home, forc'd his Father to withdraw him from thence, and unhappily prevented his further Proficiency in that Language.

Upon his leaving School, he seems to have given entirely into that way of Living which his Father propos'd to him; and in order to settle in the World after a Family manner, he thought fit to marry while he was yet very Young. His Wife was the Daughter of one *Hathaway*, said to have been a substantial Yeoman in the Neighbourhood of *Stratford*. In this kind of Settlement he continu'd for some time, 'till an Extravagance that he was guilty of, forc'd him both out of his Country and that way of Living which he had taken up;

and tho' it seem'd at first to be a Blemish upon his good Manners, and a Misfortune to him, yet it afterwards happily prov'd the occasion of exerting one of the greatest **Genius's** that ever was known in Dramatick Poetry. He had, by a Misfortune common enough to young Fellows, fallen into ill Company; and amongst them, some that made a frequent practice of Deer-stealing, engag'd him with them more than once in robbing a Park that belong'd to **Sir Thomas Lucy** of **Cherlecot**, near **Stratford**. For this he was prosecuted by that Gentleman, as he thought, somewhat too severely; and in order to revenge that ill Usage, he made a Ballad upon him. And tho' this, probably the first Essay of his Poetry, be lost, yet it is said to have been so very bitter, that it redoubled the Prosecution against him to that degree, that he was oblig'd to leave his Business and Family in **Warwickshire**, for some time, and shelter himself in **London**.

(3) It is at this Time, and upon this Accident, that he is said to have made his first Acquaintance in the Play-house. He was receiv'd into the Company then in being, at first in a very mean Rank; But his admirable Wit, and the natural Turn of it to the Stage, soon distinguished him, if not as an extraodinary Actor, yet as an excellent Writer.

...the top of his Performance was the Ghost in **Hamlet**.

[Pope added: "The highest date of any I can yet find is *Romeo and Juliet* in 1597, when the author was thirty-three years old, and *Richard the 2d* and *3d* in the next year, viz. the 34th of his age."]

The Queen was pleas'd to command him to alter it; upon which he made use of *Falstaff*.

What Grace soever the Queen confer'd upon him, it was not to her only he ow'd the Fortune which the Reputation of his Wit made. He had the Honour to meet with many great and uncommon Marks of Favour and Friendship from the Earl of *Southampton*, famous in the Histories of that Time for his Friendship to the unfortunate Earl of *Essex*. It was to that Noble Lord that he Dedicated his *Venus* and *Adonis*, the only Piece of his Poetry which he ever publish'd himself, tho' many of his Plays were surrepticiously and lamely Printed in his Lifetime. There is one Instance so singular in the Magnificence of this Patron of *Shakespear*'s, that if I had not been assur'd that the Story was handed down by Sir *William D'Avenant*, who was probably very well acquainted with his Affairs, I should not have ventur'd to have inserted, that my Lord *Southampton*, at one time, gave him a thousand Pounds, to enable him to go through with a Purchase which he heard he had a mind to.

(11) The latter Part of his Life was spent, as all Men of good Sense will wish theirs may be, in Ease, Retirement, and the Conversation of his Friends. He had the good Fortune to gather an Estate equal to his Occasion, and, in that, to his Wish; and is said to have spent some Years before his Death at his native **Stratford**. His pleasurable Wit, and

good Nature, engag'd him in the Acquaintance, and entitled him to the Friendship of the Gentlemen of the Neighbourhood. Amongst them, it is a Story almost still remember'd in that Country, that he had a particular Intimacy with Mr. *Combe*, an old Gentleman noted thereabouts for his Wealth and Usury: It happen'd, that in a pleasant Conversation amongst their common Friends, Mr. Combe told Shakespear in a laughing manner, that he fancy'd, he intended to write his Epitaph, if he happen'd to out-live him; and since he could not know what might be said of him when he was dead, he desir'd it might be done immediately.

(12) He Dy'd in the 53d Year of his Age, and was bury'd on the North side of the Chancel, in the Great Church at Stratford, where a Monument, as engrav'd in the Plate, is plac'd in the Wall. On his Grave-Stone underneath is,

> *Good Friend, for Jesus sake, forbear*
> *To dig the Dust enclosed here.*
> *Blest be the Man that spares these Stones,*
> *And Curst be he that moves my Bones.*

He had three Daughters of which two liv'd to be marry'd; *Judith*, the Elder, to one Mr. *Thomas Quiney*, by whom she had three Sons, who all dy'd without Children; and *Susannah*, who was his Favourite, to Dr. *John Hall*, a Physician of good reputation in that Country. She left one Child only, a Daughter, who was marry'd first to *Thomas Nash*, Esq; and afterwards to Sir *John Bernard* of *Abbington*, but dy'd likewise without Issue.

Appendix C
Jonson's Censure of the English Poets

In the following extract Drummond reports Jonson's censure of about eighteen contemporary writers, showing special acquaintance with Donne but not with Shakespeare. *The Works of William Drummond of Hawthornden*. Eds John Sage & Thomas Ruddiman. Scotland: James Watson, 1711, 225–26.

That **Sidney** did not keep a Decorum in making every one speak as well as himself. **Spencer's** Stanza's pleased him not, nor his Matter; the Meaning of the Allegory of his Fairy Queen he had delivered in Writing to Sir **Walter Rawleigh**, which was, That by the bleating Beast he understood the Puritans, and by the false Duessa the Queen of Scots. He told, That **Spencer's** Goods were robbed by the Irish, and his House and a little Child burnt, he and his Wife escaped, and after died for want of Bread in Kingstreet; he refused 20 Pieces sent him by my Lord Essex, and said he was sure he had no Time to spend them. **Samuel Daniel** was a good honest Man, had no Children, and was no Poet; and that he had wrote the Civil Wars, and yet hath not one Battle in all his Book. That **Michael Drayton's** Polyolbion, if he had performed what he promised, to write the Deeds of all the Worthies, had been excellent. That he was challenged for intituling one Book Mortimariades. That **Sir John Davis** played on Drayton an Epigram, who in his Sonnet concluded his Mistress might have been the Ninth Worthy, and said, he used a Phrase like Dametas in Arcadia, who said, his Mistriss, for Wit, might be a Giant. That **Silvesters** Translation of Du Bartas was not well done, and that he wrote his Verses before he understood to confer; and these of **Fairfax** were not good. That the Translations of Homer and Virgil in long Alexandrines were but Prose. That when **Sir John Harrington** desired him to tell the Truth of his Epigrams, he answered him, That he loved not the Truth, for they were Narrations, not Epigrams. He said, **Donne** was originally a Poet, his Grandfather on his Mother Side was **Heywood** the Epigrammatist. That Donne for not being understood would perish. He esteemed him the first Poet of the World for some Things; his Verses on the lost Ochadine he had by Heart, and that Passage of the Calm, That Dust and Feathers did not stir, all was so quiet. He affirmed that Donne wrote all his best pieces before he was twenty five Years of Age. That Conceit of Donne's Transformation or [Greek: Metempsychosis], was, that he sought the Soul of that Apple which Eva pulled, and thereafter made it the Soul of a Bitch, then of a She-wolf, and so of a Woman: His general Purpose was to have brought it into all the Bodies of the Hereticks from the Soul of Cain; and at last left it in the Body of Calvin. He only wrote one Sheet of this, and since he was made Doctor; repented hugely, and resolved to destroy all his Poems. He told Donne, That his Anniversary was prophane and full of Blasphemies, that if it had been written of the Virgin Mary, it had been tolerable. To which Donne answered, That he described the Idea of a Woman, and not as she was. He said, **Shakespeare** wanted Art and sometimes Sense; for in one of his Plays he brought in a Number of Men, saying they had suffered Shipwrack in Bohemia, where is no Sea near by 100 Miles. That **Sir Walter Rawleigh** esteemed more Fame than Conscience: The best Wits in England were imployed in making his History. Ben himself had written a Piece Ground for an Heroick Poem, as King Arthur's Fiction; and that **Sir P. Sidney** had an Intention to have transformed all his Arcadia to the Stories of King Arthur. He said, **Owen** was a poor Pedantick Schoolmaster, sweeping his Living from the Posteriors of little Children, and has nothing good in him, his Epigrams being bare Narrations. **Francis Beaumont** died before he was thirty Years of Age, who, he said, was a good Poet, as were **Fletcher** and **Chapman**, whom he loved. That **Sir William Alexander** was not half kind to him, and neglected him, because a friend to Drayton. That **Sir R. Ayton** loved him dearly. He fought several Times with **Marston**, and says, That Marston wrote his Father-in-Law's Preachings, and his Father-in-law his Comedies.

Appendix D

Shakespeare as Co-Author: Some Scenarios

There has been much research over the years to show that Shakespeare did not compose the works entirely on his own. However, only one play, *Two Noble Kinsmen*, named a co-author (Fletcher), but that was published in 1634, eighteen years after his death. Sir Brian Vickers in *Shakespeare Co-Author* (2002) sets out a detailed case for collaboration with various authors. Recently, Gary Taylor has announced further candidates for co-authoring, especially Middleton with the Scottish play and Marlowe on the *Henry VI* trilogy. Both Vickers and Taylor feel confident that they can define substantial sections in a play as being authored separately.

So how might co-authorship have worked? The answer is: we do not know as we have no records of how the writers actually co-operated. Among Shakespeare's biographers, only Lois Potter (2012) has even suggested where and when Shakespeare might have worked alongside another author. Here are some scenarios.

1   Joint planning; same room. This scenario involves the authors deciding on a subject and its treatment, with allocation of different sections, before settling down to develop a play. For TV shows in Britain, comedy writers often work closely in pairs, e.g. Richard Curtis & Ben Elton (on *Blackadder*) but nobody has ever suggested that one author was solely responsible for one section, or even for one character. So it would seem unlikely that Shakespeare was working alongside a co-author as there would be more cross-contributions from one author to another author's section, making it impossible to identify different contributors.

2   Joint Planning; different locations. This scenario involves an initial agreement between authors on a subject and its dramatic treatment, with allocation of different sections, but with separate writing at different locations and / or different times. Such a scenario makes sense of the different sections, but not of the notable discrepancies between the action and characterisation in different parts of the plays.

3   Shakespeare began his career by revising the work of others. Shakespeare has often been cited as the reviser of plays by other authors. In this scenario, Shakespeare need not have met or known the other author but began adapting plays from about 1591, including *Troublesome Raigne of King John* (Q 1591); *First Part of the Contention* (Q 1594); *True Tragedie of Richard Duke of York* (O 1595) *Famous Victories of Henry V* (1598), *King Lear* and of course *Hamlet*. An alternative view is that Shakespeare composed the shorter versions for the stage and later revised them into longer versions for publication (Erne *Shakespeare as a Literary Dramatist* 2003).

4   Henslowe regularly paid for the plays of dramatists such as Marlowe to be revised by other playwrights.[1] Similarly, Shakespeare might have left some shorter plays which theatre managers, perhaps much later, paid to have extended, including *Titus Andronicus* (Peele), *Pericles* (Wilkins), *Macbeth* and *Timon of Athens* (Middleton), *Henry VIII* and *The Two Noble Kinsmen* (Fletcher). In 1602 Henslowe paid William Bird and Samuel Rowley £4 for making additions to *Doctor Faustus*, which might explain why the 1616 quarto is much longer than the 1604 quarto. (*ES* iii 423–4.) Carson examines how Henslowe paid for plays to be amended by other playwrights, often after the original author had died (2005, 60–1).

Although any of the above scenarios are possible for co-authorship, it does not seem likely that Shakespeare and his various co-authors ever planned the work together.

For other detailed consideration of co-authorship with regard to the plays of Shakespeare, See E. A. J. Honigman *The Stability of Shakespeare's text,* (Lincoln, Nebraska 1965), G. E. Bentley, *The Profession of Dramatist in Shakespeare's Time,* 1590–1642 (Princeton University Press, 1971; 1986), and the studies in *Shakespeare Survey: Volume 67, Shakespeare's Collaborative Work* ed. Peter Holland (2014).

Note

1   See Roslyn Knutson 'Henslowe's Diary and the Economics of Play Revision for Revival, 1592–1603.' *Theatre Research International 10* (1985) 1–18.

Select Bibliography

Abrams, M. H. 1953. *The Mirror and the Lamp: Romantic Theory and the Critical Tradition*. Oxford: Oxford University Press.

Acheson, Arthur. 1920. *Shakespeare's Lost Years in London 1586–1592*. London: Bernard Quaritch.

Ackroyd, Peter. 2005. *Shakespeare: The Biography*. London: Anchor Books.

Adams, Joseph Quincy. 1923. *A Life of William Shakespeare*. Cambridge, MA: Houghton Mifflin.

Akrigg, G. P. V. 1968. *Shakespeare and the Earl of Southampton*. London: Hamish & Hamilton.

Allen, Don Cameron, ed. 1938. *Francis Meres: 'Palladis Tamia: Wit's Treasury'*. New York: Scholars' Facsimiles and Reprints.

Altick, Richard D. 1965. *Lives and Letters: A History of Literary Biography in England and America*. Westport, CT: Greenwood Press.

Arber, Edward, ed. 1875-94. *A Transcript of the Registers of the Company of Stationers of London 1554–1640 A.D.* 5 Volumes, London, privately printed.

Atkins, J. W. H. 1952. *Literary Criticism in Antiquity: A Sketch of Its Development*. 2 vols. London: Methuen.

———. 1966. *English Literary Criticism: 17th and 18th Centuries*. London: Methuen.

Aubrey, John. 1813. *Letters Written by Eminent Persons in the Seventeenth and Eighteenth Centuries*. (ed. T. Hearne). London: Longman, Hurst.

———. 1898. *Brief Lives Chiefly of Contemporaries Set Down by John Aubrey between the Years 1669 and 1696* (ed. Andrew Clark). Oxford: Clarendon Press.

Aune, M. G. 2006. "Crossing the Border: Shakespeare Biography, Academic Celebrity, and the Reception of *Will in the World*." In *Borrowers and Lenders: The Journal of Shakespeare and Appropriation* 2.2 (n.p.).

Baldwin, T. W. 1944. *William Shakespere's Small Latine and Lesse Greeke*. Urbana: University of Illinois Press. 2 vols..

Baker, O. L. 1937. *Shakespeare's Warwickshire and the Unknown Years*. London: Simkin Marshall.

Barton, Anne. 1984. *Ben Jonson: Dramatist*. Cambridge: Cambridge University Press.

———. 2006. "The One and Only." Review article in *New York Review of Books*.

Batchelor, John, ed. 1995. *The Art of Literary Biography*. Oxford: Clarendon Press.

Bate, Jonathan. 1997. *The Genius of Shakespeare*. London: Picador.

———. 2001. "Not such a sweet Swan of Avon." Review of *Ungentle Shakespeare* (K. Duncan-Jones). In the *Sunday Telegraph*, 21 April.

———. 2008. *The Soul of the Age: The Life, Mind and World of William Shakespeare*. London: Viking.

Bate, Walter. 1977. *Samuel Johnson*. London: Harcourt Brace Jovanovich.

Bearman, Robert. 1994. *Shakespeare in the Stratford Records*. Stroud: Sutton Publishing.

———. 2002. " 'Was William Shakespeare William Shakeshafte?' Revisited." *Shakespeare Quarterly* 53, 83–94.

———. 2003. "John Shakespeare's 'Spiritual Testament': A Reappraisal." *Shakespeare Survey* 56: Shakespeare and Comedy, 184–202.

———. 2005. "John Shakespeare: A Papist or Just Penniless?" *Shakespeare Quarterly* 56, 411–433.

———. 2012. "Shakespeare's Purchase of New Place." *Shakespeare Quarterly* 63.4, 465–486.

———. 2016. *Shakespeare's Money: How Much Did He Make and What Did This Mean?* Oxford: Oxford University Press.

Bednarz, James P. 2001. *Shakespeare and the Poets' War*. New York: Columbia University Press.

Bell, John, ed. 1774. *Bell's Edition of Shakespeare's Plays*. 9 vols. London: Bell & Etherington.

Bennett, Kate, ed. 2015. *John Aubrey, Brief Lives with an Apparatus for the Lives of Our English Mathematical Writers*. 2 vols. Oxford: Oxford University Press.

Bentley, G. E. 1945. *Shakespeare and Jonson: Their Reputations in the Seventeenth Century Compared*. Chicago: University of Chicago Press.

———. 1961. *Shakespeare: A Biographical Handbook*. New Haven, CT: Yale University Press.

Bentley, G. E. Jr. 2001. *The Stranger from Paradise, William Blake*. New Haven, CT: Yale University Press.

Benton, Michael. 2009. *Literary Biography: An Introduction*. London: John Wiley and Sons.

Bevington, David. 2010. *Shakespeare and Biography*. Oxford: Oxford University Press.

Bevington, David, Martin Butler, & Ian Donaldson, eds. 2011. *Cambridge Edition of Works of Ben Jonson*. Cambridge: Cambridge University Press.

Blaine, M. E. 2009. "Envy, Eunoia and Ethos in Jonson's Poems on Shakespeare and Drayton." *Studies in Philology* 106, 441–45.

Blayney, Peter W.M. 1996. "Introduction to the Second Edition." *The Norton Facsimile: The First Folio of Shakespeare*. New York: Norton.

———. 1997. "The Publication of Playbooks." In *A New History of Early English Drama*, eds. John D. Cox and David Scott Kastan. New York: Columbia University Press, 383–422.

Boaden, James and Abraham Wivell. 2013. *Portraits of Shakespeare, and On the Sonnets of Shakespeare*. [Reprints of essays originally published in 1824, 1827 and 1837]. Cambridge: Cambridge University Press.

Bohn, Henry. 1863. *The Biography and Bibliography of Shakespeare*. London: Bohn.

Bostridge, Mark, ed. 2004. *Lives for Sale: Biographers' Tales*. London: Continuum.

Boswell, James. 1791. *The Life of Samuel Johnson, LL.D.* 2 vols. London: Charles Dilley (Later edn. 1823;. 4 vols. London: Richardson).

Boswell, James Jr., ed. 1821. *The Plays and Poems of William Shakspeare with the Corrections and Illustrations of Various Commentators: Comprehending a Life of the Poet and an Enlarged History of the Stage by the Late Edmond Malone, with a New Glossarial Index*. 21 vols. London: Rivington and Partners (Known as the Third Variorum).

Bourdieu, Pierre. 1986. "L'illusion biographique." *Actes de la recherche en science sociale*, 62/63. Translated as "The *Biographical* Illusion." (1987) by Yves Winkin and Wendy Leeds-Hurwitz. *Working Papers and Proceedings of the Centre for Psychosocial Studies,* University of Chicago, 14, 1–7.

Bozorth, Richard R. 2005. "Auden: Love, Sexuality, Desire." In *The Cambrige Companion to W. H. Auden*. Cambridge: Cambridge University Press, 175–187.

Bradbrook, Muriel. 1978. *Shakespeare: The Poet in His World*. London: Methuen.

Brady, Jennifer, & W.H. Herendeen, eds. 1991. *Ben Jonson's 1616 Folio*. Newark, DE. University of Delaware Press.

Briggs, Julia. 2005. "Virginia Woolf Reads Shakespeare: Or, Her Silence on Master William." *Shakespeare Survey* 58: 118–28.

Brown, Cedric, ed. 1993. *Patronage, Politics and Literary Traditions in England: 1558–1658*. Detroit, MI: Wayne State University Press.

Brown, Charles Armitage. 1838. *Shakespeare's Autobiographical Poems*. London: Bohn.

Brown, Ivor. 1949. *Shakespeare*. London: Collins.

Bryson, William. 2007. *Shakespeare: The World as a Stage*. London: HarperCollins.

Buckley, Norman & Jane Buckley. 2010. *Walking with Wordsworth*. London: Francis Lincoln.

Bühler, Charlotte. 1935. "The Curve of Life as Studied in Biographies." *Journal of Applied Psychology* 19: 405–9.

Bullough, G. 1957–1975. *Narrative and Dramatic Sources of Shakespeare's Plays*. 8 vols. London: Routledge, Keegan Paul.

Burke, John J. 1995. "Filling in the Blanks of Shakespeare's Biography: A Review Essay." *South Atlantic Review* 60 (3): 103–22.

Burrow, Colin, ed. 2002. *William Shakespeare: The Complete Sonnets and Poems*. Oxford: Oxford University Press.

———. 2005. "Who Wouldn't Buy It?" Review of *Will in the World* by Stephen Greenblatt (2004). *London Review of Books* 27, 25 January 2005, 9–11.

Callaghan, Dympna. 2013. *Who Was William Shakespeare? An Introduction to the Life and Works*. Oxford: Wiley Blackwell.

Campbell, Thomas, ed. 1838. *The Dramatic Works of William Shakespeare with A Life By Thomas Campbell*. 2 vols. London: Edward Moxon.

Campbell, Joseph. 1949. *The Hero with a Thousand Faces*. Princeton, NJ: Princeton University Press.

Campbell, O. J. and E. G. Quinn, eds. 1966. *The Reader's Encyclopaedia of Shakespeare*. New York: Crowell.

Capell, Edward. 1779–1783. *Notes and Various Readings of Shakespeare*. 3 vols. London: Henry Hughs.

———, ed. 1768. *Mr William Shakespeare his Comedies, Histories, and Tragedies*. 10 vols. London: J. and R. Tonson.

Carlyle, Thomas. 1841. *On Heroes, Hero-Worship, and The Heroic in History*. London: Fraser.

Carson, Neil, ed. 2005. *A Companion to Henslowe's Diary*. Cambridge: Cambridge University Press.

Castelain, Maurice. 1904. *Ben Jonson, Discoveries: A Critical Edition*. Paris: Hachette.

Chalmers, Alexander. 1797. *An apology for the believers in the Shakspeare-papers, which were exhibited in Norfolk-Street*. London: Egerton.

———ed. 1805. *The Plays of William Shakespeare*. 10 vols. London: Rivington. (later editions in 1811 and 1823).

———ed. 1812–1817. *General Biographical Dictionary*. 32 vols. London: J. Nichols and Son.

———ed. 1817. *The British Essayists: With Prefaces Historical and Biographical*. 45 vols. London: Longman & Rees.

Chambers, E.K. 1923. *The Elizabethan Stage*. 4 vols. Oxford: Clarendon Press.

———. 1930. *William Shakespeare: A Study of Facts and Problems*. 2 vols. Oxford: Clarendon Press.

———. 1946. *Sources for a Biography of Shakespeare*. Oxford: Clarendon Press.

Cheesman, Clive. 2014. "Grants and Confirmations of Arms." In *Heralds and Heraldry in Shakespeare's England*, ed. Nigel Ramsay. Donington: Shaun Tyas, 68–104.

Chisholm, Anne. 2001. "Secrets and Lies." *The New Statesman*, 14 May 2001 www.newstatesman.com/node/140303. Accessed 31.10.2013.

Cibber, Theophilus. 1753. *The Lives of the Poets of Great Britain and Ireland*. 4 vols. London: R. Griffiths.

Clare, Janet. 2005. "The Complexion of *Twelfth Night*." *Shakespeare Survey* 58, 199–207.

Clifford, James L. 1970. *From Puzzles to Portraits: Problems of a Literary Biographer*. Chapel Hill: University of North Carolina Press.

Cockshut, A.O.J. 1974. *Truth to Life: The Art of Biography in the Nineteenth Century*. London: Collins.

Collier, John Payne. 1831. *History of English Dramatic Poetry to the Time of Shakespeare and Annals of the Stage to the Restoration*. 3 vols. London: John Murray.

———. 1835. *New Facts Regarding the Life of Shakespeare*. London: T. Rodd.

———. 1836. *New Particulars Regarding the Works of Shakespeare: In a Letter to the Rev. A. Dyce from J. Payne Collier, F. S. A.* London: T. Rodd.

———. 1838. *Traditionary Anecdotes of Shakespeare: Collected in Warwickshire, in the Year MDCXCIII. Now First Published from the Original Manuscript*. London: T. Rodd.

———. 1839. *Further Particulars Regarding Shakespeare and His Works: In a Letter to the Rev. Joseph Hunter, F. S. A. from J. Payne Collier, F. S. A.* London: T. Rodd.

———, ed. 1844. *The Works of William Shakespeare*. 8 vols. London: Whittaker & Co (New editions in 1853 & 1858). Volume 1: *The Life of William Shakespeare*.

Collins, Arthur, ed. 1746. *H. Sydney and Others, Letters and Memorials of State*. London: Osborne.

Cooper, Duff. 1949. *Sergeant Shakespeare*. London: Hart Davis.

Cooper, Tarnya, ed. 2006. *Searching for Shakespeare*. National Portrait Gallery, London and Yale Center for British Art, New Haven, CT: Yale University Press.

Cummings, Brian. 2014. "Last Words: The Biographemes of Shakespeare". In *Shakespeare Quarterly* 65, 482–490.

De Grazia, Margreta. 1991. *Shakespeare Verbatim: The Reproduction of Authenticity and the 1790 Apparatus*. Oxford: Clarendon Press.

———. 2014. "Shakespeare's Timeline." In *Shakespeare Quaerterly* 65, 379-398.

De Quincey, Thomas. 1842. 'William Shakespeare' in *Encyclopedia Britanica*. Edinburgh: A. & C. Black. 7th edn. Volume XX.

———. 1864. *Shakespeare, a Biography*. Edinburgh: A. & C. Black.

DeStefano, Barbara L. 1993. "Ben Jonson's Eulogy on Shakespeare: Native Maker and the Triumph of English." *Studies in Philology* 90 (2): 231–45.

Dictionary of American Biography. New York: Charles Scribner's Sons. 1928–36. 20 vols. Supplements 1944–95, 10 vols.

Dobson, Michael. 1992. *The Making of the National Poet. Shakespeare, Adaptation and Authorship, 1660–1769*. Oxford: Clarendon Press.

Dobson, Michael, and Stanley Wells, eds. 2001. *The Oxford Companion to Shakespeare*. Oxford: Oxford University Press.

Donaldson, Ian. 1996. "Jonson and Tother Gentleman." In *Elizabethan Theater: Essays in Honour of S. Schoenbaum*, eds. Samuel Schoenbaum, R. B. Parker, Sheldon P. Zitner. Neward, DE: University of Delaware Press, 111–129.

———. 2004. "Ben Jonson." *ODNB*. http://dx.doi.org/10.1093/ref:odnb/15116.

———. 2006. "Looking Sideways: Jonson, Shakespeare, and the Myths of Envy." In *Shakespeare, Marlowe and Jonson: New Directions in Biography*, eds. Takashi Kozuka and J. R. Mulryne, 241–58. Aldershot: Ashgate.

———. 2011. *Ben Jonson: A Life*. Oxford: Oxford University Press.

Dowden, Edward. 1874. *Shakspere: A Critical Study of His Mind and Art*. London: Henry S. King & Co (12th edn. 1901. London: Keegan Paul, Trench, Trübner & Co.).

Drake, Nathan. 1817. *Shakespeare and His Times: Including the Biography of the Poet*. 2 vols. London: Cadell & Evans.

Dryden, John. 1668. *Of Dramatick Poesie, an Essay*. London: Herringman.

———, ed. 1688. *Plutarch's Lives: Translated from the Greek by Several Hands*. 5 vols. London: Tonson.

———, 1693. *A Discourse Concerning the Origin and Progress of Satire*. London: Tonson.

Dugdale, Sir William. 1656. *The Antiquities of Warwickshire Illustrated: from Records, Leiger-Books, Manuscripts, Charters, Evidences, Tombes, and Armes: Beautified with Maps, Prospects and Portraictures*. London: Thomas Warren (Republished 1730).

Duncan-Jones, Katherine, ed. 1997. *Shakespeare's Sonnets*. London: Thomas Nelson & Sons (Arden).

———. 2001. *Ungentle Shakespeare: Scenes from His Life*. London: Thomson (Arden).

———. 2004. *Shakespeare's Life and World*. London: Folio Society.

———. 2011. *Shakespeare: From Upstart Crow to Sweet Swan, 1592–1623*. London: A&C Black (Arden).

———. 2015. *Portraits of Shakespeare*. Oxford: Bodleain Library.

Durling, D.L., and W.W. Watt. 1941. *Biography: Varieties and Parallels*. New York: Dryden Press.

Dutton, Richard. 1989. *William Shakespeare: A Literary Life*. Basingstoke: Palgrave Macmillan.

———. 2006a. "'If I am Right.' Michael Wood's *In Search of Shakespeare*." In *Screening Shakespeare in the Twenty-First Century*, eds. Mark Thornton Burnett and Ramona Wray. Edinburgh: Edinburgh University Press, 13–30.

———. 2006b. "Shakespearean Origins." In *Shakespeare, Marlowe and Jonson: New Directions in Biography*, eds. Takashi Kozuka and J.R. Mulryne. Aldershot: Ashgate, 69–83.

———. 2007. "*Shake-speares Sonnets*, Shakespeare's Sonnets, and Shakespearean Biography." In *A Companion to Shakespeare's Sonnets*, ed. Michael Schoenfeldt, 121–36. Oxford: Blackwell.

Dyce, Alexander, ed. 1857. *The Works of Shakespeare*. 6 vols. London: E. Moxon (Revised second edition in 1864–67, expanded to nine volumes, published in London by Chapman and Hall).

Eagleton, Terry. 1976. *Marxism and Literary Criticism*. Berkeley, CA: University of California Press.

Eccles, Mark. 1961. *Shakespeare in Warwickshire*. Madison: University of Wisconsin Press.

Edmondson, Paul & Stanley Wells. 2004. *Shakespeare's Sonnets*. Oxford: Oxford University Press.

———. 2012. "The Plurality of Shakespeare's Sonnets." *Shakespeare Survey* 65: 211–20.

Edwards, Philip. 1987. *Shakespeare: A Writer's Progress*. Oxford: Oxford University Press (OPUS).

Eliot, T.S. 1919. "The Sacred Wood: Ben Jonson." (Review of Smith 1919). *Times Literary Supplement*, 13 November, 637–38. Reprinted in Eliot's *Selected Essays* (1958, 147–60).

Ellis, David, ed. 1993. *Imitating Art: Essays in Biography*. London: Pluto.

———. 2000. "Biography and Shakespeare: An Outsider's View." *Cambridge Quarterly* 29: 296–313.

———. 2005. *That Man Shakespeare: Icon of Modern Culture*. Mountfield, East Sussex: Helm International.

———. 2012. *The Truth about William Shakespeare: Fact, Fiction and Modern Biographies*. Edinburgh: Edinburgh University Press.

Ellman, Richard. 1971. *Literary Biography: An Inaugural Lecture Delivered before the University of Oxford on 4 May 1971*. Oxford: Oxford University Press.

Elms, Alan C. 1994. *Uncovering Lives: the Uneasy Alliance of Biograhy and Psychology*. Oxford: Oxford University Press.

Elze, Karl, ed. 1857 *Hamlet*. Leipzig: Meyer.

———. 1888. *William Shakespeare: A Literary Biography*. London: G. Bell & Sons (Trans. L. Dora Schmitz from German original, published Halle, 1876).

Erickson. Erling A. 1993. "Biography." *World Book Encyclopedia*. Chicago: World Book, ii. 313–4.

Erne, Lukas. 1998. "Biography and Mythography: Re-reading Chettle's Alleged Apology to Shakespeare." *English Studies* 79, 430–440.

———. 2003. *Shakespeare as a Literary Dramatist*. Cambridge: Cambridge University Press.

Falconer, A. F. 1964. *Shakespeare by the Sea: A Glossary of Shakespeare's Sea and Naval Terms including Gunnery*. London: Constable.

Farmer, Richard. 1767. *Essay on the Learning of Shakespeare*. Cambridge: J. Archdeacon.

Fischer, David Hackett. 1970. *Historians' Fallacies: Toward a Logic of Historical Thought*. New York: Harper Torchbooks.

Fleay, Frederick Gard. 1886. *A Chronicle History of the Life and Work of William Shakespeare, Player, Poet, and Playmaker*. London: Nimmo.

Florio, John. 1598. *A vvorlde of wordes, or Most copious, and exact dictionarie in Italian and English, collected by Iohn Florio*. London: Edw. Blount.

Foakes, R.A., ed. 2002. *Henslowe's Diary*. Cambridge: Cambridge University Press.

Forbush, William B., ed. 2004. *Foxe's Book of Martyrs*. Peabody, MA: Hendrickson.

Foucault, Michel. 1969. "What is an Author?" In *Textual Strategies: Perspectives in Post Structuralist Criticism*, ed. Josue V. Harari, 141–60. Ithaca, NY: Cornell University Press.

Fox, Alistair. 1995. "The Complaint of Poetry for the Death of Liberality: The Decline of Literary Patronage in the 1590s." In *The Reign of Elizabeth I: Court and Culture in the Last Decade*, ed. J. Guy. Cambridge: Cambridge University Press, 229–57.

France, Peter, and William St. Clair, eds. 2002. *Mapping Lives: The Uses of Biography*. Oxford: Oxford University Press.

Franssen, Paul. 2013. "The Adventures of William Hood: Fictions of Shakespeare the Deer-Stealer." *Critical Survey* 25: 59–71.

———. 2016. *Shakespeare's Literary Lives: The Author as Character in Fiction and Film*. Cambridge: Cambridge University Press.

Freehafer, John. 1970. "Leonard Digges, Ben Johnson, and the Beginning of Shakespeare Idolatry." *Shakespeare Quarterly* 21, 63–75.

Freeman, Arthur. 2004. "The Beginnings of Shakespearean (and Jonsonian) Forgery: Attribution and the Politics of Exposure." Part I. *Library* 5: 265–93: Part II: 402–27.

Freeman, Arthur and Janet Ing Freeman. 2004. *John Payne Collier: Scholarship and Forgery in the Nineteenth Century*. 2 vols. New Haven, CT: Yale University Press.

Freud, Sigmund. 1910. *Eine Kindheitserinnerung des Leonardo da Vinci*. Leipzig und Wien: Franz Deuticke (Tr. by A. Brill, 1916. *Leonardo da Vinci and a memory of his childhood*. New York: Moffat.

Fripp, Edgar I. 1938. *Shakespeare, Man and Artist*, edited by Frederick Christian Wellstood. 2 vols. Oxford: Oxford University Press.

Fuller, Thomas. 1662. *The History of the Worthies of England*. London: Thomas Williams (Volumes 1 & 2 reprinted by John Nichols. 1811: volume 3 edited by P. A. Nuttall, 1840).

Fulton, Thomas. 2006. "Speculative Shakespeares: The Trials of Biographical Historicism." *Modern Philology* 103 (3): 385–408.

Furbank, P.N. 2000. "The Craftlike Nature of Biography." In *Biographical Passages: Essays in Victorian and Modernist Biography*, eds. Mary Lago, et al. Columbia: University of Missouri Press, 18–27.

Furnivall, F.J. 1874. *Succession of Shakspere's Works and the Use of Metrical Tests in Settling it etc.* London: Smith, Elder & Co.

Garraty, John A. 1957. *The Nature of Biography*. London: Jonathan Cape.

Garraty, John, and Mark C. Carnes, eds. 1999. *American National Biography*. 24 vols. New York: Oxford University Press, Supplement, 2002.

Gaston, Sean. 2010. "No Biography: Shakespeare, Author." In *Shakespeare and His Authors: Critical Perspectives on the Authorship Question*, ed. William Leahy, 91–103. London: Continuum.

Gebert, Clara, ed. 1933. *An Anthology of Elizabethan Dedications, Prefaces, etc.* Philadelphia: University of Pennsylvania Press.

Gifford, William. 1816. *Works of Ben Jonson with Notes, Critical and Explanatory and a Biographical Memoir*. 9 vols. London: J. C. Hotton.

Gordon, D. J. 1949. "Shakespeare's Life and Times." *Shakespeare Survey* 2, 1949, 141–144.

Gray, Austin K. 1924. "The Secret of *Love's Labour's Lost*" in *PMLA* 39, 581-611.

———. 1926. *A Chapter in the Early Life of Shakespeare: Polesworth in Arden*. Cambridge: Cambridge University Press.

———. 1928. *How Shakespeare Purged Johnson: A Problem Solved*. Cambridge: Heffer.

Gray, H. D. 1932. "The Date of Hamlet." *Journal of English and Germanic Philology* 31, 51–61.

Gras, Henk. 1989. "*Twelfth Night, Every Man Out Of His Humour*, and the Middle Temple Revels of 1597–98." *Modern Language Review* 84, 545–64.

Greenblatt, Stephen. 1980. *Renaissance Self-Fashioning: From More to Shakespeare*. Chicago, IL: University of Chicago Press.

———. 2004. *Will in the World: How Shakespeare Became Shakespeare*. London: Jonathan Cape.

Greer, Germaine. 2007. *Shakespeare's Wife*. London: Bloomsbury.

Greg, W.W. 1955. *The Shakespeare First Folio: Its Bibliographical and Textual History*. Oxford: Clarendon Press.

Gurr, Andrew. 1992. *The Shakespearean Stage: 1574–1642*. Cambridge: Cambridge University Press.

———. 1996. *The Shakespearian Playing Companies*. Oxford: Oxford University Press.

———. 2004. *The Shakespeare Company, 1594–1642*. Cambridge: Cambridge University Press.

———. 2009. "Did Shakespeare Own his Own Playbooks?" Review of English Studies 60, 206–229.

Hackett, Helen. 2009. *Shakespeare and Elizabeth: The Meeting of Two Myths*. Princeton, NJ: Princeton University Press.

Hadfield, Andrew. 2008. *Shakespeare and Republicanism*. Cambridge: Cambridge University Press.

Hallam, Henry. 1837–9. *Introduction to the Literature of Europe: In the Fifteenth, Sixteenth and Seventeenth Centuries.* 4 vols. London: J. Murray.

Halliday, F.E. 1952. *A Companion to Shakespeare.* London: Gerald Duckworth (Rev. ed., 1964. Harmondsworth: Penguin).

———. 1963. *The Life of Shakespeare.* Rev. edn. Harmondsworth: Pelican.

Halliwell(-Phillipps), J.O., ed. 1862. *Collectanea Respecting the Birth-Place of Shakespeare.* London: Thomas Richards.

———. 1847. *Important Shakespearian Discoveries: Prospectus for a New Life of William Shakespeare.* London: John Elder Smith.

———. 1848. *A Life of William Shakespeare: Including Many Particulars Respecting the Poet and His Family Never Before Published.* London: John Elder Smith.

———. 1887. *Outlines of a Life of Shakespeare.* 2 vols., 7th ed. London: Longmans, Green & Co (Other editions: 1881: 1882: 1883: 1884: 1885: 1886, 2 vols.).

Hametz, M. E. 2005. *Making Trieste Italian 1918–1954.* London: Boydell.

Harness, Rev. William, ed. 1825. *Dramatic Works of William Shakespeare.* 8 vols. London: Saunders & Otley.

Harris, Frank. 1909. *The Man Shakespeare and His Tragic Life-Story.* London: F. Palmer.

Hays, Michael L. 2016. "Shakespeare's Hand Unknown in *Sir Thomas More*: Thompson, Dawson, and the Futility of the Paleographic Argument. *Shakespeare Quarterly,* 67, 180–203.

Hazlitt, William. 1817. *Characters of Shakespear's Plays* London: Rowland.

Heinemann, Margot. 1993. "Rebel Lords, Popular Playwrights, and Political Culture: Notes on the Jacobean Patronage of the Earl of Southampton." In *Patronage, Politics and Literary Traditions in England: 1558–1658,* ed. C. C. Brown, 135–58.

Herford, C.H., P. Simpson, and E. Simpson, eds. 1925–1952. *Ben Jonson.* 11 vols. Oxford: Clarendon Press.

Higgins, Charlotte. 2009. "To Find the Mind's Construction in the Face: The Great Shakespeare Debate." *The Guardian,* 10 March 2009.

Holden, Anthony. 1999. *William Shakespeare: His Life and Work.* London: Little Brown and Co.

———. 2008. "Getting Closer to the Bard." Review of Bate *Soul of the Age* (2008) in *The Guardian,* 9 November 2008.

Holderness, Graham. 1988. *The Shakespeare Myth.* Manchester: Manchester University Press.

———. 2001. *Cultural Shakespeare: Essays in the Shakespeare Myth.* Hatfield: University of Hertfordshire Press.

———. 2011. *Nine Lives of Shakespeare.* London: Continuum.

Holland, Peter, ed. 1995. *A Midsummer Night's Dream.* Oxford: Oxford University Press.

———. 2004. "William Shakespeare: Life and Times." *ODNB.* www.oxforddnb.com/public/dnb/25200.html.

———. 2006. "Shakespeare and the *DNB*." In *Shakespeare, Marlowe and Jonson: New Directions in Biography,* eds. Takashi Kozuka and J.R. Mulryne. Aldershot: Ashgate, 139–49.

Holmes, Richard. 1995. "Inventing the Truth." In *The Art of Literary Biography,* ed. Peter Batchelor. Oxford: Clarendon Press, 15–26.

———. 2002. "The Proper Study?", in France & St Clair *Mapping Lives: The Uses of Biography*. Oxford: Oxford University Press, 7–18.

Holroyd, Michael. 2003. "The Case against Biography." In *Works on Paper: Biography and Auto-biography*. London: Little, Brown and Co, 3–9.

Honan, Park. 1998. *Shakespeare: A Life*. Oxford: Oxford University Press.

———. 2004. "Henry Wriothesley, third earl of Southampton." *ODNB*. www. oxforddnb.com/index/101030073.

———. 2009. "To Change the Picture of Shakespeare Biography." *Critical Survey* 21 (3): 103–6.

Honigmann, E.A.J. 1982. *Shakespeare's Impact on His Contemporaries*. London: Macmillan.

———. 1985. *Shakespeare: The 'Lost Years'*. Manchester: Manchester University Press.

———. 1987. *John Weever: A Biography of a Literary Associate of Shakespeare and Jonson, together with a Photographic Facsimile of Weever's Epigrammes (1559)*. Manchester: Manchester University Press.

———. ed. 1998. *Othello*. London: Thomas Nelson (Arden3).

———. 2001. "Shakespeare's Life." In *The Cambridge Companion to Shakespeare*, eds. Margreta de Grazia and Stanley Wells. Cambridge: Cambridge University Press, 1–12.

———. 2012. "Tiger Shakespeare and Gentle Shakespeare." *The Modern Language Review* 107 (3): 699–711.

Hotson, J. Leslie. 1931. *Shakespeare versus Shallow*. London: Nonesuch.

———. 1938. *I, William Shakespeare*. Oxford: Oxford University Press.

Howard-Hill, T. H., ed. 1989. *Shakespeare and 'Sir Thomas More': Essays on the Play and Its Shakespearean Interest*. Cambridge: Cambridge University Press.

Hurstfield, Joel. 1958. *The Queen's Wards: Wardship and Marriage under Elizabeth I*. London: Longmans Green.

Hunt, Maurice. 2008. *Shakespeare's As You Like It: Late Elizabethan Culture and Literary Representation*. London: Palgrave MacMillan.

James, Henry. 1903. *The Birthplace*. London: Methuen.

Jarvis, Simon. 1995. *Scholars and Gentlemen: Shakespearean Textual Criticism and Representations of Scholarly Labour, 1725–1765*. Oxford: Clarendon Press.

———. 2010. "Alexander Pope." In *Great Shakespeareans*, ed. Claude Rawson. London: Continuum, 66–114.

Jeansonne, Glen. 1989. Review of *The Craft of Literary Biography* (ed. Jeffrey Meyers, 1985). *Biography* 12: 63–64.

Johnson, Samuel. 1744. *Life of Mr. Richard Savage*. London: Roberts.

———. 1779–1781. *Lives of the Most Eminent English Poets with Critical Observations on Their Works*. 4 vols. London: C. Bathurst &c.

———, ed. 1765. *The Plays of William Shakespeare*. 8 vols. London: J. and R. Tonson.

Johnson, Samuel & George Steevens, eds.1773. *The plays of William Shakespeare*. 10 vols. London: C. Bathurst. [known as *Johnson-Steevens* 1].

———, eds.1778. *The Plays of William Shakespeare*. 10 vols. London: C. Bathurst. [known as *Johnson-Steevens* 2].

Johnson, Samuel, George Steevens & Isaac Reed, eds.1785. *The plays of William Shakespeare*. 10 vols. London: C. Bathurst. [known as *Johnson-Steevens-Reed* 3].

———, eds.1793 *The plays of William Shakspeare*. London: J. Longman. 15 vols. [known as *Johnson-Steevens-Reed* 4].

———, eds.1803. *The plays of William Shakspeare*. 21 vols. London: J. Johnson [known as the 'first variorum' or *Johnson-Steevens-Reed* 5].

Johnson, Samuel, George Steevens, Isaac Reed & William Harris, eds.1813. *The plays of William Shakespeare*. 21 vols. London: J. Nichols and Sons [known as the 'second variorum' or *Johnson-Steevens-Reed* 6].

Johnston, Freya. 2010. "Samuel Johnson." In *Great Shakespeareans*, volume 1, ed. Claude Rawson, London: Continuum, 115–59.

Jolly, Margrethe. 2014. *The First Two Quartos of Hamlet: A New View of the Origins and Relationship of the Texts*. Jefferson, NC: McFarland.

Jones, Ernest. 1949. *Hamlet and Oedipus*. London: V. Gollancz.

Jonson, Beniamin. 1616. *The Workes of Beniamin Ionson*. London: Stansby.

———. 1640-41. *The Workes of Beniamin Jonson*. 2 vols. London: Meighen.

Jorgensen, Paul A. 1956. *Shakespeare's Military World*. Berkeley, CA University of California Press.

Jowett, John. 1993. "Johannes Factotum: Henry Chettle and Greene's Groats-worth of Wit," *Proceedings of the Bibliographical Society of America*, 87.4, 453-86.

Kay, Dennis. 1991. *Shakespeare: His Life, Work and Era*. Twayne's English Author Series. London: Sidgwick & Jackson.

Kay, W. David. 1995. *Ben Jonson: A Literary Life*. London: Macmillan.

Kerrigan, John, ed. 1986. *Shakespeare's Sonnets and A Lover's Complaint*. Harmondsworth: Penguin.

Kewes, Paulina. 2002. "Shakespeare's Lives in Print 1662–1821." In *Lives in Print*, eds. Myers et al., New Castle, DE: Oak Knoll Press, 55–82.

Klause, John. 2008. *Shakespeare, the Earl, and the Jesuit*. Cranbury, NJ: Associated University Presses.

Knight, Charles. 1839–1843. *The Pictorial Edition of the Works of Shakspere*. 8 vols. London: C. Knight and Co.

———. 1843. *William Shakspere: A Biography* (Volume 8: *The Pictorial Edition*). London: C. Knight and Co.

Kolbert, Jack. 1985. *The Worlds of André Maurois*. Cranbury, NJ: Associated University Presses.

Kozuka, Takashi & J.R. Mulryne, eds. 2006. *Shakespeare, Marlowe and Jonson: New Directions in Biography*. Aldershot: Ashgate.

Kuiper, Kathleen. 2012. *The Life and Times of William Shakespeare*. New York: Rosen.

Lambert, Daniel Henry. 1904. *Cartae Shakespeareanae: Shakespeare Documents: A Chronological Catalogue of Extant Evidence Relating to the Life and Works of William Shakespeare*. London: G. Bell.

Lanier, Douglas. 2007. "Shakespeare[TM]: Myth and Biographical Fiction." In *The Cambridge Companion to Shakespeare and Modern Popular Culture*, ed. Robert Shaughnessy. Cambridge: Cambridge University Press, 93–104.

Lawson, Lesley. 2007. *Out of the Shadows: The Life of Lucy, Countess of Bedford*. London: Hambledon Continuum.

Leahy, William, ed. 2010. *Shakespeare and His Authors: Critical Perspectives on the Authorship Question*. London: Continuum.

Lee, Hermione. 2005. *Virginia Woolf's Nose: Essays on Biography*. Princeton, NJ: Princeton University Press.

Lee, Sidney. 1897. 'William Shakespeare'. *Dictionary of National Biography*, volume 51. London: Smith, Elder & Co., 348–397.

———. 1898. *A Life of William Shakespeare*. London: Smith, Elder & Co (Subsequent editions: 1898: 1899: 1904: 1905: 1908: revised and enlarged edition 1915).

———. 1900. *Shakespeare's Life and Work: Being an Abridgement, Chiefly for the Use of Students of a Life of William Shakespeare*. London: Smith, Elder & Co (2nd ed., 1907).

———. 1911. *Principles of Biography*. Cambridge: Cambridge University Press.

———. 1915. *A Life of William Shakespeare*. Revised and enlarged editon. London: Smith, Elder & Co.

Leishman, J.B., ed. 1949. *The Three Parnassus Plays*. London: Ivor Nicholson & Watson.

Lever, J. W. 1956. *The Elizabethan Love Sonnet*. London: Methuen.

———. ed. 1971. *Every Man in His Humour*. Lincoln: University of Nebraska Press.

Levi, Peter, S.J. 1988. *The Life and Times of William Shakespeare*. London: Macmillan.

Lewis, B. Roland. 1940. *The Shakespeare Documents: Facsimiles, Transliterations, Translations & Commentary*. 2 vols. Stanford, CA: Stanford University Press.

Loomis, Catherine. 2002. *William Shakespeare: A Documentary Volume*. Dictionary of Literary Biography, v. 253. Farmington Hills, MI: Gale.

Lupton. 2014. "Birth Places: Shakespeare's Beliefs / Believing in Shakespeare". *Shakespeare Quarterly* 65, 399-420.

Lynch, Jack. 2007. *Becoming Shakespeare: The Unlikely Afterlife That Turned a Provincial Playwright into the Bard*. New York: Walker & Company.

MacCabe, Colin. 2004. "The Bard as a Chat-Show Celeb." *The Independent*, 5 November 2004.

MacDonald, Robert H. 1971. *The Library of William Drummond of Hawthornden*. Edinburgh: Edinburgh University Press.

McDonald, Russ. 1979. "Othello, Thorello, and the Problem of the Foolish Hero." *Shakespeare Quarterly* 30, 51–67.

MacLure, M. *The Paul's Cross Sermons 1534–1642*. Toronto: University of Toronto Press.

Maguire, Laurie. 1996. *Shakespeare's Suspect Texts: The 'Bad' Quartos and Their Contexts*. Cambridge: Cambridge University Press.

Maguire, Laurie & Emma Smith. 2012. *30 Great Myths about Shakespeare*. Oxford: Wiley Blackwell.

Malone, Edmond, ed. 1780. *Supplement to the Edition of Shakspeare's Plays Published in 1778 by Samuel Johnson and George Steevens*. London:C. Bathurst.

———, ed. 1790. *The plays and poems: of William Shakspeare, in ten volumes*. London: Rivington and Partners.

———. 1796. *An Inquiry into the Authenticity of Certain Miscellaneous Papers and Legal Instruments Published Dec 24 MDCCXCV and Attributed to Shakspeare, Queen Elizabeth and Henry, Earl of Southampton*. London: T. Cadell Jun. and W. Davies.

Manning, John J., ed. 1991. *The First and Second Parts of John Hayward's Life and Raigne of King Henry IIII*. London: RHS.

Marcus, Leah S. 1988. *Puzzling Shakespeare: Local Reading and Its Discontents*. Berkeley: University of California Press.

Martin, Peter. 1995. *Edmond Malone, Shakespearean Scholar: A Literary Biography*. Cambridge: Cambridge University Press.

Maza, Sarah. 2004. "Stephen Greenblatt, New Historicism, and Cultural History. Or, What We Talk about When We Talk about Inter-Disciplinarity." *Modern Intellectual History* 1: 249–65.

McCabe, Richard. 2016. *'Ungainefull Arte': Poetry, Patronage, and Print in the Early Modern Era*. Oxford: Oxford University Press.

McMillin, Scott, & Sally-Beth MacLean. 1998. *The Queen's Men and Their Plays*. Cambridge: Cambridge University Press.

McPherson, David. 1974. "Ben Jonson's Library and Marginalia: An Annotated Catalogue." *Studies in Philology* 71: 1–106.

Meres, Francis. 1598. *Palladis Tamia: Wit's Treasury*. London: C. Burbie (Modern Facsimile ed. Don Cameron Allen, 1938).

Meskill, Lynne E. 2009. *Ben Jonson and Envy*. Cambridge: Cambridge University Press.

Miles, Rosalind. 1986. *Ben Jonson: His life and work*. London: Routledge & Kegan Paul.

Miller, Edward. 1959. *The Professional Writer in Elizabethan England: A Study of Nondramatic Literature*. Cambridge, MA: Harvard University Press.

Minturno, Arturo. 1563. *L'arte poetica del Signor Antonio Minturno*. Venice: Valvassori.

Miola, Robert S., ed. 2000. *Every Man in His Humour: Quarto Version*. Manchester: Manchester University Press.

Monk, Samuel H., ed. 1948. *Nicholas Rowe: Some Account of the Life of William Shakespeare (1709)*. Los Angeles, CA: Augustan Reprint Society.

Monk, Ray. 2007. "The Fictitious Life: Virginia Woolf on Biography, Reality, and Character." *Philosophy and Literature* 31: 1–40.

Mutschmann, H. and K. Wentersdorf. 1952. *Shakespeare and Catholicism*. New York: Sheed and Ward.

Murphy, Andrew. 2003. *Shakespeare in Print: A History and Chronology of Shakespeare Publishing*, Cambridge: Cambridge University Press.

———. 2010. "Shakespeare and Chronology: Edward Dowden's Biographical Readings." *Forum for Modern Language Studies* 46 (2): 130–37.

Neill, Michael., ed. 2006. *Othello*. Oxford: Oxford University Press.

Nicholl, Charles. 2007a. *The Lodger: Shakespeare on Silver Street*. London: Allen Lane.

———. 2007b. Review of *Shakespeare's Wife* by Germaine Greer (2007). *The Guardian*, 1 September 2007.

Norris, J. Parker. 1888. "The Editors of Shakespeare." *Shakespeariana: A Critical and Contemporary Review of Shakespearian Literature*, 5 January 1888, 72–75.

O'Callaghan, Michelle. 2004. "Patrons of the Mermaid Tavern." *ODNB* DOI: http://dx.doi.org/10.1093/ref:odnb/95279.

O'Connor, Garry. 1991. *Shakespeare a Popular Life*. London: Hodder.

O'Farrell, Brian. 2011. *Shakespeare's Patron: William Herbert, Third Earl of Pembroke, 1580–1630: Politics, Patronage and Power*. London: Continuum.

Orgel, Stephen and G. Blakemore Evans, eds. 2006. *The Sonnets: New Cambridge Shakespeare*. Cambridge: Cambridge University Press.

Orlin, Lena. 2014. "Anne by Indirection." *Shakespeare Quarterly* 65 (2014, 421–54).

O'Sullivan, Maurice J. Jr., ed. 1997. *Shakespeare's Other Lives: An Anthology of Fictional Depictions of the Bard*. Jefferson, NC: McFarland.

Pafford, J.H.P., ed. 1962. *The Winter's Tale* (Arden2). London: Methuen.

Parke, Catherine. N. 2002. *Biography: Writing Lives*. London: Routledge.

Parry, Glyn. 2009. "New Evidence on William Shakeshafte and Edmund Campion." *Shakespeare Yearbook* 17, 1–27.

Patterson, R.F., ed. 1923. *Ben Jonson's Conversations with William Drummond of Hawthornden*. London: Blackie & Sons.

Pearce, Joseph. 2008. *The Quest for Shakespeare*. San Franciso, CA: Ignatius Press.

Peterson, Richard. 1980. *Imitation and Praise in the Poems of Ben Jonson*. New Haven, CT: Yale University Press.

Pevsner, Nikolaus. 1967. *The Buildings of England: Hampshire and the Isle of Wight*. Harmondswoth: Penguin.

Pollard, Alfred W. 1909. *Shakespeare Folios and Quartos*. London: Methuen.

Pope, Alexander. 1723-5. *The Works of Shakespear: in six volumes collated and corrected by the former editions, by Mr. Pope*. 6 vols. London: Jacob Tonson. [Volume 1, containing the prefatory material, is dated 1725: the other volumes are dated 1723.].

Potter, Lois. 2005a. "Having Our Will: Imagination in Recent Shakespeare Biographies." *Shakespeare Survey* 58: Writing About Shakespeare: 1–8.

———. 2005b. "Review of Stephen Greenblatt's *Will in the World*." *Shakespeare Quarterly* 56 (3): 374–76.

———. 2012. *The Life of William Shakespeare: A Critical Biography*. Oxford: Wiley-Blackwell.

Price, Diana. 1997. "Reconsidering Shakespeare's Monument." *Review of English Studies* 48: 168–81.

———. 2016. "Hand D and Shakespeare's Unorthodox Literary Paper Trail." in *Journal of Early Modern Studies* 5, 329–52.

Propp, Vladimir. 1928. *Морфология сказки*. Leningrad (Translated into English as *The Morphology of the Folk Tale* by Laurence Scott. 1958. Bloomington: University of Indiana Press).

Quiller-Couch, Arthur, ed. 1921. *Merry Wives of Windsor*. Cambridge: Cambridge University Press.

Rawson, Claude, ed. 2010. *Great Shakespeareans, Volume 1: Dryden, Pope, Johnson, Malone*. London: Continuum.

Richardson, D. L. 1835. "On Shakespeare's Sonnets, their Poetical Merits, and on the question to whom they are addressed" in *The Gentleman's Magazine*, 250–6: 361–370.

Ridley, M. R. ed. 1958. *Othello*. London: Methuen (Arden2).

Riggs, David. 1989. *Ben Jonson: A Life*. Cambridge, MA: Harvard University Press.

Rowse, A. L. 1965. *Shakespeare's Southampton: Patron of Virginia*. London: Macmillan.

———. 1973. *Shakespeare: The Man*. London: Book Club Associates.

Rowe, Nicholas. 1709. *The Works of Mr. William Shakespear in Six Volumes. Adorn'd with Cuts Revis'd and Corrected, with an Account of the Life and Writings of the Author.* 6 vols. London: Jacob Tonson. [Reprinted in 1709 & 1714].

Saccio, Peter. 2000. *Shakespeare's English Kings: History, Chronicle, and Drama.* Oxford: Oxford University Press.

Sage, John, and Thomas Ruddiman. 1711. *The Works of William Drummond of Hawthornden.* Craig's-Closs, Scotland: James Watson.

Sams, Eric. 1995. *The Real Shakespeare: Retrieving the Early Years, 1564–1594.* New Haven, CT: Yale University Press.

Sarrazin, G. 1904. "Nym und Jonson." *Shakespeare Jahrbuch* 40, 213–22.

Savage, Richard, ed. 1897–1905. *The Parish Registers of Stratford-upon-Avon.* London: The Parish Register Society (Vol. 1: Baptisms, 1558–1652: vol. 2: Marriages, 1558–1812: vol. 3. Burials, 1558–1622-3).

Secord, A. W. 1948. "I. M. of the First Folio, Shakespeare, and other Mabbe Problems." *Journal of English and Germanic Philology* 47, 374–81.

Schoenbaum, Samuel. 1970. *Shakespeare's Lives.* Oxford: Clarendon Press (2nd ed., 1991).

———. 1971. "The Life of Shakespeare." In *A New Companion to Shakespeare Studies*, eds. K. Muir and S. Schoenbaum. Cambridge: Cambridge University Press, 1–14.

———. 1975. *William Shakespeare: A Documentary Life.* Oxford: Clarendon Press.

———. 1977. *William Shakespeare: A Compact Documentary Life.* Oxford: Clarendon Press (2nd ed., 1987).

———. 1981. *William Shakespeare: Records and Images.* Oxford: Clarendon Press.

Schoenfeldt, Michael, ed. 2007. *A Companion to Shakespeare's Sonnets.* Oxford: Blackwell.

Schwalm, David E. 1980. "Locating Belief in Biography." *Biography* 3: 14–27.

Scragg, Leah. 1997. "Edward Blount and the Prefatory Material to the First Folio." *Bulletin of the John Rylands Library* 97: 117–26.

Secord, A. W. 1948. "I. M. of the First Folio, Shakespeare, and other Mabbe Problems." *Journal of English and Germanic Philology* 47, 374–81.

Severn, Charles, ed. 1839. *Diary of the Rev John Ward, A.M.* London: Henry Colburn.

Shapiro, I. A. 1950. "The Mermaid Club." *Modern Language Review* 45: 6–17.

Shapiro, James S. Shapiro, 1991. *Rival Playwrights.* New York, NY: Columbia University Press.

———. 2005. *1599: A Year in the Life of William Shakespeare.* London: Faber & Faber.

———. 2010. *Contested Will: Who Wrote Shakespeare?* London: Faber & Faber.

———. 2011. "James Shapiro on Shakespeare Biographies." *Five Books*, 4 May 2011.

———. 2015. *1606: William Shakespeare and the Year of Lear.* London: Faber & Faber.

Shaw, G.B. 1901. *Three Plays for Puritans.* London: Grant Richards.

———. 1910. "Review of Frank Harris's Play *Shakespeare and His Love* (1910)." *The Nation* 8, 24 December.

Shelston, Alan. 1977. *Biography: the Critical Idiom.* London: Methuen.

Sherbo, Arthur. 1986. *The Birth of Shakespeare Studies: Commentators from Rowe (1709) to Boswell-Malone (1821).* East Lansing, MI: Colleagues Press.

Singer, Samuel Weller, ed. 1826. *The Dramatic Works of William Shakspeare.* 10 vols. Chiswick: Charles Whittingham (Reprinted 1856).

Sisson, Charles J. 1932. "Review of *The Essential Shakespeare: A Biographical Adventure* by J. Dover Wilson (1932)." *The Modern Language Review* 27 (4): 473–76.

———. 1934. *The Mythical Sorrows of Shakespeare.* Annual Shakespear Lecture of the British Academy, 21. London: Humphrey Milford.

———. 1950. "Studies in the Life and Environment of Shakespeare since 1900." *Shakespeare Survey* 3: 1–13.

Smith, Bruce R. 2007. "THWS, CWWS, WSAF, and WSCI in the Shakespeare Book Biz." Review article on recent biographies of Shakesepeare. *Shakespeare Studies* 35: 158–85.

Smith, D. Nichol. 1903. *Eighteenth Century Essays on Shakespeare.* Glasgow: James MacLehose & Sons.

Spence, Joseph. 1820. *Observations, Anecdotes, and Characters of Books and Men.* London: John Murray.

Spencer, T.J.B. 1974. "Ben Jonson on His Beloved, the Author Mr. William Shakespeare." In *The Elizabethan Theater IV,* ed. G.R. Hubbard. Hamden, CT: Archon Books, 22–40.

Spingarn, J. E. 1899. *A History of Literary Criticism in the Renaissance.* New York: Columbia University Press

Stanfield, James F. 1813. *An Essay on the Study and Compositon of Biography.* Sunderland: George Garbutt.

Stauffer, Donald. 1930. *English Biography before 1700.* Cambridge, MA: Harvard University Press.

———. 1941. *The Art of Biography in Eighteenth Century England.* Princeton, NJ: Princeton University Press.

Steevens, George. 1766. *Twenty of the Plays of Shakespeare. Being the Whole Number Printed in Quarto During his Life-Time.* London: Tonson.

Steevens, George, (ed. with S. Johnson) 1773. *The plays of William Shakespeare.* 10 vols. London: C. Bathurst. [known as *Johnson-Steevens 1*].

———, (ed. with S. Johnson) 1778. *The Plays of William Shakespeare.* 10 vols. London: C. Bathurst. [known as *Johnson-Steevens 2*].

———, (ed. with S. Johnson, I. Reed).1785. *The plays of William Shakespeare.* 10 vols. London: C. Bathurst. [known as *Johnson-Steevens-Reed 3*].

———, (ed. with S. Johnson, I. Reed). 1793 *The plays of William Shakspeare.* London: J. Longman. 15 vols. [known as *Johnson-Steevens-Reed 4*].

———, (ed. with S. Johnson, I. Reed). eds. 1803. *The plays of William Shakspeare.* 21 vols. London: J. Johnson [known as the 'first variorum' or *Johnson-Steevens-Reed 5*].

———, (ed. with S. Johnson, I. Reed, and W. Harris), eds.1813. *The plays of William Shakespeare.* 21 vols. London: J. Nichols and Sons [known as the 'second variorum' or *Johnson-Steevens-Reed 6*].

Stoddard, William Levitt. 1910. *Life of William Shakespeare Expurgated.* Boston, MA: Butterfield.

Stopes, C.C. 1922. *The Life of Henry, Third Earl of Southampton, Shakespeare's Patron*. Cambridge: Cambridge University Press.

Strachey, Lytton. 1918. *Eminent Victorians*. London: Chatto & Windus.

———. 1921. *Queen Victoria*. London: Chatto & Windus.

———. 1928. *Elizabeth and Essex: A Tragic History*. London: Chatto & Windus.

Taylor, Gary. 1989. *Reinventing Shakespeare: A Cultural History from the Restoration to the Present*. London: Hogarth Press.

———. 2014. "Empirical Middleton: *Macbeth*, Adaptation and Authorship." *Shakespeare Quarterly* 65, 239–72.

Taylor, Gary, *et al..*, 2016. *The New Oxford Shakespeare*. Oxford: Oxford University Press.

Theobald, Lewis. 1726. *Shakespeare Restored*. London: R. Franck.

Theobald, Lewis, ed. 1733. *Works of Shakespeare*. 7 vols. London: Jacob Tonson. [Other editions 1740: 1752: 1757: 1762: 1767: 1772: 1773 and 1777 (?).].

Thomas, D. 1964. *Shakespeare in the Public Records*. London: HMSO.

Thomas, Julia. 2012. *Shakespeare's Shrine: The Bard's Birthplace and the Invention of Stratford-upon-Avon*. Philadelphia: University of Pennsylvania Press.

Thompson, Ann & Neil Taylor, eds. 2006 *Hamlet* (Arden3). London: Thomson.

Trimpi, Wesley. 1962. Trimpi. *Ben Jonson's Poems: A Study of the Plain Style*. Stanford, CA: Stanford University Press.

Vickers, Brian. 2002. *Shakespeare, Co-Author: A Historical Study of Five Collaborative Plays*. Oxford: Oxford University Press.

———. '2017. "'Upstart Crow'? The Myth of Shakespeare's Plagiarism" in *Review of English Studies* 68, 244–67.

Voss, Paul J. 1998. "Books for Sale: Advertising and Patronage in Late Elizabethan England." *The Sixteenth Century Journal* 29, 733–56.

Wallace, Charles. 1910. "Shakespeare and His London Associates as Revealed in Recently Discovered Documents." *Studies of the University of Nebraska* 10: 268–77.

Walsh, Marcus. 2010. "Edmond Malone." In *Great Shakespeareans*, volume 1, ed. Claude Rawson. London: Continuum, 160–99.

Walton, Izaak. 1653. *The Compleat Angler*. London: Maxey.

Weis, René. 2007. *Shakespeare Revealed*. London: John Murray.

Wells, Stanley. 1994. *Shakespeare: A Dramatic Life*. London: Sinclair-Stevenson. Published in the U.S.A as *Shakespeare: A Life in Drama* (1995) New York: Norton: reissued in Britain as *Shakespeare: The Poet and his Plays* (1997) London: Methuen.

———. 1996. "Shakespeare's Lives: 1991–1994." *Elizabethan Theater: Essays in Honor of S. Schoenbaum*, eds. R.B. Parker and Sheldon P. Zitner. Newark, DE: University of Delaware Press, 15–29.

———. 2003. *Shakespeare for all Time*. Oxford: Oxford University Press.

———. 2006. "Sweet Master Shakespeare." In *Searching for Shakespeare*, ed. Tarnya Cooper, 13–21. National Portrait Gallery, London and Yale Center for British Art, New Haven, CT: Yale University Press.

———. ed. 2009. *Shakespeare Found! A Life Portrait at Last: Portraits, Poet, Patron, Poems*. Stratford: Shakespeare Birthplace Trust.

Wells, Stanley, & Gary Taylor, eds. 1986. *William Shakespeare: The Complete Works*. Oxford: Clarendon Press (2nd ed., 2005).

———. with John Jowett & William Montgomery. 1987. *William Shakespeare: A Textual Companion*. Oxford: Oxford University Press.

Werstine, Paul. 2013. *Early Modern Playhouse Manuscripts and the Editing of Shakespeare*. Cambridge: Cambridge University Press.

Wheler, Robert Bell. 1806. *History and Antiquities of Stratford-upon-Avon*. London: J. Ward.

———. 1814. *A Guide to Stratford -upon-Avon*. Stratford: J. Ward.

———. 1836. "Shakespeare's Marriage Licence Bond." *Gentleman's Magazine*. 266–68.

———. 1862. *Collectanea Respecting the Birth-place of Shakespeare at Stratford-on-Avon, Copied from the Manuscript Collections of the Late Robert Bell Wheler, with a Few Additions by J. O. Halliwell, F. R. S.* London: Thomas Richards.

Williams, Franklin B. Jr. 1966. "Commendatory Verses: The Rise of the Art of Puffing." *Studies in Bibliography* 19: 1–14.

Wilson, Edmund. 1938. "Morose Ben Johnson." In *The Triple Thinkers*. Oxford: Oxford University Press.

Wilson, Ian. 1993. *Shakespeare: The Evidence: Unlocking the Mysteries of the Man and His Work*. London: Headline Press.

Wilson, J. Dover. 1932. *The Essential Shakespeare: A Biographical Adventure*. Cambridge: Cambridge University Press.

Wilson, Richard. 2004. *Secret Shakespeare: Studies in Theatre, Religion and Resistance*. Manchester: Manchester University Press.

Wimsatt, William J. Jr., & Monroe C. Beardsley. 1946. "The Intentional Fallacy." *Sewanee Review* 54: 468–88. Reprinted in William J. Wimsatt. 1954. *The Verbal Icon: Studies in the Meaning of Poetry*. Lexington: University of Kentucky Press, 3–18.

Wood, Michael. 2003. *In Search of Shakespeare*. London: BBC Worldwide Ltd.

Woolf, Virginia. 1927. "The New Biography." In *Virginia Woolf: Selected Essays*, ed. David Bradshaw. Oxford: Oxford University Press, 2008, 95–100.

———. 1928. *Orlando: A Biography*. London: Hogarth Press.

———. 1939. "The Art of Biography." In *Virginia Woolf: Selected Essays*, ed. David Bradshaw. Oxford: Oxford University Press, 2008, 116–26.

———. 1979. "'Anon' and 'The Reader'," In "Virginia Woolf's Last Essays", transcribed by Brenda R. Silver. *Twentieth Century Literature* 25, 356–441.

Worden, Blair. 2006. "Shakespeare in Life and Art: Biography and *Richard II*." In *Shakespeare, Marlowe and Jonson: New Directions in Biography*, eds. Takashi Kozuka and J.R. Mulryne. Aldershot: Ashgate, 23–42.

Yates, Frances. 1934. *John Florio: The Life of an Italian in Shakespeare's England*. Cambridge: Cambridge University Press.

Index

Dates of works refer to their earliest known publication.

Printed in Great Britain
by Amazon